D0469338

When Politicians Attack
Party Cohesion in the Media

Fostering a positive brand name is the chief benefit that parties provide for their members. They do this by coordinating their activities in the legislative process and by communicating with voters. Although political scientists generally focus on the former, dismissing partisan communication as "cheap talk," this book argues that a party's ability to coordinate its communication has important implications for the study of politics. The macrolevel institutional setting of a party's communication heavily influences that party's prospects for cohesive communication. Paradoxically, unified government presents the greatest challenge to unified communication within the president's party. As this book contends, the challenge stems primarily from two sources: the constitutional separation of powers and the intervening role of the news media. In this setting, internal disputes with the president or within the congressional majority are more likely to arise. These disputes are disproportionately likely to be featured by the news media, and stories of intraparty strife become the most credible and damaging type of partisan story.

Tim Groeling is Associate Professor of Communication Studies at the University of California, Los Angeles. With Matthew A. Baum, he is the coauthor of *War Stories: The Causes and Consequences of Public Views of War*. His articles have appeared in the *Journal of Politics*, *International Organization*, *Political Communication*, *Political Behavior*, and *Presidential Studies Quarterly*, among other publications.

To Judy Groeling –
I wish you could have seen it.

COMMUNICATION, SOCIETY AND POLITICS

Editors

W. Lance Bennett
University of Washington

Robert M. Entman
The George Washington University

Politics and relations among individuals in societies across the world are being transformed by new technologies for targeting individuals and sophisticated methods for shaping personalized messages. The new technologies challenge boundaries of many kinds – among news, information, entertainment, and advertising; among media, with the arrival of the World Wide Web; and even among nations. *Communication, Society and Politics* probes the political and social impacts of these new communication systems in national, comparative, and global perspective.

OTHER BOOKS IN THE SERIES

When Politicians Attack

Party Cohesion in the Media

TIM GROELING
University of California, Los Angeles

CAMBRIDGE
UNIVERSITY PRESS

CAMBRIDGE
UNIVERSITY PRESS

32 Avenue of the Americas, New York NY 10013-2473, USA

Cambridge University Press is part of the University of Cambridge.

It furthers the University's mission by disseminating knowledge in the pursuit of education, learning and research at the highest international levels of excellence.

www.cambridge.org
Information on this title: www.cambridge.org/9780521603072

First published 2010

A catalogue record for this publication is available from the British Library

Library of Congress Cataloguing in Publication data

Groeling, Tim J.
When politicians attack : party cohesion in the media / Tim Groeling.
    p. cm. – (Communication, society and politics)
Includes bibliographical references and index.
ISBN 978-0-521-84209-9 (hardback) – ISBN 978-0-521-60307-2 (pbk.)
1. Advertising, Political.   2. Public relations and politics.   3. Political parties.
4. Communication in politics.   I. Title.   II. Series.
JF2112.A4G76   2010
324.7'3 – dc22   2010003654

ISBN 978-0-521-84209-9 Hardback
ISBN 978-0-521-60307-2 Paperback

Contents

Acknowledgments

To paraphrase a famous partisan communicator, "It takes a village to write a book." That has certainly been the case with this project, so before proceeding, I would like to thank all of the village people.

The origins of this book stretch back farther than I like to admit. Although I have been fascinated by the topic of partisan communication for most of my adult life, the topic really came into focus during my graduate education at the University of California, San Diego (UCSD). In particular, the seed of this book was planted during a seminar on Media and Politics taught by my mentor, Sam Kernell. Sam and the other participants in the seminar – particularly Daniel Hallin and Michael Schudson – channeled my broader interest in the media into a more focused research agenda.

Other instructors at UCSD – particularly Mathew McCubbins and Gary Jacobson – piqued my interest in and refined my thinking about Congress. Gary Cox, Arthur Lupia, and Mathew McCubbins helped me to recognize the central dilemmas that people face as they try to act collectively. Speaking of acting collectively, I owe a tremendous debt to my fellow graduate students at UCSD. Matt Baum, Jamie Druckman, Daniel Kaufman, Thomas Kim, Adam Many, Marc Rosenblum, David Shirk, Mark Sniderman, and others motivated me and helped me maintain my sanity throughout my graduate career. Other faculty and staff at UCSD provided tremendous assistance along the way, including Neal Beck, Amy Bridges, Penny Cumby, Elisabeth Gerber, Alan Houston, Peter Irons, Steve Lincoln, Keith Pezzoli, Glenn Smith, Martha Stacklin, Rosalind Streichler, and Christine Vaz. Of course, I would never have been accepted at such a fine graduate school in the first place without my excellent DePauw University instructors, including Ken Bode, Robert Calvert, Nafhat Nasr, Phil Powlick, Ralph Raymond, Richard Roth, and especially Bruce Stinebrickner, who nudged my professional career onto the right path at several critical junctures.

I owe a tremendous debt to the members of my dissertation committee, who helped nurture this project from its infancy. Gary Cox, Dan Hallin, Gary Jacobson, and Michael Schudson steered me out of blind alleys, clarified my thinking, and pushed me toward a final product of which I can be proud. My dissertation chair, Sam Kernell, however, provided the most help. Sam was involved in every stage of this book's development, and it is no understatement to say that without him, you would probably not be reading this text today.

I also have benefited tremendously from the support of the faculty and staff here at the University of California, Los Angeles (UCLA). Even before I was hired, the then-Chair of the Communication Studies program, Neil Malamuth, was endlessly supportive and enthusiastic, and he helped move heaven, earth, and faculty committees to advance my research. My colleague and coauthor, Matt Baum, assisted me in literally countless ways and has served as a guide and model for my academic career. My UCLA colleagues in the Department of Political Science – particularly Tim Groseclose, Barbara Sinclair, Lynn Vavreck, and John Zaller – also provided great feedback. My Department of Communications Studies colleagues, including Greg Bryant, Kyu Hahn, Martie Haselton, Kerri Johnson, and Francis Steen, broadened my thinking and perspective on the research. In many ways, Paul Rosenthal was helping with the book before I even knew the book would exist: Without the archive of television broadcasts he collected in the 1970s and 1980s, the Baum and Groeling data collection used in Chapters 3 and 5 would be far less complete and persuasive. Of course, I am deeply and continually indebted to the UCLA Department of Communication Studies staff – particularly Jane Bitar, Sylvia Merschel, and Rima Yoohanna – without whom my work at UCLA would have quickly spiraled into chaos, disorder, and despair.

Similarly, I am indebted to several sources for the data used in this book. I relied heavily on content-analysis data collected by the Center for Media and Public Affairs. The director, S. Robert Lichter, first provided preliminary versions of these data, and I have found it to be increasingly valuable since then. In addition, the online resources of LexisNexis and ProQuest have broadened my access to historical news data in ways that were unthinkable when I began the research.

As alluded to previously, however, the most invaluable data assistance I received was in the context of Matt Baum's and my 25-year content analysis of evening-news coverage surrounding foreign-policy crises, which was supported in part by a grant from the Institute on Global Conflict and Cooperation. It goes without saying that Matt's boundless and insightful analysis regarding these data was phenomenally valuable, and our work on that project informed much of my thinking herein. Lori Cox Han and Diane Heith motivated us to conduct the empirical research, for which I will always be tremendously appreciative. Our two graduate assistants, Phil Gussin of UCLA and Delynn Davidson of UCSD, provided assistance with energy and keen insight.

Of course, the content analysis would never have gotten off the ground without the help of our army of student content-analysts at UCLA and UCSD. We thank Jeff Barry, Alexandra Brandt, Ross Bul, Stephanie Chambers, Frank Chang, Tim Chettiath, Connie Choe, Francis Choi, Blaire Cirlin, Jenny Cocco, Elizabeth Cummings, Sarah Davis, Jennifer Dekel, Betty Fang, Brette Fishman, Kristin Gatfield, Rita Ghuloum, Christina Gibson, Angela Gill, Daniel Gordon, Sasha Gorelick, Anjana Gupta, Kazue Harima, Julia Heiser, Marchela Iahdjian, Sangeeta Kalsi, Robert Kelly, Angela Kim, Jihyun Kim, Alain Kinaly, Daniella Knelman, Priya Koundinya, Lauren Kubota, Jennifer Lee, Frank Martinez, Joe Mason, Jennifer Murakami, Kim Newin, Maya Oren, Leeja Patel, Andrea Peterson, Kate Pillon, Brittney Reuter, David Rigsby, Brooke Riley, Justin Ryan, Dean Sage, Sundeep Sahni, Michael Sefanov, Taleen Serebrakian, Sara Shamolian, Paula Simon, Eric Simpson, Erin Skaalen, Ashley Skipwith, Katherine Steele, Julia Tozlian, Jenny Triplett, Caroline Van Der Harten, Phuong Vu, Spencer Westcott, Shira Wheeler, William Whitehorn, Barri Worth, Jordan Yurica, and Jennie Zhu. I also benefited tremendously from the meticulous and insightful research assistance of Davide Baruzzi, Amber Escamilla, Ashley Eure, Andrea Evans, Patrice Fabel, Kuros Ghaffari, Mallory Gompert, Sandra Hanian, Dina Knudsen, Meredith McNaughton, Daniel Prager, Clare Robinson, Alyson Tufts, Elisabeth Turner, Kate Wagner, and many others.

In addition, I want to thank all of the students and scholars who provided feedback on papers related to this book at various conferences – specifically John Aldrich, Scott Althaus, Dunia Andary, Andrew Bargen, Andrew Barrett, Adam Berinsky, Jon Bond, Meena Bose, Richard Brody, Jeffrey Cohen, Cary Covington, Ann Crigler, David Crockett, George Edwards, Matthew Eshbaugh-Soha, Steven Farnsworth, Richard Fleisher, John Frendreis, Brian Gaines, David Harding, David Holian, Jennifer

Hora, William Horner, Kathleen Hall Jamieson, Montague Kern, Glen Krutz, Chappell Lawson, Daniel Lipinski, John Maltese, Michal Mezey, Catherine Needham, Daniel Ponder, Brandon Prins, Markus Prior, David Rankin, Russell Renka, Brian Roberts, David Rohde, Jon Schaff, Brian Schaffner, Patrick Sellers, Robert Shapiro, L. Earl Shaw, Steven Shull, Sarah Sled, Robert Spitzer, Terry Sullivan, and Raymond Tatalovich. Similarly, I was exceptionally influenced by the feedback I received at a 1999 conference at Texas A&M University on "Congress and the President in a Partisan Era." The conference was an exceptionally important influence on my thinking and eventually led to an interesting volume from Congressional Quarterly (CQ) Press. I want to thank Brenda Carter and her CQ colleagues for all of their help on prior projects and advice when I was putting this one together.

Of course, the people at Cambridge University Press deserve my highest appreciation for believing in this book and steering it through to completion. From the beginning, Robert Entman was the book's "guardian angel" in guiding it through the publication process with care and enthusiasm. W. Lance Bennett and Lew Bateman provided valuable feedback and insight that immeasurably improved the project, as did two anonymous reviewers. The editorial and production staff at Aptara, Connie Burt and Barbara Walthall, took the manuscript through proofs and final production.

I incessantly imposed on kind souls including Matt Baum, Jamie Druckman, Sam Kernell, and John Zaller to read and comment on various elements of the book.

My father and my wife Vicki provided loving support and tireless editing throughout the grueling process required to bring this text to completion. And, as always, my daughters Laura and Carrie make it all worthwhile.

Introduction: Singing from the Same Hymnbook

Party Cohesion in the Media

> Communications is where it's all at. It's not what you're doing but the perceptions that are so important.
>
> – Representative John Boehner (R-OH), speaking on Medicare Reform in 1995[1]

Incumbent Senator Lincoln Chafee (R-RI) entered the 2006 election in a relatively enviable political position. Chafee was the scion of a Rhode Island dynasty that had produced numerous governors and senators, including his father and immediate predecessor in the Senate, John Chafee. After being appointed to complete his deceased father's term in 1999, Chafee captured 57% of the vote in his own right in the 2000 election. Reflecting the same independent streak demonstrated by his father, Chafee repeatedly defied the Republican leadership on key issues, favoring the relatively liberal positions of his constituents over those of the national party.[2] After fending off a right-wing challenger in the 2006 primary election, Chafee seemed well positioned to appeal to moderate voters in his relatively liberal state, with polling showing that more than half of voters thought his positions on the issues were "about right" and nearly two thirds approved of the way he was handling his job as senator.[3]

---

[1] Maraniss and Weisskopf (1996, 142).

[2] For example, Chafee broke ranks with his fellow Republicans on Bush's 2001 tax cut, the so-called partial-birth–abortion ban, the Iraq War authorization, a proposed Flag Desecration Amendment, the Medicare prescription-drug benefit, the nomination of Samuel Alito to the U.S. Supreme Court, and other policies.

[3] Of the respondents, 63% approved of Chafee's job performance, 17% believed he was "too liberal," and 25% believed he was "too conservative" (CNN 2006).

Despite all of those advantages, Chafee lost the election to his Democratic opponent, Sheldon Whitehouse. Chafee's actions in office, as well as his ultimate defeat, present an interesting window into the conduct of modern American politics. In particular, they demonstrate the degree to which partisanship has come to dominate not only the conduct of politics within the legislature in Washington but also the information that the American public uses in evaluating politics – and politicians.

TALKING OUT OF THE SAME SIDES OF THEIR MOUTHS

Although political scientists often dismiss the statements of politicians as "cheap talk," politicians certainly behave as though they believe that "talk matters." In fact, politicians sometimes behave as if talk were *all* that mattered.[4] Even outside of the talk-heavy world of campaigns and elections, modern politicians issue news releases, leak damaging information about enemies, appear in front of network cameras, stage elaborate photogenic events, and conduct the public's business in front of television cameras. They do so not from vanity but rather from strategy: All of these efforts are intended to directly or indirectly influence the public's perception of the politician and his or her party.

Fostering a positive party "brand name" is the chief collective good provided by parties. Parties foster a positive image through coordinating their activities in the legislative process and their communication with voters. Although political scientists generally emphasize the former activity and dismiss the importance of partisan communication, I argue that a party's ability to coordinate communication has important implications for the study of American politics (Chapter 1). In particular, for members of the presidential party, the failure to coordinate messages can significantly damage their leader's standing in public opinion (Chapter 5) and actually undermine the attractiveness and stability of unified government (Chapter 6).

A party's success or failure in collective communication is heavily influenced by the macrolevel institutional setting of that communication.

---

[4] Of course, the clearest indication of the value that politicians attach to communication is evident in the tremendous resources devoted to campaign advertising. TNS Media Intelligence, which systematically tracks advertising purchases, estimated that candidates and other political groups spent $1.7 billion on advertising in the 2004 election cycle and between $2.5 billion and $2.7 billion in the 2008 election (Atkinson 2008). The fundraising necessary to support such massive spending, in turn, consumes massive quantities of politicians' time and attention – almost a third of all senators' time, according to one estimate (Hollings 2006).

Specifically, in unified government, the president undermines his party's ability to successfully communicate with voters. Thus, unified government paradoxically presents the greatest challenge for unified collective communication for the president's party and places that party at far greater electoral risk than it faces in divided government. These challenges stem primarily from two sources: the constitutional separation of powers (Chapter 6) and the intervening role of the news media (Chapter 2). In this setting:

- Important internal disputes with the president or within the congressional majority are more likely to arise (Chapter 6).
- These disputes are disproportionately likely to be featured by the news media in stories initiated by the president (Chapter 3) and by Congress (Chapter 4).
- The resulting stories of intraparty strife are among the most credible and damaging types of partisan story, particularly among independent and presidential-party viewers (Chapter 5).

All else being equal, moving to divided government decreases both the likelihood that collective communication in the presidential party will break down and the attractiveness of such stories for the news media. When combined with the postwar surge in influence of nonpartisan broadcast media, this thesis may explain the relative instability of unified government in the modern American context (Chapter 6 and Conclusion). In setting out this argument, the book proceeds as follows.

CHAPTER-BY-CHAPTER OVERVIEW

Chapter 1: "McParty": Cohesion and the Party "Brand Name"

Although considerable ink has been spilled examining individual politicians' efforts to use publicity or media campaigns to serve their political ends, far less is known about how the political parties collectively establish their reputations and images with the public. Whenever individuals collectively pool their efforts to produce a good, they face myriad potential collective-action problems, such as costs associated with coordination, conformity, and/or "free riding" (Olson 1965; Ostrom 1990). Scholars including Cox and McCubbins (1993), Kiewiet and McCubbins (1991), Rohde (1991), and Rohde, Aldrich, and Tofias (2007) explain how and why parties organize to reduce the costs of collective action as they pass legislation. Yet, we still have little understanding of the parties' efforts to foster a valuable party image through their collective communication with voters, especially across branches of government. As mentioned previously, scholars often dismiss such rhetoric as cheap talk that is unlikely to be seen or believed by voters. This perception persists despite substantial evidence that the parties take collective communication very seriously.

Some scholars argue that one party or the other has an institutional advantage in such efforts. For example, Entman (2005) concluded that the "fundamental ideological, organizational, behavioral, and financial differences between the Democrats and Republicans [make] only the latter a consistent, full-fledged partisan force in American national politics," whereas Taylor (2005) argued that Republicans enjoy a consistent "edge" in American politics because of factors such as their disproportionate electoral advantages in smaller states and areas with a growing population, superior party organizing, campaign fundraising, issue ownership of key policy areas, and message support by right-leaning think tanks and news outlets.[5] Others contend that emotional or conceptual strengths of appeals packaged by Republican candidates systematically give them the advantage in elections against more cerebral arguments from Democrats.[6]

Although I accept that various factors might converge to give one party substantial or even dominant advantages in the short term, I view the American parties as malleable entities. Each party recently has become far more ideologically cohesive and disciplined as New England and the South have realigned, and congressional districts have become more gerrymandered (Jacobson 2005). Moreover, each party can observe the strategies and techniques used by the other and try to adapt. For example, despite the assumed Republican Party advantage in campaign finance, Barack Obama's fundraising in 2008 crushed that of his Republican rival, bringing in more than *twice* as much money as the George W. Bush and Al Gore campaigns in 2000 – *combined* (Salant 2008). Republicans learned from Gore's surprisingly effective "get-out-the-vote" effort in 2000

---

[5] However, consistent with my subsequent argument, Taylor (2005, 245) explicitly argued that the Republicans would be unable to translate these conditions into a durable electoral majority, in part because of the adaptability of the Democratic Party, which allows that party to "transform itself to meet the wants of the electorate."

[6] For example, in his 1996 book, *Moral Politics: What Conservatives Know That Liberals Don't*, George Lakoff argued that part of the reason why Republicans enjoyed electoral success was because they had a better understanding of how to relate politics to key metaphors or concepts held by voters. Similarly, Drew Westin argued in his 2007 book, *Political Brain: The Role of Emotion in Deciding the Fate of the Nation*, that since at least the 1980s, Republicans have better understood and used emotional appeals than Democrats in pursuing their policy and electoral goals.

and then exceeded that effort in 2004 – only to see their efforts swamped by the Obama campaign's massive 2008 effort. In the 2004 election, Democrats had an early lead in 527-group support, which was later matched by Republicans in the same cycle.

More directly related to this study (see Chapter 1), the Republicans' apparently dominant advantage in message and branding cited by the authors mentioned herein was the result of conscious development and considerable effort by Newt Gingrich and his allies. In turn, the Democrats' recent success in this area was – at least, in part – the consequence of a deliberate and well-funded effort by liberal activists and fundraisers to create liberal think tanks, media centers, and "training camps for young progressives" (see Nichols 2005 for a discussion of the origins of the "Phoenix Group," which spearheaded this effort). Similarly, the Bush Administration's famous "message discipline" was consciously and successfully emulated by the Obama campaign. Of course, the fact that each party achieved unified control of government in the last decade is the most obvious sign that neither has a permanent hold on the reins of power.

However, while the parties exhibit an ability to mimic successful strategies and tactics, their innovations are bounded by the institutional context of American politics. In Chapter 1, I use the metaphor of parties as franchises not only to identify the incentives to brand parties collectively (which apply to all electoral parties) but also to emphasize that both American parties are exceptionally weak in their formal powers to control franchisees compared to business franchises or parties in other countries.

Understanding how and why franchises cooperate to foster their brand names enables me to trace how parties attempt to accomplish those same goals. I will also examine the corresponding difficulties that franchise operations encounter in those efforts and the institutions they have created to address these problems. The franchise problems and solutions are particularly instructive as I examine the relatively limited powers that parties possess in the United States to force members to "toe the party line."

To refine and illustrate this larger point, I provide a short case study of the 1994 Republican "Contract with America," as well as two similar Republican Party initiatives in 1980 and 1992 and a Democratic Party effort in 2006. These cases reinforce the conclusion that parties – not only individual politicians – are important units of analysis when studying modern political communication.

Chapter 2: Man Bites President: The Mediation of Partisan Communication

Even in this era of technological and communication revolutions, very little of the communication by politicians and parties is directly consumed by the citizenry; instead, most of it is delivered to voters as a condensed, highly edited package called "news."[7] Some authors argue that reporters' preferences, organizational needs, or efforts determine the news (Abramson 1990; Althaus 2003; Arterton 1984; Cater 1959; Cronkite 1998; Donohew 1965; Gans 1979; Gieber 1956, 1960; Janowitz 1975; Katz and Lazarsfeld 1955; Lichter, Rothman, and Lichter 1986; Linsky 1986; Page 1996; Patterson 1996; Schramm 1949; Singer 1997; Smoller 1990; Snider 1967; Weaver et al. 1981; Westley and MacLean 1957; White 1950; Wolfsfeld 1991). Others argue that the news media are passive conduits for information chosen by politicians (Bennett, Lawrence, and Livingston 2006; Cohen 1963; Entman and Page 1994; Hallin 1986; Kingdon 1989; Lasorsa and Reese 1990; Sigal 1973; Westlye 1991; Zaller and Chiu 2000).

In Chapter 2, I argue that politicians can exercise some control over the news-making process by carefully choosing their words; however, if they hope to hear those words on the news, they also must anticipate and adapt to the preferences and routines of journalists, who have traditionally stood between them and their public.[8]

I construct a model of the communication process that provides insight into how politicians and journalists interact to produce political news. In building this model, several well-established axioms of newsworthiness are presented that I argue encapsulate journalists' preferences over a variety of political-news content. I then build on the Chapter 1 discussion of party-message discipline to construct a typology of partisan messages. Finally, I construct a two-factor model of news outcomes based on the probabilities of politicians making particular statements and journalists broadcasting those statements. This model allows predictions to be made

---

[7] Even in the heat of the 2008 presidential primary contest, a Pew (2008b) study showed that only 14% of Americans received e-mail messages from political groups or organizations about the campaign, and only 8% reported visiting candidate websites. In contrast, 40% reported "regularly" learning something about the campaign from local TV news and 38% from cable news programs.

[8] As discussed in the book's Conclusion, however, new media are increasingly eroding the relatively monolithic control of the "mainstream media" on mass communication. It is interesting that this transition apparently has been accompanied by greater partisanship in both professional and amateur news.

regarding which stories are most or least likely to appear in a variety of media and institutional contexts.

Based on this analysis, I contend that even ideologically "balanced" journalists can have a predictable and significant influence on the partisan composition of political news. In particular, the model predicts that:

- The news media undermine the presidential party's ability to support its chief executive.
- Conflicts or disagreements between the president and his congressional party are extremely likely to be broadcast if available to the media.
- The nonpresidential party has equivalent "message success" regardless of the content of its statement and is only slightly less newsworthy when moving to minority-party status in unified government.

Chapter 3: Breaking the "Eleventh Commandment": Party Cohesion in Presidential News

In what was called his "eleventh commandment," Ronald Reagan famously warned his fellow Republicans, "Thou shall not speak ill of a fellow Republican."[9] Chapter 3 tests the Chapter 2 predictions by examining network evening news broadcasts and other data. The two main data sources for this analysis provide content analyses of the evening news, spanning thousands of individual broadcasts and statements.

To test the predictions of the model, I first determine the frequency with which the president, his party, and the nonpresidential party support or criticize one another in the news. The results confirm that parties repeatedly have broken Reagan's eleventh commandment. Although both parties predictably attack one another, the content analyses highlight remarkable public discord within the presidential party across several presidencies, with negative evaluations comprising about two thirds of all broadcast presidential evaluations by members of his own party. The preponderance of negative evaluations is difficult to explain as a "fair" sample by journalists unless the presidential party actually disagrees twice as often as it agrees with the president.

However, evaluating the theory using only news-content analysis is difficult because the analyses can only measure stories that actually appear

---

[9] Although the term has become closely identified with Reagan, in his autobiography, Reagan actually gave credit for the prohibition to Gaylord Parkinson, Chair of the California Republican Party, who invoked it during the contentious 1966 Republican gubernatorial primary (Reagan 1990, 150).

on the news. As such, it is difficult to distinguish cases in which parties chose not to make a statement from those in which a statement was made but was rejected by the news media. To address this concern, three methods are used to investigate the news media's independent influence. In the first method, I use *Congressional Quarterly*'s presidential-support scores as a proxy to measure congressional support of the president (as opposed to support as shown in the media). In the second method, I use presidential approval ratings as a proxy for the presidential party's willingness to criticize the president. Finally, I conduct a case study of coverage of the North American Free Trade Agreement (NAFTA) ratification debate, in which news media expectations regarding support and opposition from the presidential party may have shifted. All three methods support the notion that the media typically appear to over-represent criticism and under-represent praise of the president by his congressional party.

Overall, the patterns of intraparty evaluations discussed here correspond well to the needs of the news media, which typically have the final say over which party messages are transmitted to the public. Members of the presidential party appear to have extremely limited capacity to praise the president in the news media, even when they control the legislature. Conversely, when they are willing to criticize the president, they find journalists an eager conduit for their words.

Chapter 4: Life in the Shadows: The President's Legislative Party as Newsmaker

Chapters 2 and 3 examine the difficulties that the parties face in controlling their communication through the news media. Specifically, those chapters highlight the obstacles faced by members of the presidential party in Congress as they attempt to praise their chief executive. In Chapter 4, I turn to stories on Congress's home turf.

The chapter begins by situating this inquiry in the broader research on congressional news. Next, the conditions that might be expected to enhance rhetorical unity within the congressional parties are examined, including ideological and pragmatic connections between partisans and the presence of party-communication institutions. This is followed by an examination of how institutional control of Congress and the presidency can influence a legislative party's ability to communicate unified messages to the public. I argue that although a congressional party should receive greater coverage when it is in the majority (i.e., the Majority Hypothesis), the president harms his congressional comrades by supplanting them as the party's principal spokesperson in the news media and by increasing the stature and newsworthiness of the nonpresidential party (i.e., the Presidential Substitution Hypothesis).

To test these hypotheses, I examine news messages by and about members of Congress. By examining evening news coverage of the congressional parties, I find that the nonpresidential party appears to receive a substantial bonus in its volume of coverage beyond what might have been predicted by its majority or minority status. Also consistent with my predictions, the presidential party has great difficulty gaining coverage of self-praise when faced with an opposing majority and a president of its own party. In contrast, the majority party in divided government faces an ideal environment for self-promotion. Consistent with both hypotheses, the presidential party's gain from its majority status in unified government is largely offset by its association with the president, leading to near-parity with the nonpresidential party.

I find that although members of the presidential party apparently treat one another slightly better than they treat their president in their aggregate presentation in the news, they still fail to present consistent and favorable messages to the public. Conversely, the nonpresidential party actually benefits from the presence of a "hostile" president, even when it is in the minority.

Chapter 5: When Politicians Attack: The Political Implications of Partisan Conflict in the Media

Previous chapters determined that partisans often face great difficulty in getting the media to report them as supporting their comrades, while internal disputes – especially those erupting within the governing party – generally receive prominent coverage. Chapter 5 moves beyond the examination of how such messages are selected by politicians and the media and instead focuses on the effects of those messages on public opinion. Although prior research provided basic insights about the potential effects of different types of elite messages, this chapter examines exactly when and how partisan conflict in the media affects public opinion about the president.

I begin by developing a typology of partisan messages in the media, determining the likely effects of those messages based on their general content and the credibility of the speaker. Specifically, I argue that partisan messages are more credible to a viewer when (1) the speaker shares the viewer's party affiliation; and (2) the message imposes some cost on the speaker. I then derive several testable hypotheses regarding the likely credibility of different types of partisan messages for different viewers, followed by a test of those predictions using the massive collection of content analysis data first explored in Chapter 2, data on presidential approval, and the results of two experiments. Consistent with my predictions, I find that:

- Presidential-party criticism of the president is exceptionally damaging to his standing, particularly among his fellow partisans in the electorate and independents.
- Praise from the opposing party should be the most beneficial type of message for the president among members of the nonpresidential party and independents.

Finally, these findings are linked explicitly to each party's seemingly paradoxical convention-speaker choices in 2004 and 2008, as well as liberal activists' subsequent efforts to defeat former Democratic vice-presidential candidate Senator Joe Lieberman (I-CT) in his reelection bid.

Chapter 6: With Enemies Like These: The Silver Lining of Divided Government

Among many influential scholars of American politics, the Constitution's system of competing institutions often has been viewed as a debilitating sickness, with unified party government prescribed as a cure. For example, Woodrow Wilson observed that to achieve "harmonious, consistent, and responsible party government" one needed to connect the president as closely as possible with his party in Congress.[10]

A central point of this book is that unified government presents its own severe challenges for the governing party. In fact, a party controlling the presidency might communicate a consistent brand name as well or even better if its members were relegated to the minority in Congress.[11] In addition, as discussed previously regarding the case of Lincoln Chafee, there are situations in which there are intense pressures for elements of the party to "go it alone" and distance themselves from their peers. Although such incentives have been observed at the individual level in cases such as

---

[10] Wilson, quoted in Ranney (1954).

[11] An important caveat to this statement is the assumption that achieving – and maintaining – unified government with a supermajority in the Senate is exceptionally challenging in current American politics.

members "running against Congress" or distancing themselves from the party, this behavior also can occur at the institutional level. To the degree to which different branches of a party are willing to attempt to establish their own party image with the public, the advantages that Wilson and others ascribed to unified party government are diminished.

Chapter 6 begins with a brief case study of the short-lived Republican unified government of 2001. The recent history of unified and divided government in the American context is briefly discussed, followed by the Republicans' disastrous experience with unified government following the 2004 election. Next, the scholarly literature on party government is examined, with particular attention to the recent debate regarding the legislative productivity of unified versus divided government. This discussion highlights the useful way in which divided government credibly allows each party to avoid responsibility for governmental failures in contrast to the accountability that accompanies unified control of government. The latter situation is exacerbated by the ability of the minority party in the Senate to block the efforts of the "governing" party through the filibuster power, putting any governing party without supermajorities in the Senate in the uncomfortable position of sharing power with the minority party without sharing any blame for failure.

I then return to the main focus of this book: partisan communication. In doing so, I conclude that divided government "uncircles" the presidential-party "firing squad" and reins in the most damaging types of messages about the presidential party: intraparty criticism. By presenting a credible common foe, the Democratic majority helped the Republicans rally their rhetoric, decreasing such intraparty criticism and sharpening cross-party attacks.[12]

I then conclude Chapter 6 with a case study of the 1996 presidential election, in which Bill Clinton and the opposing Republican Congress shaped their respective party "brand names" at the cost of their out-of-power peers. Clinton's technique of "triangulation" has been widely

---

[12] Although the September 11 attacks also helped Bush rally his fellow Republicans to his side, the switch to divided government had already produced noticeable differences in Republican rhetoric. According to the 2001 Center for Media and Public Affairs (CMPA) daily content analysis (see Chapter 3) – even when I exclude post–9/11 evaluations and evaluations by Jeffords himself (whose inclusion biases the results more strongly in my predicted direction) – there was a substantial decrease in intraparty Republican criticism and an increase in preferred Republican messages *after* Jeffords left the party, despite the fact that Jeffords's Republican tenure included Bush's "honeymoon" period following the inauguration.

noted; however, it is also important that the increasing distance between the electoral fortunes of presidential and congressional party members did not occur *despite* the common bond of party but rather *because* of it. Prior to 1994, the Democratic majorities in the House and Senate regularly and aggressively competed with Clinton to define and articulate "Democratic" policies in health care, the budget, trade policy, foreign and military affairs, and other arenas. When relegated to the minority in 1994, congressional Democrats lost much of their independent ability to initiate news or affect legislative outcomes. The congressional Democrats' "junior" status within the party thus allowed Clinton to repudiate long-standing Democratic policy positions (most notably through the far-reaching Welfare Reform Act) with remarkably little public opposition from his party.[13]

Conclusion: Uncircling the Firing Squad: Party Cohesion in a New Media Era

This book identifies a profound irony of American politics, at least within the realm of partisan communication: Unified party control of government often begets party discord, particularly in the media. To make matters worse, the book also shows the dire consequences that political parties face when they "circle the firing squad" and attack one another.

Although parties inevitably suffer from internal squabbles, in unified government both the president and his legislative party have legitimate claims of authority to represent their party. Given the differing preferences that inevitably arise (see Chapter 1), fellow partisans must jockey to get their preferred items on the agenda. Making matters worse, any friction in the governing party is exceedingly newsworthy and exceedingly damaging to the public support for the president and his administration. In divided government, conversely, the presidential party in Congress is demoted to junior partner in this relationship, heavily dependent on the president to represent and fight for its interests in conflicts with the majority party.

Because the presidential party has suffered the most from party factional warfare, it potentially has the most to gain by changing it. Unfortunately, as James Madison observed in Federalist #10 (1787), cures for the mischief of faction are generally worse than the disease. I contend

---

[13] As discussed in Chapter 3, Clinton's fellow Democrats were far more assertive in their disputes over issues such as NAFTA when they were in the majority.

that a more promising solution for the presidential party may stem from changes in the media environment. Specifically, I argue that the presidential party may be able to present a more accurate and helpful image to the public through channels of communication other than the traditional news media.

In particular, the most promising future for parties may actually be in a return to the past, at least in terms of the news media: The fact that our modern era of divided government coincides almost precisely with the rise of television news and decline of local newspaper partisanship is likely no coincidence. In fact, I argue that prevailing standards of balance and newsworthiness prior to the 1950s allowed far greater opportunities for a news organization's "preferred" party to engage in self-praise and diminished opportunities for defecting party members to be heard.

In the Conclusion, I discuss how an expansion of news outlets and evolution in standards of newsworthiness may serve to strengthen the ability of parties to communicate cohesively and that such changes may already be underway. In particular, the rise of niche, ideologically tilted mass-media outlets (e.g., the Fox News Channel) and new forms of digital outreach and mobilization on the part of the parties may enhance their ability to present positive and consistent messages, even in cases of unified government.

I

"McParty"

Cohesion and the Party "Brand Name"

.

> The strategy and marketing behind "Contract with America" is no different
> from "It's the Real Thing" for Coca-Cola or "Just Do It" for Nike.
>
> – Mary Sharkey (1994)

INTRODUCTION: "BRANDING" THE REPUBLICAN PARTY

In the midst of a busy campaign calendar, Representative Newt Gingrich (R-GA) and almost every other Republican candidate for federal
office gathered on the steps of the Capitol building for an elaborately
staged rally. During the event, the assembled Republicans pledged to
onlookers and representatives of the news media that, if elected, they
would pursue a specific, multipoint legislative agenda. All three network
evening-news broadcasts gave the rally prominent coverage, as did major
national newspapers.[1] When asked by reporters about the purpose of
the event, Gingrich conceded, "Yes, it's a media event, but it's also an
attempt at accountability." Gingrich then contrasted his own party's display of unity with the "alienation" of congressional Democrats from their
president. Unlike the out-of-power Republicans, Gingrich said, the ruling
Democrats "attack and blame each other" (Cattani 1980).

---

[1] The rally was covered within the first 10 minutes of each network's broadcast and in
the lead story segment on ABC and NBC, according to the Vanderbilt television-news
abstracts. According to LexisNexis, the event received front-page coverage in the *The
Christian Science Monitor* and less prominent coverage in the *The Washington Post* and
The New York Times.

14

FIGURE I.I. The 1980 Republican "Governing Team Day" Ceremony. Photo courtesy of the Ronald Reagan Presidential Library Foundation.

A few weeks later, the unified Republicans achieved a stunning electoral victory in the 1980 election: Not only did Ronald Reagan convincingly defeat the incumbent Democrat Jimmy Carter for the presidency, Republicans also won the Senate for the first time since 1952 and gained 33 seats in the House of Representatives. Although it is impossible to solely credit the "Governing Team Day" rally and pledge-signing with the Republicans' success, Gingrich apparently was impressed enough to return to the tactic more than a decade later with the famous 10-item "Contract with America."[2]

---

[2] In a televised interview with C-SPAN's Brian Lamb, Gingrich gave lobbyist Charles McWhorter credit for the genesis of the Contract:

"McWhorter came by to see me in 1980 and said, you know, you ought to do an event on the Capitol steps. Get every candidate out there with Reagan and Bush, and Bill Brock had sent him over, Brock liked the idea, and the Campaign committee said that they would put it together, the Reagan–Bush team signed on, and actually the forerunner of the Contract with America was a Capitol steps event in October of 1980, which was the first time, I believe, in American history, that all of the federal candidates stood on the steps together, and said, you elect us and we'll do these things. And so, Charlie McWhorter, through Bill Brock, actually became the creator of the model that we used 14 years later to be the Contract with America" (C-SPAN 1999).

Journalists covering the September 1994 Contract signing characterized it as a "publicity stunt," "hokum," a "made-for-television ceremony," a "photogenic rally," and even "duplicitous propaganda."[3] Still,
many journalists and commentators who criticized the legislative program of the Contract conceded that it had helped to clearly define the
choices in the upcoming elections.[4]

The Republicans consciously viewed the Contract with America as
a marketing tool. Rather than conceiving of the Contract as a "wish
list" of legislative preferences, Gingrich and his political action committee (GOPAC) viewed their strategy as "fundamentally and essentially a
communications plan" (Seelye, Engelberg, and Gerth 1995 [emphasis in
original]). In internal correspondence, GOPAC strategists argued that
because they did not control the media, they had to create their own
"propaganda machine" that could supply their "activists and potential
followers with ideas, information, and rhetoric" (Seelye, Engelberg, and
Gerth 1995). The Contract, then, served less as a Republican legislative
agenda than as a convenient list of poll-tested "talking points" that could
coordinate the campaign rhetoric of candidates across the country. As
one journalist observed, "The GOP 'contract' represents an attempt to
give Republican House candidates a national theme to run on. The GOP
often has sought to link its House candidates together under national election themes. . . . This year's effort represents a new level of coordination"
(Goodsell 1994).

Although the Republicans had successfully bogged down much of the
Democratic agenda prior to the 1994 election, they did not pin their hopes
solely on attacking and defeating the majority's initiatives. In the words
of one journalist, the Republicans were anxious to avoid being labeled
"the party that only says 'no'" (Goodsell 1994). Because their minority
status had prevented them from passing much of their own legislation,
Republicans instead used the Contract to help establish what they argued
was a positive electoral strategy. One journalist covering the Contract
ceremony noted, "For Republicans, the event was an opportunity to say
that they stand for something. Usually, Democrats complain that the
minority party never wants to accomplish anything and tries instead to
derail the Democrats' ideas" (Zuckman 1994). Gingrich himself argued

---

[3] These quotes appeared, respectively, in Martin (1994), Sharkey (1994), Fletcher (1994),
Cooper (1994), and an unsigned editorial in *The New York Times* on September 28,
1994.
[4] Unsigned Commentary (1994).

to his troops that President Clinton's standing with the American people was already so low "that our job is to go out and offer a clear, positive alternative...to say, 'look, we're different'" (Best 1994).[5]

In contrast to such Republican unity, congressional Democrats in 1994 sought to distance themselves from their unpopular president.[6] To do so, they tried to "switch the campaign debate from an unpopular Clinton" to the Contract with America by blasting its terms and supporters.[7] With both parties focusing their rhetoric on the Contract, campaigns across the country could converge on a common set of issues and themes, helping to further turn the election away from purely local politics.[8]

[5] Democratic Congressional Campaign Committee Chair Rahm Emanuel (D-IL) echoed this sentiment in the lead-up to the 2006 midterm election when he said that rather than just criticize Republicans' missteps or the policies of the status quo, "Democrats have an obligation to lay out to the country what [our] ideas are." He then laid out five key-issue stances for Democrats that year: "One, we make college education as universal for the 21st century that a high school education was in the 20th.... Second, we get a summit on the budget to deal with the $3 trillion of debt that's been added up in five years and structural deficits of $400 billion a year. Third, an energy policy that says in 10 years, we cut our dependence on foreign oil in half and make this a hybrid economy. Four, we create an institute on science and technology that builds for America like, the National Institutes has done for health care, we maintain our edge. And five, we have a universal health-care system over the next 10 years where if you work, you have health care" (Russert 2005b).

[6] In fact, to the horror of his fellow Democrats, Clinton actually challenged voters to turn the November midterm elections into a referendum between his policies and those embodied by the Contract. This decision was characterized by the *Los Angeles Times* as "a high-risk strategy that flies directly against the desires of many of his party's candidates.... Across the country, Democratic candidates have been distancing themselves from Clinton, trying to focus the voters on local concerns, not broad, national themes. In private meetings, many strategists have urged that the White House avoid precisely the sort of argument Clinton made Friday" (Lauter 1994, 1). Although the Republicans' unified opposition to Clinton certainly had a role in his unpopularity, one of the central ironies of this text is that during his brief period of unified government, Clinton was especially damaged by criticism by the same Democratic members of Congress who then scrambled to distance themselves as they approached the disastrous 1994 midterm election.

[7] Cooper (1994). The Democrats were generally successful at inserting their perspective into journalistic accounts of the Contract's signing ceremony. Almost all of the day's stories (i.e., 35 of 39) reported the White House view that the Contract would increase the deficit. Sound bites from Laura Tyson, Leon Panetta, and others denouncing the Contract as "Voodoo Two" also were common. The Democrats heavily criticized the fact that the GOP held a $5,000-per-plate fundraising dinner almost immediately after the Contract with America signing ceremony. In an attempt to highlight the Republican reform "hypocrisy," they sent tuxedo-clad Democratic staffers into the crowd during the ceremony with oversized novelty checks made out to Republicans.

[8] A search of the Major Newspapers Index of LexisNexis for "Contract with America" in 1994 produced 2,627 stories, 711 of which appeared on or before the election and 39 in

The 1994 election produced a historic victory for Republican candidates. Republicans achieved control of both chambers of the legislature for the first time since they had ridden into office on Eisenhower's coattails in 1952. In each case that a Republican congressional incumbent faced a Democratic challenger, the Republican won.[9] Moreover, in 35 House and 2 Senate races, Democratic incumbents were sent packing by Republican challengers. The GOP celebrated a net gain of 53 seats in the House, the largest win by either party since the late 1940s. The net gain of seven seats in the Senate was a stunning and unexpected result as well.

As I will discuss in this and subsequent chapters, the victories by Gingrich and his unified Republican party were not isolated incidents. Instead, their efforts represent the clearest success from treating parties as "brands" that are developed through conscious marketing. The Gingrich victories, along with the similar success of Democrats in the 2006 midterm election, highlight the huge potential benefits that parties can reap when they successfully coordinate their media messages – and the exceptional branding difficulties modern American parties face when achieving so-called unified control of government.

PARTIES, AMERICAN-STYLE

In contrast to the cohesive party vision pursued by Gingrich and others, the conventional view of American politicians is that of independent office-holding entrepreneurs who succeed or fail largely through their own efforts to raise money and wage strong campaigns (Agranoff 1976; Arterton 1984; Wattenberg 1996). Once in office, they stake out positions on issues and engage in constituency service to strengthen their prospects of reelection and possibly moving to higher office (Fenno 1978). Whether by cause or effect, America's independent office-holding politicians are not nearly as loyal to their political parties as their counterparts throughout Europe and in other strong party systems.

Relatively speaking, America's elected officeholders are a self-reliant breed; however, they too have always found reason to associate with a political party. Indeed, politicians have seized on the party as an instrument of collective action since the first days of the Republic.[10] Despite

---

the day following the Capitol-steps rally. These results include stories from only the 58 newspapers in the index, thereby substantially under-representing the actual number of stories across different media outlets.

[9] See Tables 1.9 and 1.14 in Stanley and Niemi (1998).

[10] The Framers of the Constitution were not enamored with the notion of party, much less a single party controlling the executive and legislative branches of government. George

being viewed by the Founders as "sores on the body politic" (Hofstadter 1969), implementation of the U.S. Constitution was followed almost immediately by the development of parties working and campaigning together to control the governing apparatus.[11]

Traditionally, social scientists struggling for a metaphor to understand how party members worked together likened parties to clubs, sports teams, bureaucracies, interest groups, corporations, or other social organizations. Although each comparison yields interesting predictions, I propose instead that parties function in a manner more closely resembling franchise businesses such as McDonald's.[12] In such businesses, a common corporate "brand name" links and benefits independent entrepreneurs scattered throughout the country. Similarly, political parties attempt collectively to foster a valued brand name to aid in campaigning and governing.[13]

By understanding how and why franchise businesses organize to foster their brand names, one may better understand how parties attempt to perform this same goal. This chapter investigates parties' logic for doing

---

Washington warned in his Farewell Address about the "baneful effects of the spirit of party" (Washington 1796). Thomas Jefferson stated flatly, "If I could not go to heaven but with a party, I would not go there at all" (cited in Aldrich 1995). James Madison's *Federalist #10* (1787) and *#51* (1788) explicitly argued that one of the benefits of the new Constitution was that it would mitigate against the violence of faction (or party) in society and in government. By increasing the size and diversity of the electorate and spreading governmental power across institutions, Madison and the Framers hoped to make it difficult for a single "cabal" to dominate society and government. Hofstadter (1969) noted the paradox that the "co-founders of the first American party system on both sides, Federalists and Republicans, were men who looked on parties as sores on the body politic."

[11] By the end of the Second Congress (1791–1793), most members identified with either the Federalists or Republicans. In the next two years, voting in the legislature began to polarize along party lines (Martis 1989, cited in Aldrich 1995).

[12] This metaphor, of course, does not originate with this text nor does the fascination with McDonald's as a corporate exemplar of a strong franchisor. Using McDonald's as an example, McCubbins first suggested the metaphor more than a decade ago. Grynaviski (2002) explicitly compared the Bucktail Party in 19th-century New York to a franchise like McDonald's. An article by Carty (2004) explored the metaphor in the context of comparative party systems, promoting the comparison of "franchise contracts" as a means of categorizing party organizations – again invoking a comparison to McDonald's. My analysis makes several contributions to this existing literature, including (1) incorporation of the literature on brand management; (2) explicit recognition of the role played by party communication in branding, as opposed to an exclusive focus on the legislative outputs of a party; and (3) recognition of the relative weakness of American parties' central control over their franchisees, particularly across branches of government.

[13] Of course, prior to civil-service reforms, political patronage provided a more tangible distributional benefit for many party supporters.

so, as well as the obstacles inherent in the American party system that impede their pursuit. I will also examine the corresponding difficulties that franchise operations encounter when trying to coordinate their brand name and the institutional adaptations they apply to mitigate these problems. The franchise problems and solutions are especially instructive as the chapter examines the relatively limited powers that parties possess in the United States to force members to "toe the party line" – particularly when compared to their European counterparts. The chapter concludes by discussing the evaporation of the last vestiges of Gingrich's "Republican Revolution" following President Bush's 2004 reelection, which illustrates the difficulties that parties face in maintaining a consistent brand name, particularly across branches of government.

WHAT IS A BRAND NAME?

There are various definitions of *brand name*. David Ogilvy, famed founder of the Ogilvy advertising empire, defined a brand name as the "intangible sum of a product's attributes: its name, packaging, and price, its history, its reputation, and the way it's advertised."[14] This concept reveals three main dimensions of a brand (Barwise, Dunham, and Ritson 2000), as follows:

- the underlying concrete attributes of the product
- the manner in which that product is presented to the public
- the image that the public holds in mind concerning the product

Each of these three dimensions is examined carefully in the political science and public-opinion literature regarding parties. However, these studies tend to view each of the three dimensions in isolation from one another. For example, some scholars focus primarily on how parties can shape their underlying reality by producing a valued record of competence through their actions in the legislature (Aldrich 1995; Aldrich and Rohde 1996; Cox and McCubbins 1993; Kiewiet and McCubbins 1991; Rohde 1991). Other scholars, particularly those who study campaigns, advertising, or rhetoric, are most concerned with the second dimension: the manner in which parties present themselves to the public through their words (Entman 1989; Franz and Goldstein 2002; Geer 1998; Hart 2000; Jamieson 1984, 1992; Jarvis 2005; Spilotes and Vavreck 2002; West 2001). Public-opinion scholars studying parties, in turn, focused

---

[14] Master-McNeil, Inc. (2003).

primarily on the third dimension – that is, examining whether people's views of the party are coherent and persistent, and how such perceptions affect voting choices (Abramson, Aldrich, and Rohde 2002; Campbell et al. 1960; Nie, Verba, and Petrocik 1976).

The primary function of a brand name is to differentiate sellers' products or services from those of their competitors. To illustrate this point, I begin with a hypothetical scenario. Imagine that you and your family are hungry while driving on an unfamiliar stretch of an interstate highway. Exiting the highway, you see two signs, one of which tells you to turn right for "Tom's Fine Restaurant" and the other indicates that you should turn left for "Alex's Cafe." Which way do you turn? How confident are you that your choice will be correct? Absent some other cue, such as the quality of the workmanship on the sign or a line of ambulances proceeding from one of the restaurants, it is difficult to see how the choice could be anything but ambivalent.

Now compare the situation to one in which one of the signs points to "McDonald's." Suddenly, despite the fact that you have never before ventured down this stretch of highway, you probably have enough information to make your choice with confidence. The fact that one restaurant is a McDonald's means you already know most of the items that are likely to be on the menu. In fact, you probably know the approximate cost, the exact ingredients, and – perhaps most important – whether you like at least some of the items offered.[15] Moreover, you also likely know other significant details about the restaurant, such as whether it uses Styrofoam to package its burgers (not anymore), how fast the service is (quite fast), and even where the bathrooms are located (to the right of the front counter, in the back).

Attaching a brand name to one competitor instantly clarifies the choice of restaurants, even when the other alternative remains unknown. Similarly, the attachment of a "Republican" or "Democrat" brand name to candidates for political office instantly identifies them as more electable than those wearing other party labels.

More important, parties also can help elected politicians overcome enormous communication costs with their constituency, particularly for members of Congress or other party members other than national leaders. No matter how diligently they practice constituent service and other

---

[15] Most adults of my generation, on request, can sing the exact ingredients of the Big Mac™ sandwich. We also have well-informed musical opinions about whether Burger King employees are upset by special orders.

home-style techniques (Fenno 1978), these politicians know that they cannot capture the attention of a sizable share of the electorate. Party membership offers an efficient way to advertise a politician's stand on issues to a far-flung, inattentive constituency. Voters might know nothing about two candidates except their party label; however, based on this simple information, they can probably construct a complex picture of their candidate's likely stands and competence on such issues as tax cuts, abortion rights, defense spending, and social-service support (Petrocik 1996; Petrocik, Benoit, and Hansen 2003). Recognizing the cheap information contained in party labels, voters rely on them – sometimes exclusively – in their candidate choices (Abramson, Aldrich, and Rohde 2002; Campbell et al. 1960; Nie, Verba, and Petrocik 1976).

How Are Valuable Brand Names Fostered?

According to a review of the business-brand–promotion literature conducted by Needham (2002), successful strategies for building a brand require four related components: simplicity, consistency, authenticity, and connection to audience aspirations.[16]

Simplicity
In an ideal world, consumers would have an incentive to research their options extensively before making a choice, particularly when their choices are personally expensive or consequential. However, in a world in which attention and information are costly, it usually makes more sense to reach decisions that are merely "good enough" – often by relying on shortcuts or heuristics.[17]

Rather than presenting every possible piece of information relating to a product in excruciating detail, producers can assist consumers in reaching decisions by highlighting a subset of information. Marketing experts argue that effective brands present "a few high-quality pieces of

---

[16] In subsequent work, Needham (2005) further refined her concepts, expanding her analysis to include six separate categories. The new listing also begins with "simplicity" but separates "aspiration" into "aspiration and values" and divides "consistency and authenticity" into "reassurance, uniqueness, and credibility."

[17] Ignorance about an issue is said to be "rational" when the cost of sufficiently educating oneself about the issue to make an informed decision outweighs any potential benefit that one could reasonably expect to gain from that decision; therefore, it would be irrational to waste time doing so. See Downs (1957); Lupia (1994); Popkin (1991); Simon (1957); and Sniderman, Brody, and Tetlock (1991).

information" and avoid "bombarding consumers with large quantities of information and ironically causing confusion" (De Chernatony and McDonald 2000, quoted in Needham 2005). McDonald's exemplifies this simplicity through its concentration on a narrow range of food offerings and a specific niche in the marketplace.[18] It also focuses its mass-media advertising on short and simple slogans or themes, such as "You deserve a break today" and "I'm lovin' it."[19]

Newt Gingrich and his fellow Republicans certainly hoped to accomplish a wide range of goals if they achieved majority control of the House in 1994. However, rather than detailing each of their desired legislative proposals or outcomes, they focused on a manageable and understandable subset of ten items. Moreover, instead of addressing those ten points as isolated objectives, the Republicans further simplified their agenda for mass consumption by consolidating it into a document they termed the "Contract with America."

Consistency

Another way to enhance the value of a brand name is to ensure that the information associated with it is consistent. Ralph Waldo Emerson's often-cited dismissal of "foolish consistency" as the "hobgoblin of little minds, adored by little statesmen and philosophers and divines" pointedly fails to identify exactly which types of consistency are, in fact, foolish.[20] If humans have difficulty processing information in general, they find processing dissonant or contradictory information to be especially tricky (Festinger 1957). Unless it is the party's goal to obfuscate its true position (Franklin 1991), consistent communication aids the party by increasing the probability that inattentive or moderately attentive viewers will

---

[18] McDonald's continues to be under intense pressure from some franchises to vary its menu. In addition to famous failures like the "McPizza," recent regional variations include the "McBrat bratwurst sandwich in the upper Midwest, McLobster Roll in New England, a hot-mustard-laden Homestyle Burger in Texas and, for Ohioans, the Brutus Buckeye Burger, a stomachful with three burger patties, three cheddar slices, lettuce, tomato and onion" (Upbin 1999). Some competitors, such as In-N-Out Burger, have done a better job of avoiding complexity in their menu offerings (see www.in-n-out .com/menu.asp). In-N-Out Burger has an interesting response to pressure for additional menu items, offering "secret" menu options that do not appear on the regular menu (see www.in-n-out.com/secretmenu.asp).

[19] See en.wikipedia.org/wiki/McDonald's_TV_campaigns_and_slogans for a complete and updated list of all major McDonald's TV campaigns and slogans from the last four decades.

[20] Quoted in Bartlett (1919).

receive its message (Zaller 1997) and that – all else being equal – the message will be believed.[21]

Recognizing the value of consistency, McDonald's is almost pathological in its pursuit of uniformity. Since the late 1950s, the chain has published an operations and training manual that details the proper operation of each restaurant. It specifies such arcane details as the thickness of each french fry (0.28 inch), the weight of an uncooked hamburger patty (1.6 ounces), the proper oil temperature for cooking french fries (335 degrees), and even the acceptable variations in sandwich toppings (the tartar sauce on the Filet-o-Fish™ can be replaced with ketchup but not mayonnaise or Special Sauce™) (Schlosser 2001).[22]

Consistency is arguably even more valuable in politics. A stable, consistent brand name is essential if a party aims to inform voters. As Representative Lindsay Graham (R-SC) observed, "The only time you get in trouble as a politician is to send mixed signals" (Sawyer 1996). For example, one of the most common campaign tactics in modern politics is to label an opponent a "flip-flopper." In the 2004 presidential election, both campaigns devoted a prominent page on their website describing alleged "flip-flops" by their opponent on major issues.[23] During the 2004 Republican National Convention, delegates even waved flip-flop beach sandals to emphasize John Kerry's alleged shifts (Stanley 2004).

Ann Lewis, Director of Communication for Bill Clinton's successful 1996 reelection campaign, specifically criticized the Kerry campaign's

---

[21] An unsavory proponent of this perspective was Hitler's chief propagandist, Joseph Goebbels, who argued that "The most brilliant propagandist technique will yield no success unless one fundamental principle is borne in mind constantly . . . it must confine itself to a few points and repeat them over and over." Indeed, an unsigned 1933 article in *Printers' Ink* explicitly recognized this link when it – while noting its authors had "no brief for Hitler's ideas in any form" – spoke approvingly of his propaganda efforts as having "depended almost entirely on slogans made effective by reiteration, made general by American advertising methods" (1933, 78).

[22] To ensure uniformity, each store must abide by McDonald's "formulas and specifications for menu items, methods of operation, inventory control, bookkeeping, accounting and marketing, trademarks and service marks, and concepts for restaurant design, signage and equipment layout" (McDonald's Corporation 2004).

[23] See Bush–Cheney '04, Inc. (2004), "John Kerry's Flip Flops," 16 April, www.georgewbush.com/KerryFlipFlops, accessed August 6, 2004; and Democratic National Committee, "The Bush Record: Top 10 Bush Flip Flops," www.democrats.org/specialreports/top10flipflops, accessed August 6, 2004.

The campaign to reelect George W. Bush even compiled an 11-minute video detailing John Kerry's alleged flip-flops on the issue of Iraq over the course of his career and in the current campaign: "Kerry Iraq Documentary." Republican National Committee (2004), www.kerryoniraq.com; accessed August 6, 2004.

message discipline, complaining that they had "a different message every two or three weeks" (Associated Press 2005). In contrast, the Chair of the Democratic National Committee, Howard Dean, praised Bush's message discipline, saying that Bush "gets on, he says a quick message, 20 seconds, repeats it four times a day, for 100 days in a row. We've got to learn to do that" (Russert 2005a). Just four years later, it became clear that at least some Democrats had learned to do exactly that. In fact, the dramatic reversal of message discipline across the parties – which pitted the tightly controlled, consistent, and thematic messaging of the Obama campaign with the almost wild gyrations of the McCain camp – led one journalist to ask, "Have the political parties switched roles this election? The normally hapless Democrats have become an imperious, on-message political machine. The habitually martial GOP, which stays on message like drill sergeants stay on GIs, lacks an overarching message this year . . . " (Erbe 2008).[24] By most accounts, the Obama White House in general (and Chief of Staff Rahm Emanuel in particular) "insists on discipline" and argues that staffers "can disagree, but you're not going to air the disagreements publicly and you're not going to undercut your sibling – or you'll pay for it at the dinner table" (Baker and Zeleny 2009).

Consistency also is vital for politicians in those circumstances when they cannot control the channel through which their messages are conveyed. Unfortunately for politicians, most of the partisan messages viewed by the public are filtered through the news media. To make matters worse, disagreement within a party is far more newsworthy than consistency (see Chapter 2). To achieve their desired message consistency, parties generally have had to pay huge advertising costs to bypass the news media's filters. In 1994, however, Gingrich explicitly recognized the Contract with America as exactly the sort of "propaganda tool" that would allow his allies to power a consistent message through the news media's filters.[25]

---

[24] Repeated gaffes by Barack Obama's running mate, Joe Biden, were a notable exception to this successful message control, with embarrassing statements that undercut the campaign's position on "clean" coal power, implied Hillary Clinton might have been a better choice for Obama's running mate, and warned that Obama would face an "international, generated crisis" in his first six months in office. However, the campaign reasserted control by cutting off Biden from questions from both the media and the public. Biden himself wistfully remarked, "I learned to just go, 'Mm, mm, mm, mm.' Walk down the line. I don't say anything anymore" (Coraso 2008).

[25] Note that as discussed in the Conclusion of this book, two factors recently allowed parties to communicate more efficiently with their partisans in the electorate. In particular, I argue that both the return of overtly partisan mass-media outlets (which had largely faded after the rise of television news) and the popularization of the World Wide Web have given parties more sympathetic – and affordable – outlets for their communication.

Authenticity

For Needham (2002), the "authenticity" of a brand indicates its ability to symbolize the "internal values" of the product or its producer. Thus, a company must not only continually repeat the same messages; the messages also must be internally consistent and connected to some empirical reality for the good being offered. In the case of McDonald's, the corporation ensures this connection through extensive annual inspections of individual restaurants.[26] Failure to pass an inspection can lead to the immediate closure of a store.[27]

In politics, authenticity most clearly implies that a record of accomplishments backs up a party's brand name. As previously discussed, most political science literature concerning party image uses this reputational motivation for collective action. According to this view, parties work together to build a valuable record to which they can point in the coming election (Cox and McCubbins 1993).

However, Gingrich's successes in 1980 and 1994, as well as the Democratic Party successes in 2006 and 2008, highlight the limitations of this view. Specifically, Gingrich and the 2006 Democrats scored their impressive electoral victories when their parties had almost nonexistent legislative records, having languished in the chamber's minority for years (or decades, for Gingrich). In Gingrich's case, the Republicans cannily used the Contract and the Governing Team Day documents to clearly commit to a program they would accomplish *if elected*, and those documents (at least, in the case of the Contract) guided their actions once they took office.[28] In 2006, Democrats combined withering allegations

---

[26] According to Love (1986, 145–6), Kroc "introduced a level of supervision that was unknown in the fast-food industry." Beginning in 1957, McDonald's instituted regular, detailed inspections of their franchisees. Using a seven-page, single-spaced "field service report," individual franchises were evaluated on "the cleanliness of the store, the quality of its food, the times and temperatures followed in cooking, and the time it took to serve customers." By the 1960s, these reports determined whether franchises would be granted licenses for additional stores. By the 1980s, McDonald's employed nearly 300 inspectors (called "field service consultants") and devoted nearly $19 million to these inspections.

[27] Love (1986, 61) argued that franchise conformity was a "bedrock" requirement for Kroc. In a tape-recorded message to his early partners, Kroc exclaimed "Now, dammit, we are not going to stand for any monkey business [from franchisees]. These guys want to sign a franchise, by God, it is a matter of buyer beware. Once they sign it, they are going to conform and we are going to hold to it that they do conform."

[28] Within the first 93 days of the congressional session, Congress voted on all ten of the Contract items. However, only two (i.e., a curb on unfunded mandates on the states and the application of federal labor laws to Congress) were approved by the Senate and

of Republican mismanagement of the Iraq War and corruption with their own positive "New Direction for America" agenda that included "health care, economic security, college affordability, energy independence, and retirement security" (Preston 2006).

Connection to Audience Aspirations

According to Bunting (2001), brand names no longer simply convey information about the product; rather, they attempt to link it to a broader philosophy or ideology. Although it is often hyperbolic, brand managers want consumers to think that not only are they better off for having bought a product but also that *the world* is better off.

From the earliest days of Ray Kroc, McDonald's has identified its core ideology using the initials QSC: Quality, Service, and Cleanliness.[29] Brands that imply world-changing ideological impacts include Macintosh computers (best exemplified by the famous "1984" Super Bowl ad and the "Think Different" campaign), Coca-Cola (the "I'd like to buy the world a Coke" ad), Saturn ("A New Kind of Car Company"), and Google ("Don't be evil"), as well as various companies that explicitly link their products to policy goals (e.g., The Body Shop's support of AIDS research and opposition to animal testing).[30]

Political parties have both an easier and a more difficult time than corporations fostering a consistent ideology. Unlike "corporate ideology," political ideology is a well-developed concept that has been studied extensively.[31] In particular, Gingrich spent considerable time prior to the

---

signed into law by Clinton. By the end of the 104th Congress, the remainder of the Contract items had been blocked by Republicans in the Senate, vetoed by Clinton, or ruled unconstitutional by the U.S. Supreme Court.

[29] McDonald's was particularly zealous in its dedication to cleanliness, devoting fully half of its store operation's manual to detailed cleaning regimens. According to Love (1986, 143), the manual specified that "every day the windows had to be cleaned, the lot hosed down, and the garbage and waste cans scrubbed. Every other day, all stainless steel in the store, including such typically ignored areas as exhaust stacks, had to be polished. Every week, the ceiling of the store had to be washed. Mopping floors and wiping counters became nearly a continuous process, and the cleaning cloth became an essential tool for every crew member. 'If you've got time to lean, you've got time to clean' was perhaps the first Krocism that infiltrated the entire system and shaped its operations philosophy." Kroc also established an intensive inspection regime to ensure that his franchisees executed these instructions to the letter.

[30] For examples, see www.thebodyshop.com/bodyshop/values/against_animal_testing.jsp, www.thebodyshop.com/bodyshop/values/defend_human_rights.jsp, and www.thebody shop.com/bodyshop/values/protect_our_planet.jsp.

[31] There are literally thousands of texts on the subject of political ideology. For example, a text for the phrase "political ideology" across the 64 journals indexed in the political

1994 election pushing his party to pursue a more aggressive, conservative, and consistent ideology. He also used GOPAC resources to recruit, train, and support like-minded politicians to his banner (Herrnson 2003). Perhaps most important, the Republicans made a concerted and public attempt to deliver on the promises of the Contract after they were elected.

Unfortunately for partisans (see the next section), conflicts over the direction of ideology within a party are inevitable, even within so-called unified parties. As addressed in Chapter 6, these disputes become more difficult to resolve when a party is in power and the disputes are tied to actual policy.

GENERAL THREATS TO BRAND NAMES

Whenever the costs and benefits of a brand are shared among individuals, there is a tendency for those individuals to minimize costs and maximize benefits, even if doing so harms the brand name. For example, if the general public has a positive image of the McDonald's brand, there is an incentive for individual owners in the chain to increase their own profitability by raising prices and/or devoting fewer resources to costly ingredients, maintenance, and cleanliness. As in Hardin's "The Tragedy of the Commons" (1968), if enough stores follow this logic, the common value of the brand eventually will be damaged beyond repair.

Even stores that are not trying to free-ride off the brand may prefer to "customize" their store to the local conditions by making changes that are inconsistent with the overall brand. For example, a local McDonald's manager might prefer to serve Big Macs with mayonnaise instead of Special Sauce or to get better contract terms from Pepsi instead of Coca-Cola. Although each change may be relatively minor, the aggregate effect of such variations from the brand diminishes the informational value for consumers and, therefore, for other stores that invested in the brand.

Specific Threats to Party Brand Names

In *Federalist #10*, James Madison (1787) observed that "As long as the reason of man continues fallible, and he is at liberty to exercise it, different opinions will be formed." Although the Republican and Democratic parties are increasingly cohesive ideologically (Bond and Fleisher 2000;

science section of JSTOR returned 2,999 hits. The same search in Amazon.com's book section returned 40,881 hits. (Searches conducted January 2, 2009.)

Jacobson 2005, 2008), it should not be surprising that conflicts still simmer within each regarding the content of their brand names.

Many of the disputes arise from fundamental disagreements in the coalitions that unite to form the parties. For example, the modern Republican Party has been described as a "motley coalition of defense hawks, religious activists, and economic conservatives" (Hook 2004), and the Democrats' internal coalitional splits have been derided at least since Will Rogers quipped, "I'm not a member of any organized party. I'm a Democrat." Although these coalitions joined together to pursue common aims, there always will be cleavages that threaten to wedge apart fellow partisans.

For example, in the years since the September 11, 2001, attacks, Democratic partisans have been deeply divided on issues of foreign policy. Some Democrats, particularly those associated with the centrist Democratic Leadership Council (DLC), argued that their party needed to support a more hawkish foreign policy. Following the attacks, then-Senator Joe Biden (D-DE) criticized a "small faction" of his party that was unwilling to support even the occasional use of force: "There are some really bright guys and women in my party who underestimate the transformative capability of military power, when coupled with a rational policy that is both preventative and nation-building in nature" (Goldberg 2005). Fellow Senator Evan Bayh (D-IN) went further, arguing that the Democrats would continue to fail electorally if they failed to increase their foreign-policy credibility: "If the American people don't trust us with their lives, they're unlikely to trust us with much else. . . . We have to brand more effectively. It's marketing" (Goldberg 2005).

However, following the invasion of Iraq, many Democrats increasingly attacked the Bush Administration's foreign policy. Their fire also was directed at Democrats that they viewed as supporting Bush, including members of the DLC. "I can't tell the difference between the positions the DLC puts forward and Republican policy," said Jack Blum, counsel for the liberal Americans for Democratic Action (Lambro 2005). Senator Joe Lieberman's (I-CT) 2006 reelection travails provide perhaps the clearest example of the potential implications of such disputes: Largely because of his support of the Bush Administration's foreign policy, Lieberman was defeated in the Democratic primary by an antiwar challenger who was supported by activists within the party (Chapter 5 discusses Lieberman's continuing conflicts with Democrats unhappy with his public stances). For their part, Republicans also publicly savaged their fellow partisans over issues like the Iraq War (Groeling and Baum 2008), social security reform (Klein 2005b; Stevenson and Toner 2005), and even the candidacy of 2008 Republican vice-presidential nominee Sarah Palin (Buckley 2008; Parker 2008).

The temptation to customize the brand is particularly strong in electoral politics, where the penalty for failing to heed constituents' preferences is ejection from office. For politicians, the ideal party brand name is one that communicates perfectly that for which a candidate stands (which presumably is a position that a majority of the voters in that candidate's district will support). If the correspondence between the brand name and the candidate's ideal positioning is close, the candidate can run an inexpensive, effective campaign by swearing fealty to his or her political party. However, on issues for which the brand name diverges significantly from the constituency's preferences – for example, Republicans in pro-choice districts – the candidate faces the constant temptation to defect from the "party line." This tension is exacerbated when defection provides the party member with greater personal exposure and opportunities to customize his or her brand name in the news media (see Chapter 2).

The American system's separation of powers further complicates a party's attempts to build a valued brand name. Specifically, the president and members of his legislative party face very different constituencies when they stand for election. The most obvious difference is the size and composition of the districts: Although every voter in a senator's state or a member's district is also in the president's district, the process of aggregating those voters can produce a very different electorate overall.

This is especially true in the case of so-called gerrymandered congressional districts, into which dense concentrations of partisans have been packed to ensure victory by that party's candidate. Recently, this process has led to more polarized congressional districts, representatives, and parties (Jacobson 2004), which in turn are less in step with their party's presidents (Rae 1998). In addition, politicians serving in these offices confront different electoral calendars and, therefore, a different time horizon for their political calculations. These difficulties are compounded by the fact that every voter in the American federal system has at least four different national elected partisan officials representing their district: a House member, a Senator, the Vice President, and the President.

Further muddling the situation for partisans, Jacobson argued, is the fact that the expectations or criteria used by citizens to make their vote choices can vary systematically according to the level of office. Thus, if presidents are selected primarily on the basis of their ability to provide collective goods like low tax rates, a strong economy, balanced budgets, low inflation, a strong defense, or smaller government, they may prefer a different brand name than members of Congress rewarded for "bringing home the bacon" to voters in their districts (Jacobson 1990).

This tension was clearly illustrated by Gingrich's first attempt to revive the Governing Team Day strategy that had worked so well for the Republican Party in 1980. In 1992, Gingrich met at the White House with then-president George H. W. Bush to discuss the party's strategy for November. Well before the conventions, national polls showed President Bush locked in a tight race with Bill Clinton and Ross Perot. In their meeting, Gingrich proposed that congressional Republicans and the president join forces and offer the American public a comprehensive conservative program of action.

Many of the components of the new plan closely mirrored those in the 1980 pledge, including reduced federal spending and a tax cut.[32] In addition, the proposed legislative program promoted term limits for federal elected officials and welfare reform. Gingrich also suggested that Bush again appear with congressional Republicans in a signing ceremony on the Capitol steps to highlight their common agenda.

Bush demurred. According to Robert Teeter, Bush's campaign chairman, as Bush continued to sink in the polls, he came to regard a Capitol ceremony with Gingrich and other Republicans "not necessarily to be a plus" (Seelye, Engelberg, and Gerth 1995). As for the new contract itself, Bush remained uncommitted to Gingrich's 100-day legislative agenda. According to one Gingrich aide, the proposal gradually "evolved into the inevitability that it's not going to happen" (Seelye, Engelberg, and Gerth 1995). In any case, Bush's declining popularity made him a less attractive election partner to congressional Republicans. Far from forming a common front, many congressional Republicans began to distance themselves from Bush.[33] By the end of the election, congressional Republicans had

---

[32] According to Cattani (1980), the original 1980 pledge included cuts in Congress's own operating budget and committees; cuts in government "waste"; a 10% cut in individual tax rates; incentives for private investment in inner cities; and an increase in defense spending.

[33] In some cases, Republicans actually advertised their greater similarities to Clinton than to Bush. The *Los Angeles Times* reported shortly before the election that "From New York to Oregon, in at least five different states where Bush badly trails the Democratic presidential nominee, Republican Senate hopefuls are hedging their bets by emphasizing similarities between their views and the Arkansas governor's on issues such as the death penalty and the line-item veto" (Brownstein 1992).

actually appeared more often in the news to criticize rather than praise Bush.[34]

STRATEGIES FOR CONTROLLING "AGENCY LOSSES" TO THE BRAND NAME

The risk that members might defect from the party brand name to suit their own ends is a specific manifestation of what economists and political scientists generally refer to as *agency loss*. Agency loss is a danger in any situation in which a person or organization (i.e., the *principal*) delegates responsibility to another person or organization (i.e., the *agent*), who then has incentive to use that power for his or her own ends (Kiewiet and McCubbins 1991; Mirrlees 1976). Although these losses are a risk in any principal–agent relationship, scholars have identified four general mechanisms through which they can be constrained (albeit at a cost), as follows:

- contract design
- screening
- monitoring and reporting requirements
- institutional checks

For this analysis, the relevant principals and agents in the relationship must be identified. For the remainder of the book, the "agents" are individual partisan officeholders at the national level of government who join an existing party and alter its brand name through their words and deeds.[35] However, these same officeholders are also the primary governmental stakeholders and beneficiaries of the party branding, which complicates the analysis. The next section examines how economic institutions manage principal–agent relationships and how franchise businesses in particular might serve as a useful metaphor that helps one better understand these relationships within parties.

---

[34] See Chapter 5 for a complete analysis of these patterns of intraparty praise and criticism. As his congressional colleagues had feared, Bush still lost the general election to Bill Clinton. Despite their concerns about being dragged down by Bush (or perhaps as the result of their distinct message), congressional Republicans actually ended up with a net gain of 10 seats in the House and held even in the Senate.

[35] For simplicity, I exclude partisans at other levels of government or in the electorate from this analysis. The problems identified here become *more* severe as greater numbers of speakers or stakeholders become involved in defining the party brand name.

INSTITUTIONS AS BRAND-AIDS

Since ancient times, brand names have been used to serve commercial interests.[36] Today, businesses are still the most common and successful stewards of brand names. Because of this continued connection to brands, it is tempting to use corporations as the model when examining the branding behavior of political parties.

Cox and McCubbins (1993) persuasively argued that collective-action problems in politics closely resemble many that occur in the private sphere. Therefore, they look to the "theory of the firm" (Alchian and Demsetz 1972) as a guide to explain how parties might solve these problems. In this metaphor, parties correspond to business entrepreneurs who have the following three distinguishing features:

• They are experts in monitoring worker production and preventing shirking.
• They have the right to hire, fire, and negotiate compensation for individual workers.
• They have a claim on all profits produced by their firm.[37]

Cox and McCubbins then argued that parties have an incentive to delegate the monitoring and sanctioning power to a central agent (in this case, the party leadership within the legislature), which has personal incentives to maximize the general welfare of the legislative party by bolstering the collective-party image.

However well it applies to parties within a legislature, the metaphor of party-as-firm has important limitations when applied more broadly. For example, although the leadership of a congressional party certainly has negotiating leverage over a president sharing the party label, it has nothing approaching the ability to hire – much less fire – its chief executive.[38] Compensation for workers in firms also tends to be more direct than in parties: In laying out his theory of party organization, Schlesinger (1984) explicitly argued that while parties and firms both were constrained by

---

[36] According to a glossary provided by branding specialists, Master-McNeil, Inc. (2003), "Branding dates back to ancient times, when names or marks appeared on such goods as bricks, pots, ointments and metals. In medieval Europe, trade guilds used brands to provide quality assurance for customers and legal protection for manufacturers."

[37] See Cox and McCubbins (1993, 92).

[38] As discussed in Chapter 5, members of the president's party in the legislature can severely damage the president through their criticism; however, such criticism generally also damages the overall party's image with the public.

markets, parties were distinct in that the outputs of business firms consisted largely of private goods (as opposed to the collective goods produced by parties) and that workers in firms were compensated directly for their work (rather than indirectly by the achievement of shared goals). Cox and McCubbins argued that the party leadership within the legislature can influence the collective output of the chamber by committee "stacking" (i.e., ensuring a favorable balance of supporters in the membership) and control of the legislative agenda; however, there is much less evidence of the type of private goods that firms normally provide to their workers. What is needed, then, is a party metaphor that combines the central coordination and monitoring function of the firm with collective – rather than private – good outputs. As noted previously, I argue that a specific type of business (i.e., the franchise) provides exactly this type of metaphor.

A *franchise* is a legal arrangement that begins after a company (i.e., the franchisor) has established a valuable brand name. The company then "contracts with a party [the franchisee] that wants to use the name on a nonexclusive basis to sell goods or services."[39] This contract generally charges a flat fee and grants supervisory powers to the franchisor; in turn, it grants the independent franchisee business a monopoly on the brand name within a specified geographic area (i.e., the "territory") and the rights to any profits in excess of the franchise fee. Therefore, as discussed previously, the franchisees that join have a collective benefit from maintaining the brand name but also an individual incentive to shirk responsibilities and thus maximize their local revenues.

The next section illustrates how McDonald's uses contract design, screening, monitoring and reporting requirements, and institutional checks to manage the company's relationship to its franchisees. I then examine how parties in general (and Gingrich and his allies in particular) attempt to use these same mechanisms in their relations with individual party officeholders.

Controlling Agency Loss at McDonald's

McDonald's is perhaps the most well known and successful example of a franchise operation. More than two thirds of the corporation's revenue comes from franchises or affiliates (McDonald's 2003) and it is not an exaggeration to say that McDonald's success as a worldwide corporation

---

[39] Definition adapted from the Washington School of CPAs (n.d.).

stems primarily from its successful implementation of franchising. By offloading most of the costs of the construction, maintenance, and management of new stores onto the franchisees, the McDonald's Corporation was able to expand nationwide (and worldwide) far more rapidly than its competitors (Olsen 2003). In addition to rewarding the parent company with fees and rents, the franchisees also provided continual reinvestment into the corporate brand name by contributing to McDonald's product advertising and promotion, enabling the company to spend $1.2 billion annually on advertising.[40] However, despite (or perhaps because of) the benefits that McDonald's has accrued through the actions of its franchises, it is particularly aggressive in ensuring that its franchises' actions further the corporate interest.

The primary tool that McDonald's uses to control franchises is the unusually detailed and onerous contract that every franchisee must sign. These agreements, in turn, lay the groundwork for other mechanisms of institutional control. For example, license agreements allow for inspections to ensure that franchisees adhere to McDonald's standards. In severe cases of disobedience, the company retains the right to revoke the franchise before the end of the 20-year license. This "death-penalty" option, although seldom exercised, serves as a powerful example for other franchisees.[41]

---

[40] 2001 data cited in Olsen (2003). Their 2008 advertising budget was estimated to be $1.15 billion (Advertising Age 2008).

[41] The contract gives the corporation the right to examine the franchisee's "accounts, books, tax returns, food products, preparation methods, food quality, and appearance" (Michigan Court of Appeals 2000). Moreover, it requires franchisees "to use McDonald's layout designs, maintain the building in conformance with blueprints, and obtain written consent before altering, converting, or adding to the building" (Michigan Court of Appeals 2000). One of the most famous cases involved Sandy Agate, who operated a series of successful McDonald's franchises in the 1970s. In 1975, Agate decided to buck the corporate policy of serving Coca-Cola and instead served Pepsi. Agate was soon informed that his 20-year franchise would not be renewed, and he elected to sell his franchise (Love 1986, 85). In another case, a franchisee (i.e., Bob Ahern) failed McDonald's inspections and then challenged the loss of his franchise in court. McDonald's won but could not evict Ahern because he was one of the few franchisees to own the property on which his restaurant was located. According to Love (1986, 408–9), "At 5:00 A.M. on the day after the court's decision, Shelby Yastrow, McDonald's general counsel, showed up at Ahern's store with a crew to remove the Golden Arches and the McDonald's sign.... Ahern renamed his hamburger restaurant Berney's, but he soon found new respect for the power of the McDonald's name and the wrath of its managers against those who were thought to have abused it. McDonald's opened a lavish new franchised unit – complete with an indoor Playland – a block and a half from Ahern's place. Berney's was out of business within the year."

In a move designed to give McDonald's even greater leverage over franchisees, the corporation historically has maintained ownership of the land on which most franchises are located, which also assists in the corporation's goal of screening out "bad" owners by limiting their franchise to a single restaurant.[42]

Controlling Agency Loss within Parties

Classic "strong" parties of the European model actually approximate strong franchisors like McDonald's rather well. British cabinet members, for example, traditionally have maintained collective (rather than individual) responsibility over the policies of their government and have been expected to publicly support a policy, even if they privately fought it "tooth and nail" in the Cabinet (Kingdom 1999, 404). If a minister speaks out in the House against the government's recommendation, he or she can be dismissed (Robins and Jones 1997, 74). British parties also exercise some control over parliamentary debate and discussion, including the famous British "Question Time," by planting questions, coaching answers, and crowding out undesired topics (Kingdom 1999, 387). For

---

[42] This practice originated in the early days with Ray Kroc, the "father" of the corporation:

Rather than sell blanket geographic franchises, which would grant the holder the right to build as many or as few stores as he chose in a particular area, Kroc sold only individual franchises, for a low fee of $950. This insured that operators unwilling to play by his rules could open no more than one outlet. As a landlord, Kroc could compose legal documents guaranteeing further control. And by writing leases that would force tenants to conform to corporate policy, he could more easily insure that the look, feel, and taste of McDonald's would be identical in Bangor, Maine and Butte, Montana (Schlosser 2001, 95).

Kroc would test the commitment of prospective franchisees by offering them locations far from home and by forbidding them from operating any business except the franchise. "New franchisees had to start their lives anew with just one McDonald's restaurant. Those who contradicted or ignored Kroc's directives would never get the chance to obtain a second McDonald's" (Schlosser 2001, 95). Although the corporation clearly holds the upper hand in most of its interactions with franchisees, the franchisees have continued to challenge it on a number of issues. They have banded together to fight what they view as market over-saturation as well as a variety of costly corporate initiatives, such as an effort to enforce "value" pricing and made-to-order food preparation. Other efforts include individual (Baumann 1997) and collaborative lawsuits (Alexander 2003) and lobbying for greater legal protection against the company (*Los Angeles Times*, 22 May 1997). All legislative attempts to promote greater franchise rights appear to have failed thus far, most recently with the defeat of the Small Business Franchise Act (SBFA) of 1999 (see www.franchisee.org/legislative.htm).

rank-and-file members, speaking out against the party can significantly damage their career:

"Those [members of Parliament] yearning to ascend the 'greasy pole' must define their role in conformity with a culture of obedience.... If they seek the limelight with a controversial article or challenging speech, they run the risk of incurring displeasure.... The reason for such obedience is ambition: a career is advanced through the patronage of those above" (Kingdom 1999, 357, 373).

Perhaps most important, European parties have traditionally maintained control over who runs under their brand name and in what district.[43] In the 1960s, for example, Labour Party rebels were warned, "although every dog might be permitted one bite, he should not forget that his constituency 'license' would need renewing."[44]

Conversely, American parties appear to be franchises with particularly weak central control over their membership. At the state or local level, parties traditionally try to recruit strong candidates for office (Sabato and Larson 2002); however, short of grooming competitive primary challengers, they can neither prevent people from capturing their party's nominations nor prohibit them from associating with the name brand.[45]

---

[43] For example, the British Labour Party expelled George Galloway in October 2003 when it concluded that his actions opposing the war in Iraq broke the party rule that banned "bringing the Labour Party into disrepute by behaviour that is prejudicial or grossly detrimental to the party" (BBC 2003). Galloway later returned to Parliament as a member of the Respect Coalition (BBC 2005).

[44] In this case, four of the seven left-wing members opposing Prime Minister Wilson were not selected as candidates in their home district in the next election (Kingdon 1989, 375).

[45] This current weakness stands in marked contrast to the power once held by state and local party organizations, which often could dictate their preferred slate of candidates and go so far as to arbitrarily rotate party members into and out of congressional seats. (See Reynolds 2006 for a discussion of the prior candidate-selection powers of state and local party organizations.) A contemporary example of this phenomenon was the candidacy of James L. Hart, who sought the Republican nomination in a safe Democratic district in Tennessee in 2004. Hart, who had no Republican primary opponent on the ballot, publicly endorsed the practice of eugenics shortly before the August primary election, leaving Republican officials scrambling to organize a write-in campaign for a more mainstream candidate. The write-in campaign failed, making Hart the official Republican candidate in the election (Jackson 2004). Chapter 5 discusses how liberal activists successfully opposed Senator Joe Lieberman (I-CT) in the 2006 Democratic primary for his seat. However, it is worth noting that many prominent Democrats actually campaigned for Lieberman in his primary defeat, including Barbara Boxer, Bill Clinton, Hillary Clinton, Joe Biden, Barack Obama, Daniel Inouye, Evan Bayh, Diane Feinstein, Ben Nelson, and many others.

If a member is elected, there is no contractual relationship between that member and the party, and defectors are unlikely to suffer for opposing the party in any but the most exceptional circumstances.[46] As was previously discussed, Cox and McCubbins (1993) convincingly demonstrated that parties can strongly influence Congress's legislative output by delegating to the party leadership, stacking the membership of key committees, and controlling the legislative agenda. However, even these strong legislative parties have difficulty controlling a president of the same party.[47] They also have little power to enforce their branding decisions on other party members outside the legislative and executive branches – and even less power to control which messages about their party reach the public through the news media.

Unlike voting or other forms of political action, "partisan talk" is a type of action for which there are surprisingly few institutions or venues for collective behavior: In almost all cases, partisan talk takes the form of individuals speaking.[48] National politicians enjoy considerable individual opportunities to present their own messages, all of which further their goal of fostering greater exposure and name recognition with their constituents. "Senator A" says something provocative on the Senate floor; a colleague issues a press release applauding or disputing her statement; others stake out their position on Sunday talk shows; and a lucky few

---

[46] An example of such exceptional circumstances was the Democratic Party's struggle over civil rights. For example, in 1949, the chairman of the Democratic National Committee, Senator J. Howard McGrath (D-RI) warned that "Dixiecrats" who were not cooperative with the Democratic Party's platform would be denied patronage by President Truman (*Los Angeles Times* 1949). McGrath further argued that there would be no "future value to the party" if those Democrats failed to go along with the party platform.

[47] In response to Mayhew's (1974) contention that "national swings in the congressional vote are normally judgments on what the president is doing . . . rather than what Congress is doing" (28), Cox and McCubbins (1993) somewhat weakly argued that although clearly related to swings in the aggregate House vote, presidential popularity and macroeconomic factors fail to explain much of the observed variation in partisan fortunes and that these factors might be influenced by congressional parties.

[48] The parties' quadrennial nominating conventions are the single largest exception to this rule. Although they once served as venues for bitterly contested battles within parties for the nomination, conventions are now treated like multiday choreographed "infomercials," wherein carefully scripted messages and displays of rhetorical unity are the order of the day. Even the traditional battles over the content of the party platform have been sanitized to minimize the voicing of dissent within the convention. See Novak (2004) for a description of (and complaints regarding) Republican efforts to short-circuit internal debate and conflict over their platform. As I argue in the Conclusion chapter and elsewhere (Groeling and Engstrom 2009), the demise of the partisan press deprived political parties of another venue for coherently communicating a party brand to the general public.

even end up talking to the nation on the evening news. Some "leak" information; still others speak discreetly "off the record."

These types of communication present party members with few occasions in which institutional rules require the party to speak with a single voice. Unlike actions such as votes, for which collective-decision rules typically are well developed, the competition to define party images through talk is inherently open. Every time that party members speak to the press, they must fight the temptation to craft messages that match the preferences of their particular constituency rather than their party as a whole. The risk, of course, is that such "cafeteria communication" will undermine the consistency and value of the party's image with the public. Decrying the Democrats' inability to present a clear plan for the country, one commentator argued that the root of the problem was "a political culture that flourishes among Democrats that allows them to act as if they're independents rather than members of a political party" (Freedburg 2002).

It is not surprising that parties strive to hide internal dissent from public view just as they do with internal party deliberations over votes.[49] However, there are few examples of collectively imposed rules that enforce the conformity of speech in the legislative setting, and even fewer that apply across the legislative and executive divide. Political talk exposes a potential "Achilles' heel" of party action in the American context: There is great temptation for members to defect and scant means for the collectivity to prevent such defections. Moreover, the few tools available to parties for rewarding or punishing members for their communication efforts typically are costly and often run the risk of undermining the ultimate goal of cohesive party messaging.

For example, in 2009 Senators Max Baucus (D-MT) and Charles Grassley (R-IA) were involved in very public and protracted negotiations to find a bipartisan compromise on one of the Obama Administration's key legislative initiatives: health-care reform. Because the compromises under discussion departed significantly from the preferred stances of each party, both senators faced threats "that they might lose their leadership positions if they conceded too much to the other side" and face primary

---

[49] For example, majority-party leaders have used tools such as their scheduling and committee-assignment powers to discreetly kill bills that could publicly divide the party. In 2004, then-Republican Speaker of the House J. Dennis Hastert (D-IL) went even further, announcing a new policy in which legislation would be brought to the floor for voting only if it passed approval by a "majority of the majority" – meaning only if a majority of the Republicans supported it (Babington 2004).

challengers in subsequent elections (Brownstein 2009). Similarly, moderate Democrats hesitant to support provisions of the Democrats' healthcare reform plan were targeted in hostile advertising in their home districts sponsored by pro-reform political groups (Condon 2009; O'Brien 2009a). These ads eventually were repudiated by President Obama and others, who argued that the party was ill-served by damaging the electoral chances of its own members.[50]

In addition, there is considerable confusion and competition in deciding who can and should speak for a party. Even if the legislative parties were able to "corral" their membership into a common position on an issue, they must be concerned about other officials who share their party label weighing in on the issue.[51] This is especially true when the other officials occupy the "bully pulpit" of the presidency. As demonstrated in the case of Gingrich's attempts to coordinate the Republican brand with Bush in 1992, control of the presidency both aids and complicates a party's ability to cohesively communicate a party message. While presidents have the luxury of serving four-year terms, the entire House of Representatives and a third of the Senate are always less than two years away from facing the voters' wrath.

Similarly, following his successful 2004 reelection bid, George W. Bush put Social Security reform at the top of his domestic agenda and made it a "test of his political clout" (Stevenson and Toner 2005). From the start, Bush's fellow Republicans, especially those facing their own reelection campaign in 2006, were at best wary of and at worst hostile to Bush's agenda (Hernandez 2005; Weisman and VandeHei 2005). As Representative Zach Wamp (R-TN) put it shortly after Bush's 2004 reelection, "Congress needs to stand up and hold its ground.... Any time you have a second-term president, you have an agenda the administration wants – and Congress says, 'You don't have to face reelection; we do'" (Hook 2004). A prominent Republican criticized the Bush Administration's hubris, saying, "They thought because they had slain the Kerry

---

[50] See Hecht (2009) for a state-level example of a party attempting to discipline members for undermining the party's valued brand. For an example of less costly social sanctioning of a member, see Raju (2009), which discusses the Republican reaction to the perceived extremity of Senator Jim DeMint's (R-OH) rhetoric. For an example of a "carrot" rather than a "stick," see Thrush (2009), in which Democrats appeared to provide fundraising benefits to members for their support.

[51] Subsequent chapters discuss how parties increasingly rely on centrally produced talking points or briefing materials to allow disparate members to coordinate their messages with the public.

dragon they could claim a mandate and do what they wanted to. Now they have to sell things, whether it's Iraq or stem cells or John Bolton – let alone Social Security – on their own merits" (Stevenson 2005).

Republicans were particularly concerned about tackling Social Security, long-dubbed the "Third Rail" of American politics for its tendency to kill those careless enough to touch it: "Many Republicans know the party lacks credibility on the Social Security issue.... For us to wade out there and take that on makes the party politically vulnerable," Representative Robert S. Walker (R-PA) presciently observed (Vieth and Hook 2004).

For their part, congressional Democrats rallied around their leadership and became even more united despite their minority status. As Republicans fought among themselves about the wisdom of potential reforms, House Minority Leader Nancy Pelosi demanded that Democrats unanimously oppose any GOP proposals and even "ordered Democrats not to work on bills or even hold press conferences with Republicans whom the party is trying to defeat in November" (Bacon 2006). Pelosi also was absolutely unwilling to have her party put forward any alternative reform proposal. When some Democrats asked when they might be advancing such a plan, her reply was reportedly sharp: "Never. Is never good enough for you?" When Representative Robert Wexler (D-FL) publicly proposed raising Social Security taxes, Pelosi "immediately chewed him out over the phone" and ensured his plan received only one other Democratic vote (Bacon 2006).

As Democrats surveyed the smoking aftermath of the failed Republican reforms, they took heart in the parallels that they observed between Clinton's and Bush's unified governments: "one party in control of Congress and the White House; a furor over ethics; a huge piece of long-promised domestic legislation seemingly dead in the water (now Social Security, then health care); increasing fault lines in the majority; and a surprising unity in the minority" (Toner and Hulse 2005). The historic 2006 defeat suffered by the Republicans served as a fitting "bookend" to Gingrich's 1980 and 1994 victories, as the out-of-power party turned legislative weakness into rhetorical unity and electoral success at the expense of a governing party dragged down by an unpopular chief executive.

CONCLUSION

It is worth noting that Newt Gingrich, who generally received favorable "ink" in this chapter, did not last long as Speaker of the House. After his stunning success in 1994, Gingrich was unable to achieve further gains for his party and instead watched his hard-fought majority gradually dissolve. After a particularly disastrous government shutdown in 1995 and disheartening losses in the wake of the Monica Lewinsky scandal, Gingrich was pushed in 1998 from the Speaker position he had earned just four years before. For its part, the principles embodied in the Contract with America retained their relevance within the Republican Party – if for no other reason than to stress how far the GOP strayed from its core principles while in power (Klein 2005a).

Although Gingrich's two successes were not flukes, they resulted from relatively specific circumstances. As discussed in subsequent chapters, it is no accident that Gingrich's two historic victories precisely coincided with the first two instances since the 1960s that the Democrats controlled both the presidency and Congress. Similarly, the Democrats' 2006 triumph occurred under Republican unified government. Indeed, the central paradox of this book is that achieving unified institutional power across branches of government can disastrously undermine the value of the party brand name and expose party members to increased risks at the polls. It is a lesson that Democrats should take to heart as they now take the reins of power for the first time in more than a decade.

2

Man Bites President

The Mediation of Partisan Communication

> It's true: The news media are biased. We're biased in favor of change, as
> opposed to the status quo. We're biased in favor of bad news, rather than
> good news. We're biased in favor of conflict rather than harmony.
>
> – David Shaw, *Los Angeles Times*[1]

INTRODUCTION

In the midst of then-Vice President Al Gore's post-election challenge to
George W. Bush's victory in Florida, Gore telephoned his running mate,
Joe Lieberman, as well as congressional leaders Representative Richard
Gephardt (D-MO) and Senator Tom Daschle (D-SD). This conference
call would not have been unusual except for one detail: Most such calls
are not broadcast live on television by CNN.[2]

In an obviously scripted conversation, Gore and Lieberman began by
stiffly relating recent developments in their vote-challenge campaign and
offering thanks to the congressional Democrats for their continued support. The congressional leaders, in turn, played their part by repeatedly
emphasizing the "overwhelming support" for Gore's challenge among
Democratic members of Congress.[3]

---

[1] David Shaw (2003), "Media Matters: The More Pernicious Bias Is Less Substance,
More Fluff." *Los Angeles Times*, 19 January; www.latimes.com/news/custom/showcase/
la-ca-shaw19jan19.story.

[2] CNN's Frank Sesno self-consciously noted that this "was not an intimate little conversation" but rather was intended for public consumption. If so, it succeeded, as CNN and
other news channels repeated the tape of the conversation throughout the day.

[3] Transcript #00112702V54 (2000), CNN Live Event/Special, 27 November. LexisNexis:
4 December.

This incident is noteworthy not so much because of the content of the conversation, which was exactly the sort of support for Gore one would expect to hear from his fellow Democrats; rather, it is interesting because of the almost embarrassing lengths that Gore and company went to in an attempt to get the support covered in the news media. Why would the Democratic leaders feel obliged to engage in amateur theatrics to get their message broadcast?

The short answer is that Gore and his team did what they believed was necessary to make an unappealing story more palatable to journalists. According to a post-election insider account of the incident in *The Washington Post*, Gore's advisers realized that the conversation appeared "staged and corny," but they nevertheless were intent on using the event to send the message that "the party was rallying behind Gore."[4] Implicit in the advisers' reasoning is the notion that without the elaborate stagecraft, the desired message of intraparty support for Gore would not have reached citizens at all.[5]

Politicians and the News Media

Citizens observe very little of what politicians do and say. Indeed, with the possible exception of debates, politicians' extensive efforts to reach citizens directly through advertising, speeches, and similar activities are likely to be consumed only by a small subset of potential viewers. Instead, the most common means of contact between national party members and their constituents is through the chopped, formed, and pressed packages called "news." As discussed in the Introduction chapter, politicians and parties believe that their political success critically depends on the messages that the public receives through mass media. Because of this dependency, politicians and parties have spent increasing amounts of time and resources in an attempt to manage their image and statements in the news media.

The likelihood that politicians will succeed in these attempts remains a matter of continued scholarly debate. Some authors argue that the attitudes, strategies, or efforts of journalists or news organizations largely

---

4 In particular, Democrats were eager to preempt stories that highlighted impatience with Gore's challenge among rank-and-file Democrats. Gore advisers Chris Lehane and Mark Fabiani are given credit for devising the call (Kurtz 2000).

5 In the same account, Kurtz (2000) noted, "The cable networks kept replaying the phone call, with Gore stiffly reciting his talking points from his dining room, and that, the media advisers felt, *was better than nothing*" [emphasis added].

determine the content of the news in opposition to or independent from powerful political elites (Althaus 2003; Arterton 1984; Cronkite 1998; Donohew 1965; Gans 1979; Gieber 1956, 1960; Janowitz 1975; Katz and Lazarsfeld 1955; Lichter, Rothman, and Lichter 1986; Page 1996; Patterson 1996; Schramm 1949; Singer 1997; Snider 1967; Weaver et al. 1981; Westley and MacLean 1957; White 1950; Wolfsfeld 1991). Journalists perceive their role as "watchdogs" guarding the public against powerful interests. Their organizations have traditionally controlled the final, crucial steps in the news process – deciding what is news and delivering it to the public. These "gatekeepers" and "agenda-setters" are thus active participants in determining the final content of that news.[6] In the extreme, news outlets are viewed as a "fourth branch of government," able to independently use their connection with the public to rally opinion and force political change or reform – often in direct opposition to political elites (Abramson 1990; Cater 1959; Linsky 1986; Smoller 1990).

However, other scholars argue that journalists should be viewed as relatively passive conduits for information that is chosen individually or collectively by politicians or other elite sources (Bennett 1990; Bennett, Lawrence, and Livingston 2006; Cohen 1963; Entman and Page 1994; Hallin 1986; Kingdon 1989; Lasorsa and Reese 1990; Sigal 1973; Westlye 1991; Zaller and Chiu 2000). Although disputes among the elite sources or particularly dramatic events might allow journalists some discretion, these scholars generally view the media as passive and nonstrategic, like a conveyor belt faithfully delivering the views of elites (Bennett, Lawrence, and Livingston 2006; Zaller and Chiu 2000).[7]

Here, I contend that while politicians can and do exercise some control over their image in the news through what they choose to do and say, they must generally account for and adapt to the preferences and routines

---

[6] As Cater (1959, 7) elegantly stated, "The reporter is the recorder of government but he is also a participant. He operates in a system in which power is divided. He as much as anyone, and more than a great many, helps to shape the course of government. He is the indispensable broker and middleman among the subgovernments of Washington. He can choose from among the myriad events that seethe beneath the surface of government which to describe, which to ignore."

[7] The view that journalists "index" their coverage to reflect opinion in dominant institutional power blocs may not be inconsistent with the argument that journalists base their coverage on shared norms or professional values. In fact, Bennett (1990) persuasively argues that indexing can be viewed as a professional norm that serves a useful function for journalists (but, arguably, not the public).

of journalists if they hope to have their statements appear on the news.[8] In the case of Gore and his fellow Democrats, they feared that their basic story (i.e., "Democrats say they support their fellow Democrat Gore") would not be sufficiently "newsworthy" to receive wide coverage. They therefore resorted to theatrics to get their message across to the public.

In this chapter, I argue that Gore and his fellow Democrats were correct to doubt the attractiveness of their unadorned message of party unity: Common standards of newsworthiness make such statements of intraparty support extremely unattractive for journalists.[9] In the

---

[8] This approach is consistent with the exchange analysis of Grossman and Rourke (1976), as well as Gans (1979), Paletz and Entman (1981), and Cook (1998), and to portions of the "gatekeeper" literature that view journalists and editors as constrained by their audience's preferences (see, e.g., Westley and MacLean 1957) or the "newsworthiness" of the event being covered (Galtung and Ruge 1965). It is also at least somewhat consistent with Entman's (2004) cascading activation model, in that the sequence of this analysis begins with the executive branch – with Congress in a role of designated respondent – and posits an active role for both journalists and the general public in the flow of communication. However, Entman's model focuses more broadly on the propagation and acceptance of frames rather than evaluative partisan statements. A key focus of his model is whether the frames advanced by the president and his administration are congruent with the dominant cultural schema (e.g., the Cold War paradigm prior to the collapse of the Soviet Union) and whether journalists may or may not be free to advance critical counterframes. As I discuss later, because my model predicts the choice of which partisan comments to include in a story – rather than the frame used to interpret them or the statements made by journalists or other sources – Entman's analysis is mostly orthogonal to the analysis presented herein.

[9] This argument represents perhaps my theory's greatest divergence from the indexing theory's predictions regarding political power and press coverage. Similar to indexing, I premise my argument on the newsworthiness of powerful political actors (see the Authority Axiom in this chapter) and argue that when the presidency and Congress are controlled by opposing parties, press coverage reflects that disagreement and allows reporters substantial freedom to select favorable or negative coverage from the warring sources. (However, see Chapter 4's discussion of the comparative obscurity of the president's legislative party in times of divided government.) In addition, my predictions for press coverage in instances in which the president and opposing party are unified behind a policy also should reflect that of indexing (i.e., dominant coverage of the consensus), although my argument would predict that even a small group of dissenters within either party should receive considerable coverage. In the case of unified government, however, I depart from one of the core notions of indexing: that members of "institutional power blocs likely to influence the outcome of a situation" (Bennett 1990, 107) should receive more coverage and attention than ineffectual blocs or those out of power. In fact, as discussed later in this chapter, I argue that the presidential party in Congress – which is clearly the dominant and decisive power in instances of unified government – actually has less control over the messages it delivers to the public than do members of the out-of-power minority party. Moreover, after providing empirical evidence for these paradoxical patterns of coverage, I argue that the undesirable party messages to which the media are drawn are precisely those that have the greatest impact on public opinion – further undermining the ability of

following sections, I construct a model of the communication process to provide insight into how partisan sources and journalists interact to produce political news. In building this model, I first present several axioms of newsworthiness that I contend encapsulate widely held journalistic preferences regarding news content. Building on the Chapter 1 discussion of party brand names and message discipline, I then construct a typology of partisan messages to predict which stories are most likely to be offered by partisans and accepted by journalists in various media and institutional contexts.

Based on this analysis, I show that even ideologically "balanced" journalists can have a predictable and significant influence on the partisan composition of political news. Most important, the evidence presented here indicates that the news media weaken the ability of the president's party in Congress to present its preferred branding and praise its chief executive, particularly in the case of unified government. These predictions are then tested empirically in Chapters 3 and 4 through an examination of partisan responses to news initiated by the president and members of Congress, respectively.

WHAT IS NEWSWORTHY?

Journalists receive attention first because they have the last word in the content of political news.[10] Excluding crises or ceremonial events such as the State of the Union Address, journalists stand between politicians and their ultimate goal – that is, communication with citizens.[11]

---

the governing party to steer public opinion, even as it controls the levers of government. My predictions may be observationally equivalent to Entman's cascade model (2004), at least in instances in which the president is unpopular, as elites and journalists choose to oppose or distance themselves from the president. My argument diverges from Entman's in instances in which the president is popular, where I still expect to see disproportionate coverage of opposition from Congress, particularly from within his own party.

[10] Of course, citizens have the choice not to consume a particular news source. However, one of the difficulties that television-news consumers face in deciding whether to allocate their attention to a news story is that they are generally unable to determine its quality until after they have already consumed it (Hamilton 2004; McManus 1992). As discussed in this book's Conclusion chapter, the rise of new media has undercut the agenda-setting power of traditional media and increasingly offers consumers news that favors a specific partisan viewpoint.

[11] Changes in the media environment occasionally allow politicians to circumvent the press and communicate with the public directly. Three significant historical examples are paid advertising, partisan-affiliated newspapers, and the congressional franking privilege.

Moreover, journalists – at least in the modern era – strongly value their professionalism and independence from politicians (Janowitz 1975), as well as their ability to exercise control over their "journalistic voice" in the news (Zaller n.d.).

Scholars have identified certain characteristics of stories or sources that make them more desirable for journalists as they select the final news product. In this section, I examine several of those characteristics in more depth and present axioms of newsworthiness that summarize their influence on the content of the news. I argue that in general, journalists are more likely to air a story if it is novel, conflictual, and balanced, and if it involves authoritative political actors.

The following discussion provides an empirical and common-sense foundation for these axioms, all of which are grounded in both intuitive logic and prior studies of journalism. For example, Graber (1997, 118–22) identifies four elements that make stories more likely to appear in American news: (1) novelty and excitement, (2) familiarity and similarity, (3) conflict and violence, and (4) neglect of major societal problems. Because my model is generally agnostic about the subject of the evaluation, Graber's fourth element does not apply here. Her discussion of the first three elements, however, maps closely to my Novelty, Authority, and Conflict Axioms.

Although Graber criticizes the news for relying on the aforementioned characteristics, the Project for Excellence in Journalism (PEJ) ironically reiterates many of them in its criteria for evaluating news quality. PEJ examines local newscast quality by measuring their adherence to "simple values: community relevance, focus on the significant, covering a broad range of topics, authoritative sourcing in stories, presenting more than one point of view, citing multiple sources, level of enterprise, professionalism – or understandability of a story – and level of sensationalism – defined as the repetition of gore, violence, thrilling action or implied disgrace, with the intention of luring an audience to the story rather than to convey information" (Project for Excellence in Journalism 2002).

Paid advertising remains a ready (if costly) tool, but the latter two options have been undercut by the decline of partisan newspapers in the 19th (Hamilton 2004) and 20th (Groeling and Engstrom 2009) centuries and by increasing restrictions on the franking privilege (Roff 2009). Newer innovations include e-mail, websites, and web-based video resources such as YouTube channels. Until recently, these alternatives generally have been more expensive, less credible, and narrower in audience than the "mainstream" press. The Conclusion chapter of this book further discusses recent trends in new media.

For PEJ, a good story focus means – among other things – that the newscast covers "unusual" events (which corresponds to my Novelty Axiom). Its point-of-view criterion measures the "balance, fairness, and credibility" of a story chiefly by noting "whether the story had multiple points of view" (which corresponds to my Balance Axiom). Finally, PEJ (2002) noted, "Newscasts should be authoritative to be credible. A good yardstick is the quality of one's sources" (which corresponds to my Authority Axiom).[12]

Novelty

The first and most obvious characteristic of newsworthiness is that it places a premium on stories that are actually *new*. Informing readers or viewers of unexpected, inconsistent, novel, or surprising information is the core value provided by news organizations. In fact, without novelty it makes little sense to speak of "news" organizations at all. As ABC's John Cochran observes, "We do try to find places where we can surprise people.... If you can find a surprise, you've got to find a way to get them in the tent" (Kurtz 1998). Graber (1997, 118) acknowledges this same tendency when she notes, "Sensational and novel occurrences often drown out news of more lasting significance that lacks excitement." Hutchings (2003) argues that such unexpected information also should be especially valuable for citizens in a democracy as they try to hold their representatives accountable.

Journalists search for the sensational and new in politics in a relatively narrow segment of society and (as I discuss in my Authority Axiom) particularly within the rarefied air of official Washington (Bennett 1990; Graber 1997; Hallin 1986; Lippmann 1920; Sigal 1973). However, although journalists' routines, beats, and norms constrain the actors likely to appear in their stories, reporters strongly resist attempts by political actors to deliver "scripted," consistent messages to the public. CBS's Chief White House Correspondent noted in regard to covering the 2004 Republican National Convention that conventions "are so heavily scripted these

---

[12] I made an explicit decision here not to derive the axioms from another assumed set of first principles, such as an appeal to a profit motive, preferences over political outcomes, likelihood to enhance public information, and so forth. Several excellent studies do this type of analysis (see, e.g., Bovitz, Druckman, and Lupia 2002; Hamilton 2004) from such first principles; however, extending my model in this way would provide little additional explanatory power and would substantially complicate the narrative presented herein.

days... our job... is to find the inconsistency here, to find the people who aren't quite agreeing with the script that's going on on any given convention night, to get behind the story"[13] (Kurtz 2004).

Similarly, journalists looking for news at Bush press conferences described their interactions with the president as a "contest between Bush's desire to repeat his previously articulated views ('sticking a tape in the VCR,' as one frequent Bush questioner put it), and the reporters' quest to elicit something that will contribute to democracy, not to mention getting them on television or the front page" (Allen 2004). As CNN's Dana Bash stated, "Bush, like most skilled politicians, will tend to answer the way he wants, no matter what the question. The hardest thing is to ask the question in a way he can't do that" (Allen 2004).

This leads me to propose what I call the *Novelty Axiom*, as follows:

> *Novelty Axiom*: All else being equal, journalists prefer stories that contain new, inconsistent, or unexpected information to stories presenting old, consistent, or expected information.

Conflict

The second characteristic of "good" news, ironically, is a preference for bad news. Authors including Cappella and Jamieson (1997), Patterson (1996), Robinson (1976), and Sabato (1991) observe that while negativity and conflict have long been staples of American journalism, the news media have increasingly embraced "attack journalism" and cynicism since the 1960s. Regardless of whether the shift is attributed to

---

[13] Following is the full exchange between the host and Roberts (Kurtz 2004):

Kurtz: Is there a tension, John Roberts, between the show, the infomercial that the parties put on at events like this and the media's attempt to kind of cut through the propaganda, to provide a reality check, if you will?

Roberts: Oh, definitely. I mean, these things are so heavily scripted these days, I mean, how long has it been since a convention really meant anything politically? That our job, as Debra said, is to find the inconsistency here, to find the people who aren't quite agreeing with the script that's going on on any given convention night, to get behind the story. That's what we do, is we try to get the story behind the story. One of the most important things covering the White House is, always to keep in mind, here's what they're telling us, now what aren't they telling us? And our goal over the next four days is going to be to find out what they're not telling us.

Kurtz: Perhaps the only unscripted moment will be whether the balloons above us on the roof here will drop on time, as they apparently did not in Boston.

underlying changes in competition, standards of performance, public attitudes, post–Watergate/Vietnam cynicism, or other causes, there seems to be a consensus within the scholarly literature that negativity dominates modern news coverage.[14]

Although not all politicians go as far as Former Vice President Spiro Agnew did in characterizing the media as "nattering nabobs of negativism," recent politicians appear to share the view that the press favors negativity and conflict in its story choices.[15] Early in his first year in office, President Bill Clinton already had concluded that for the media, "success and lack of discord are not as noteworthy as failure."[16] This estimation was shared by Clinton's nemesis, Newt Gingrich, when he said, "The number one fact about the news media is they love fights. . . . You have to give them confrontations. When you give them confrontations, you get attention. . . . "[17]

Journalists themselves bluntly describe their preference for conflict. In an interview on CNN's *Reliable Sources*, media critic Howard Kurtz asked a reporter about covering an apparent disagreement between President George W. Bush and his Vice President, Dick Cheney.

> *Kurtz*: Debra Saunders, will journalists be looking for conflict on issues like abortion and gay marriage, for example? Dick Cheney coming out and saying that he personally doesn't favor the constitutional amendment banning gay marriage that the president does. Will that be a storyline here?
>
> *Debra Saunders, San Francisco Chronicle*: Well, journalists are always looking for conflict. That's what we do (Kurtz 2004).

---

[14] See empirical studies such as those of Lichter and Amundson (1994), Lichter and Noyes (1995), Robinson and Sheehan (1983), and Rozell (1994), as well as several publications from the CMPA. For a contrarian view, see Chapter 5 of Zaller (n.d.), in which Zaller argues that studies of negativity overstate their results by comparing only the proportion of positive/negative stories and excluding "neutral" stories. Groeling and Kernell (1998) find evidence that journalists' decisions to air presidential-approval polls in the early 1990s reflected responsiveness to both changes and negativity in those results. Groeling (2008) finds considerable cross-party and cross-network differences in newsworthiness of such negativity between Fox and the three traditional networks.

[15] In the same speech, Agnew complained about "professional pessimists" whose theme song was "every silver lining has a cloud." In the same alliterative vein, he also characterized his stereotypical liberal critic as a "prophet of doom," the "troubadour of trouble," the "disciple of despair," and the "hopeless hypochondriacs of history." The speech is available in mp3 format at www.earthstation1.com/Spiro_Agnew.html.

[16] Clinton press conference, May 7, 1993. Clinton made the statement in response to a reporter's question as to why his job approval had dropped by 15 points in two months.

[17] Quoted in Osborne (1984).

This apparent journalistic preference for conflict or negativity leads me to propose the *Conflict Axiom*, as follows:

> *Conflict Axiom*: All else being equal, journalists prefer stories in which polit-
> ical figures attack one another to stories in which political figures praise one
> another.[18]

Balance

In this section, I discuss what determines *whose* views are likely to be considered newsworthy. Many bestselling tomes and polemics (and the occasional scholarly study) have considered whether the media favor lib-eral or conservative points of view in their coverage. The Conclusion chapter includes historical detail about this debate; here, I eschew it by remaining agnostic regarding any inherent "liberal" or "conservative" bias in the news. Instead, I follow the tradition of Tuchman (1972) and others, who argue that journalists have a strong incentive to use proce-dures or strategic "rituals" of objectivity in doing their jobs, if for no other reason than to undercut these bias accusations.[19] The main ritual that Tuchman and others discuss is presenting "both sides of the story."[20] Tuchman (1972, 665) gave the specific example of a reporter's response to a Democratic senator's claim that "A" is true:

> ... since the senator's claim to truth cannot be verified, the news consumer may accuse both the reporter and the news organization of bias (or of "favoring" the senator) if an opposing viewpoint is not presented. ... Although the reporter cannot himself confirm the truth of the senator's charge, he can contact someone who can. For instance, he can ask the Republican secretary of defense whether the senator's charge is true. ... Presenting both truth-claim "A" attributed to the senator and truth-claim "B" attributed to the secretary of defense, the newsman

---

[18] A potential objection to this axiom is the notion that cross-party praise (e.g., Senator Harry Reid [D-NV] praising George W. Bush) may be more newsworthy than cross-party criticism (e.g., Reid criticizing Bush). I argue that if this is true, it is actually a case of the Novelty Axiom having a relatively greater weight in this situation rather than a refutation of the Conflict Axiom. The interaction of the axioms is discussed at length later in this chapter.

[19] Because being perceived as a biased news outlet severely undercuts an outlet's credibility (Baum and Groeling 2008), even journalists who are truly biased may choose to conceal their bias as much as possible to maintain their credibility (and thus their influence).

[20] Another proponent of this view is Leon Sigal, who concurs that "in matters of contro-versy, [journalists] attempt to balance sources with conflicting perspectives, if not within a single story, then from one story to the next as coverage continues over time" (Sigal 1986).

may then claim he is "objective" because he has presented "both sides of the story" without favoring either man or political party.

News organizations, particularly broadcasters, have long followed this "balancing" practice. For many years, broadcast stations were required by the "equal time" provision of the Federal Communications Commission (FCC) Section 315 to treat competing candidates and parties equally in the allocation of free and paid air time.[21] Moreover, this balancing tendency is particularly evident in presidential addresses such as the State of the Union Address or weekly radio addresses. After airing the president's speech, broadcasters grant the opposing party time for "rebuttals" or "responses" to the Address. In such cases, the networks do not (1) screen the responses to ensure that they are sufficiently adversarial, (2) consider the opposing party's majority or minority status in making this decision, or (3) search for members of the president's party who might also oppose his speech. Instead, representatives from the opposing party are granted the airtime simply because of their membership in a party other than the president's.

Therefore, I propose the *Balance Axiom*, which states the following:

> *Balance Axiom*: All else being equal, journalists prefer stories that include both parties' views to stories that present only the views of members of a single party.[22]

Authority

The final dimension of newsworthiness predicts which political actors are likely to be considered newsworthy, regardless of any requirements for partisan balance. Graber (1997, 116) argued that the "gatekeeping process winnows the group of newsworthy people to a very small cadre of familiar and unfamiliar figures . . . predominantly political figures." Sigal

---

[21] See the Conclusion chapter for a discussion of how the FCC's so-called fairness doctrine evolved over time.

[22] It can be argued that journalists prefer to balance the views presented in a story rather than simply have a "quota" that rewards representation from each of the two parties. In other words, if there is dissent within a party, might not the media actor be happy to ignore the other party altogether and achieve balance by citing the intraparty dissidents? I exclude such formulations from the Balance Axiom for two reasons: (1) the main appeal of such internal disputes is already captured by the Novelty Axiom; and (2) such focus on a single party still leaves the journalist open to attack for bias by members of the ignored party. As a practical matter, if I were to assume that intraparty critics could satisfy the need for balance in a story, that assumption would actually strengthen, not weaken, the predicted newsworthiness of intraparty criticism.

(1986, 20) wrote that "by convention, reporters choose authoritative sources over other potential sources" and that "the higher up an official's position in government, the more authoritative a source he or she was presumed to be, and the better his or her prospects for making the news." Lippmann (1920) concurs, arguing that:

> The established leaders of any organization have great natural advantages. They are believed to have better sources of information. The books and papers are in their offices. They took part in the important conferences. They met the important people. They have responsibility. It is, therefore, easier for them to secure attention and speak in a convincing tone.[23]

This leads to the following *Authority Axiom*:

> *Authority Axiom*: All else being equal, journalists prefer sources with greater rather than lesser authority to be included in their stories.

Many scholars examined the "pecking order" of sources (Balutis 1977; Graber 1997; Robinson and Appel 1979; Tidmarch and Pitney 1985); as might be expected, due to his status as "the most powerful man in the world" – at least during the 20th and 21st centuries – the "list is headed by the incumbent president" (Graber 1997, 116).[24] Both institutional and individual politicians' newsworthiness rankings reflect the institutional authority of the sources. This leads me to propose the related *Presidential Authority Axiom*, as follows:

> *Presidential Authority Axiom*: All else being equal, journalists prefer to use the president as a source rather than any other political actor.

Within Congress, members of one party are institutionally and electorally more important than the other: members of the majority party.[25] Through its control of the institutions and procedures of Congress, the

---

[23] Quoted in Sigal (1986, 20).

[24] This president-centric coverage is in sharp contrast to the more prominent role of Congress in 19th-century news (excluding news of presidential elections and wars). See Kernell and Jacobson (1987).

[25] Some scholars draw a distinction in the authority of members of the House of Representatives and the Senate, arguing that senators are more important (Hess, 1986). Similarly, Robinson and Appel (1979, 415) conclude that "The Senate gets more coverage than the House because the Senate contains fewer heads." Although such distinctions between the houses of the legislative branch are probably important in some contexts, in the interest of parsimony, I choose to exclude them from this analysis. Similarly, although I do not dispute that some members are more "telegenic" than others, I argue that a telegenic member of the majority party would have an easier time receiving coverage than a telegenic member of the minority party, all else being equal. As Cook (1989) argues, while at one time "doing something out of the ordinary may once have been sufficient

majority party can shape the legislative process. Proposals favored by the majority are much more likely to become law, and proposals opposed by the majority are unlikely to advance in the legislative process. From this, I derive my final newsworthiness axiom, the *Majority Party Axiom*, as follows:

> *Majority Party Axiom*: All else being equal, journalists prefer to use as sources members of the majority congressional party rather than members of the minority party.

In the preceding sections I discussed the basic factors of newsworthiness that journalists consider as they choose among potential stories. In the next section I examine the categories of partisan messages from which journalists choose as they assemble the news, as well as the likelihood that each type of message will be offered by partisans.

ON MESSAGE: A TYPOLOGY OF PARTISAN MESSAGES

In Chapter 1, I discussed how the desire to build positive brand names motivates party members to convey simple, repetitive, and coherent messages that reflect their basic party ideology – mirroring the strategies employed by franchise businesses building brand names. Although parties can choose to emphasize a wide variety of messages in their communication with voters, in this chapter I will focus on four basic categories of partisan statements:

- Statements that attack the other party (cross-party attacks).
- Statements that support one's own party (intraparty praise).
- Statements that support the other party (cross-party praise).
- Statements that attack one's own party (intraparty attacks).

Generally speaking, if parties hope to build a valuable and distinct brand name with voters, their messages about themselves should be consistently positive and their messages regarding the other party should be consistently negative. Thus, in this chapter I assume that the parties prefer to broadcast messages from the first two categories (i.e., cross-party attacks and intraparty praise) and to avoid presenting messages from the last two categories (i.e., cross-party praise and intraparty attacks).

to win publicity . . . now gaining a subcommittee chair may be a necessary precondition to make the national news."

TABLE 2.1. *Types of Partisan Messages*

	Valence of Message	
Party of Source and Target	Negative	Positive
Same	*Intraparty criticism*	Intraparty praise
Different	Cross-party criticism	*Cross-party praise*

This typology serves as a unifying, meaningful, and parsimonious message metric for the hypotheses and empirical analyses of news content in subsequent chapters. Table 2.1 illustrates this categorization by dividing partisan messages according to their valence and whether their source and target are members of the same party.

If Party A is the source of the messages in Table 2.2, it typically prefers to avoid presenting damaging messages (i.e., messages in which its members criticize themselves and praise the opposing party, indicated with italics) and seeks instead to concentrate on providing beneficial messages (i.e., praising fellow partisans and criticizing members of the opposing party).

As I discussed in Chapter 1, there are situations in which party members' preferences vary from this simple characterization. For example, parties occasionally may wish to enhance their "bipartisan" image by rationing praise across the aisle. In addition, individual members sometimes face a serious incentive to defect from their fellow partisans, including the temptation to engage in "cafeteria conformity" with the national party brand or to "distance" themselves from unpopular fellow partisans.[26]

Because it underlies much of the remainder of this book, I pause here to explain my analysis's focus on this subset of partisan remarks. The choice of which types of partisan rhetoric to examine obviously excludes several types of statements – indeed, anything short of explicit praise or criticism – from many potentially important political actors (i.e., nonpartisan figures or partisans below the national level) that might alter the public's perception of the parties.

---

[26] A good indicator of such pressure on members occurs when their opponent runs advertisements that "morph" the image of the member into that of other members of that party. As former Dallas Mayor Ron Kirk, who lost a 2002 Texas Senate race, plaintively declared in his speech seeking to head the Democratic National Committee, "I know the frustration you feel to be burdened by a national party that you have to run from" (Shapiro 2005).

TABLE 2.2. *Party A's Preferred Partisan Messages, If Party A is the Source of the Message*

Target	Valence of Message	
	Negative	Positive
Party A	*Does not prefer*	**Prefers**
Party B	**Prefers**	*Does not prefer*

The theory I present here explains not only how journalists and politicians interact to construct political news, but also how the political and institutional settings of that interaction can influence the outcome. The theory also predicts the credibility of such messages to different subsets of the population. While it is clearly preferable to construct a theory and gather data that encompass all consequential forms of rhetoric from all media across time, such a massive endeavor would lack focus and clarity and consume a sizable portion of our nation's GNP. Instead, this analysis focuses on a consequential, easily identifiable, and discrete subset of information that can be reliably tracked and quantified over time and across the news-making process and that is linked to clear, testable predictions of public-opinion changes.[27]

---

[27] Such data avoid many of the analytical complications associated with other potential types of rhetoric or news content. For example, aggregating all partisan rhetoric across every medium would raise real issues of comparability and scaling. Would criticism of the president from his own party's Speaker of the House on the network evening news be the same as similar criticism from a precinct captain of his party appearing only in a small local newspaper? Similarly, tracking the origin or use of a particular term, issue, or story is typically quite difficult, much less aggregating such data across long periods. A story on health-insurance problems in 2009 plausibly might be the result of an emphasis on that issue by the White House, legislation moving through Congress, efforts by the medical industry or other interest groups, objective changes in the industry, or even a reporter falling ill or just watching the movie *Sicko* on television. Indeed, in a 2009 interview, *Sicko* director Michael Moore said, "Two years ago, I tried to get the health-care debate going, and it did eventually, and now where are we? We may not even have it. What am I supposed to do at a certain point?" (Germain 2009). Framing is also a tempting target for my analysis. However, the shifting meaning of frames across cultural settings (see, e.g., Entman's [2004] and Althaus's [2003] discussions of how the end of the Cold War affected foreign-policy frames), media presentations (Druckman 2004), and even analysts (Druckman 1999) can produce massive variation in their informational and persuasive impact. Moreover, unless clear sourcing information is provided and the frame is especially novel and syntactically distinct, it is difficult to track the origin and impact of diverse frames within a system and across time. Finally, although expanding my chosen type of rhetoric (i.e., praise or criticism of partisan targets) to include a broader number of sources, targets, and news outlets seems preferable, the cost of gathering such

Because my objective is to study party cohesion in the media, the messages I choose to analyze here have an additional advantage: These messages are so clear, unambiguous, and prominent that this subset of partisan rhetoric can be viewed as a "best case" for the parties. If parties can collectively maintain cohesive control over their message, that ability should be most evident in precisely these types of evaluations. By selecting a subset of rhetoric over which the parties have such clear preferences, I can focus greater attention on the mediating role that journalists' preferences play on the predicted outcomes.[28] The next section maps this typology of preferences onto the preferences of journalists as they construct stories.

PUTTING IT TOGETHER: BUILDING STORIES FROM MESSAGES

As I discussed in the section that introduced the Balance Axiom, reporters generally avoid overtly expressing their own opinions in stories. This is because explicitly expressing their own opinion – especially by criticizing a political party – leaves reporters extremely vulnerable to charges of bias. By "objectively" using a source to deliver and interpret the partisan information in a story, journalists can avoid being tarred with such claims of bias (Janowitz 1975; Tuchman 1972).

Similarly, once a reporter has allowed one partisan view to be expressed in a story, he or she is under pressure to present "both sides of the story" (which is the basis for the Balance Axiom). Failing to do so again exposes the reporter to charges of favoring one party over the other. Cook (1998) argues that journalists can influence story balance by "weaving" in collected comments and quotes. If a source attempts to present only one side of an issue or control a story, a journalist can respond by seeking out critical sources for balance (Cook 1998). Following Cook, I argue that the fundamental task for journalists who cover partisan issues is one of aggregation rather than pure creation: Journalists must survey the available partisan comments or positions, evaluate them on the basis of their content and source, select the "best"

---

data and the difficulty in aggregating it across such diverse sources, targets, and media mean that it must be set aside for another day on practical grounds.

[28] In other words, when the Presidential-Party Criticism Hypothesis later predicts that the presidential party in the legislature will be disproportionately unlikely to appear in the news praising the president, this will be true *despite* the fact that the party is assumed to be *trying* to praise the president.

messages, and then integrate them into an overall story package that is newsworthy.[29]

Narrowing the Scope: President-Initiated News

Of course, there is almost no limit to the stories that can be assembled from various partisan messages – for example, a Democratic mayor might be included in a story responding to presidential actions; several Republican governors might be seen criticizing a Democratic governor's actions, and so forth. Although the nature of the American political and party systems ensures that there are always hundreds – if not thousands – of potential partisan sources available for a given story, all sources are not created equal: According to the Presidential Authority Axiom, the president is a uniquely powerful and attractive source for American journalists.

Therefore, for the purposes of the hypotheses derived in this chapter, my analysis is limited to news stories initiated by a *presidential* message or action. In this situation, the media already have started constructing a story about the president and are now attempting to complete the story by getting reactions or commentary from other political actors. (In Chapter 4, I will apply the same theory to stories initiated by congressional party members.)[30]

It is easy to see why the media tend to present large amounts of presidential news. The president is often referred to as the most important man in America or even the world. Presidents are the embodiment of the executive branch of government and are viewed as America's highest-ranking elected officials.

---

[29] Most of the discussion that follows implicitly assumes that only one congressional party will be included in a presidential-story package. Theoretically, there is reason to believe that in most cases, the limited carrying capacity of television news restricts the number of sources that can appear in a single story. Empirically, the evening-news content analysis in Chapter 3 confirms that the vast majority of president-initiated stories include evaluations from only one congressional party. For example, for President George H. W. Bush and his administration, only 14 of the coded stories included evaluations from both congressional parties.

[30] In fact, the reverse process often occurs. Long-time congressional correspondent Steve Gerstel recalls writing congressional story after congressional story for United Press International (UPI), only to see the story "topped" (and his byline replaced with a White House reporter's) with a new lead from the White House if the president reacted to the congressional action in his story (Povich 1996).

Presidential dominance of the news has been demonstrated repeatedly in empirical studies of news content. One study of the *CBS Evening
News* found that 20% of a typical news broadcast dealt with presidential
news, and an astounding 97% of the broadcasts from 1969 to 1985 contained some mention of the president (Smoller 1990, 45). Other authors
found similar results by studying the *CBS Evening News* as well as *The
New York Times* and *Time* magazine (Grossman and Kumar 1981, 258).
Another study concluded that the president received about three times as
much attention on the three major networks' evening-news broadcasts in
the mid-1990s as did Congress and the U.S. Supreme Court combined
(Graber 1997, Table 9.1).

Congress: The Greek Chorus of Presidential News

If the president is well suited to initiate political stories, then congressional
sources are extremely well positioned to respond to the president. Because
of the separation of powers established by the U.S. Constitution, most
presidential initiatives require congressional acquiescence in one form or
another to succeed.[31] The news media often attempt to cover Congress
as an "institutional counterweight" to the president.[32] In fact, Kernell
(1997) argues that modern presidents often "go public" through the mass
media precisely to influence congressional votes and actions. Thus, by
presenting congressional reactions to presidential initiatives, journalists
can provide citizens with important information regarding the likely fate
of such initiatives.

In addition to their role in determining the fate of presidential initiatives, senators and representatives are important political actors in their
own right. The congressional contingent of the nonpresidential party represents the most important federal officeholders of that party, especially in
the case of divided government (e.g., situations in which the presidential
party lacks the majority in at least one of the two congressional chambers).
Legislators are also among the best-known national politicians available

---

[31] As was shown in September 1999, Congress often asserts an oversight role, even in cases
of purely executive prerogatives. At that time, President Bill Clinton offered pardons to
several Puerto Ricans jailed for their participation in terrorist activities. Despite the fact
that Congress has no constitutional role in presidential pardons, a House committee
investigating the pardons attempted to subpoena documents relating to the decision,
which was rebuffed by assertions of executive privilege. Similar congressional outcry
followed Clinton's eleventh-hour pardons of fugitive financier Marc Rich and others in
2001.

[32] Hess (1991, 103).

to the media.[33] By using such famous figures in their stories, media actors can substantially reduce the effort they devote to providing background and context to their viewers. Leading congressional figures also are exceptionally likely to be tied in the public mind to their party and therefore should exercise disproportionate influence on how the public perceives that party's brand name.

Finally, Congress is a well-established "beat" for the Washington media. Although the number of reporters on the congressional beat has varied substantially over the years, most national news organizations dedicate at least a portion of their resources to gathering the expected news coming out of Congress. Legislative parties, committees, and individual members all possess institutional resources designed to convey messages to reporters, which makes them among the most important "franchisees" contributing to their party's branding with the public (see Chapter 1).

Given these considerations, the news media typically include a congressional component in presidential stories. In fact, because of the manner in which the president dominates national political news, a sizable proportion of congressional news is also presidential. Figure 2.1 shows that when stories mentioned Congress on ABC's *World News Tonight*, they generally mentioned the president as well.[34] In addition, a content analysis undertaken by the CMPA (see Chapter 4) shows that congressional parties spend more time evaluating the president and his administration than one another in the news.[35]

---

[33] Opposition-party presidential candidates are an important exception to this rule, as are prominent governors and members of previous administrations.

[34] Search of LexisNexis; transcripts are unavailable for a comparable date range for other networks. For results at the story level, I used the following search terms: "(president or Clinton or white house) and (capitol hill or rep. or representative or senate or senator or Sen. or congress) and show (world news tonight) and not type (show)." Because LexisNexis did not index ABC at the story level for most of 1992, the figure for that year probably overstates the number of stories with both actors appearing. Also, the stories involving Hillary Clinton or former President George H. W. Bush might skew the totals. However, except for 1992, this search is likely to undercount stories in which Congress responds to a separate president-initiated story (often used when a Capitol Hill correspondent packages a separate story to complement another story by the White House correspondent). The 2006 and 2007 searches also were changed to reflect the new name of the program (i.e., *World News with Charles Gibson*).

[35] The tallies cover 1981, 1992–1995, and 2001, and include only those statements in which a positive or negative evaluation is made. Chapter 4 presents more information on CMPA's coding. In this period, congressional Democrats and Republicans made 3,507 evaluations of the presidential administrations (2,745 of which were directed personally at the president). In contrast, the congressional parties evaluated themselves or one another only 2,861 times.

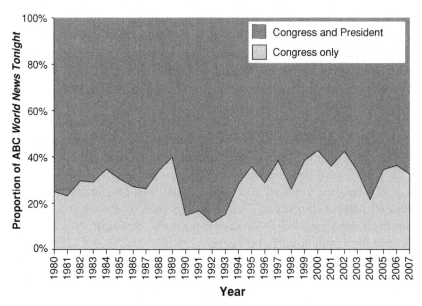

FIGURE 2.1. Congressional news is presidential news.

Therefore, I limit the remainder of the analysis in this and the following chapter to mining this particularly rich vein of partisan information:
stories in which congressional sources are responding to presidential messages or initiatives.

Making the Choice: Selecting Congressional Responses to Presidential News

A practical concern with this model of responses to presidential news
is that journalists might not observe the individual statements of any
specific member of Congress. Furthermore, as I discussed in Chapter 1,
the weak central powers of American parties make it very difficult for a
party to ensure that all of its "franchisees" are communicating the same
preferred messages. However, it seems safe to assume that journalists
have easy access to messages that represent a congressional party's *preferred* viewpoint. As I will discuss in Chapter 4, in recent years both legislative parties have set up formal institutions to facilitate and coordinate
their messages to journalists. For example, the House Republican Conference regularly produces "fact sheets," "issue briefs," "issue features," and
"talking-point" documents for its members. Although individual party

members seek to depart from the "party line" in many instances, for the purposes of this model, I will assume that a member's likelihood of offering a particular message corresponds to the party's collective preferences over such messages.[36]

This section, therefore, revisits my journalistic preference axioms and applies them to possible congressional responses to presidential news. The intent of this exercise is not to make precise predictions about how journalists will react in a single news story but rather to point out broader patterns that tend to disproportionately feature (or ignore) certain subsets of partisan messages.

Implications of the Novelty Axiom

Consistent with the journalistic notion that "man-bites-dog" stories are more newsworthy than "dog-bites-man" ones, the Novelty Axiom rewards the press for choosing partisan statements that are unexpected or unusual. In the specific case of congressional responses to presidential news, each party can offer only two of the four message types. In other words, members of the president's party cannot evaluate him across party lines because they share his party affiliation; thus, their messages about the president can take the form of only *intraparty* praise or criticism. The other legislative party, in turn, can offer only *cross-party* praise or criticism when talking about the president.

Table 2.3 applies the Novelty Axiom to these messages, predicting that journalists should be happier airing unusual stories of presidential-party infighting than those showing harmony. Similarly, stories including praise from the nonpresidential party should be preferred to "politics as usual" – that is, criticism across the aisle.[37]

---

[36] Again, this assumption is intended to provide a "best-case scenario" for the unity of a party's messages. A key point of this chapter is to show how the news media's preferences produce disproportionate levels of criticism by the presidential party, *even if they are assumed to be trying to praise the president*.

[37] It is possible for the media to have expectations that run counter to those suggested by party affiliation. In other words, I acknowledge that there are instances in which journalists may expect the presidential party's members to oppose the president or expect the nonpresidential party to support the president. In such cases, the novelty payoff would presumably flip. In the empirical analysis in Chapter 3, I examine Democratic opposition to and Republican support of the ratification of NAFTA to test for exactly this sort of flipped expectation. Results of this test support the notion that reporters' expectations can flip in such circumstances, leading them to treat intraparty support as novel. Of course, this remains the exception rather than the rule for partisan communication.

TABLE 2.3. *Journalist Novelty Payoffs across Partisan Message Types*

Message Type	Journalist Novelty Payoff
President praised by his party	low
President criticized by his party	high
President praised by other party	high
President criticized by other party	low

Implications of the Conflict Axiom

The Conflict Axiom assumes that journalists prefer stories in which political figures attack one another to stories in which these figures praise one another (all else being equal). Applying this axiom to the partisan-story typology yields fairly straightforward results, as shown in Table 2.4: Messages containing cross-party or intraparty criticism of the president provide a higher conflict payoff than messages praising him.

Implications of the Balance Axiom

The Balance Axiom assumes a journalistic preference for stories featuring representation of both parties' viewpoints, regardless of the content of their respective messages (all else being equal). To provide balance to the overall story in instances of presidential news, wherein the president is already featured, journalists should prefer nonpresidential-party statements (Table 2.5).

Implications of the Authority Axiom

Consistent with the Authority Axiom, each story I examine here contains a message from the president – the single most authoritative source in American politics. However, when deciding among messages from the legislative parties, journalists also weigh the congressional source's

TABLE 2.4. *Journalist Conflict Payoffs across Partisan Message Types*

Message Type	Journalist Conflict Payoff
President praised by his party	low
President criticized by his party	high
President praised by other party	low
President criticized by other party	high

TABLE 2.5. *Journalist Balance Payoffs across Partisan Message Types*

Message Type	Journalist Balance Payoff
President praised by his party	low
President criticized by his party	low
President praised by other party	high
President criticized by other party	high

authority. This case relies on the Majority Party Axiom, which assumes that members of the congressional majority party are more authoritative than members of the minority party (all else being equal).[38] Application of this axiom to the message types in Table 2.6 illustrates how the transition from unified to divided government alters the authority of each party.[39]

ANALYSIS AND HYPOTHESES

Table 2.7 applies these story-characteristic preferences to four types of partisan evaluations of the president, which then determines which types of stories are most likely to gain airtime.[40] Regarding these evaluations, Table 2.7 shows that praise of the president by his own party is of little interest to journalists, especially during periods of divided government.

[38] Obviously this assumes away some potential exceptions, such as the case in which a minority party official is a candidate for president (e.g., when Senator John McCain became his party's nominee in 2008). However, in the aggregate the assumption should hold. Chapter 4 discusses how the president typically undercuts the newsworthiness of his own party by serving as a more authoritative substitute.

[39] In unified government, the president's party has majorities in both houses of Congress. This analysis generally avoids treating the House and Senate separately. However, in cases of divided government in which the presidential party controls only one house of Congress (as was the case with the Senate Republicans after the 1980 election of Ronald Reagan), media attention likely will be disproportionately focused on the chamber controlled by the nonpresidential party.

[40] A caution to this analysis is that it is not clear what relative weights journalists place on novelty, conflict, balance, and authority. For example, it is possible that journalists value novelty in a story so much that they are willing to include it, even if doing so means the story does not include conflict, balance, or authority. Even so, Table 2.7 provides information about which subsets of stories are dominated by others. For example, journalists should *always* prefer presidential-party criticism of the president to comparable presidential-party praise. In game-theoretic terms, this is equivalent to viewing the selection of presidential praise as a weakly dominated strategy for journalists: In most categories, they are better off choosing presidential-party criticism, and in no case are they actually made worse off.

TABLE 2.6. *Journalist Authority Payoffs across Partisan Message Types and Unified/Divided Government*

Message Type	Journalist Authority Payoff, Divided Government	Journalist Authority Payoff, Unified Government
President praised by his party	low	high
President criticized by his party	low	high
President praised by other party	high	low
President criticized by other party	high	low

This is because praise of the president by a member of his own party is neither novel nor conflictual and certainly does not add to the partisan balance of a story. In contrast, criticism of the president by his fellow party members is highly attractive to journalists, especially during unified government. After all, by definition, criticism is conflictual – and it is certainly unexpected that two politicians sharing a common party bond would publicly attack one another.

Conversely, evaluations of the president by the nonpresidential party tend to be at least somewhat newsworthy regardless of which party controls the Congress, although they are particularly newsworthy during periods of divided government. If such comments praise the president, they are considered novel; if they are critical, they fulfill the journalistic desire for conflict. Including comments by the opposition party also consistently adds balance to stories about the president and his policies. Finally, journalists' preference for authoritative sources tends to overrepresent the majority party in Congress. If the majority happens to share

TABLE 2.7. *Message Attractiveness to Journalists*

Message Type	Journalist Payoff From			Authority	
	Novelty	Conflict	Balance	Unified Government	Divided Government
President praised by his party	low	low	low	high	low
President criticized by his party	high	high	low	high	low
President praised by other party	high	low	high	low	high
President criticized by other party	low	high	high	low	high

TABLE 2.8. *Probability of Stories Airing on the News*

Message Type	Likelihood Partisan Will Say	Likelihood Media Will Choose[41]	Likelihood a Given Newscast Will Include
President praised by his party	most likely	least likely	unlikely
President criticized by his party	least likely	likely	more likely
President praised by other party	least likely	likely	more likely
President criticized by other party	most likely	likely	very likely

the president's party affiliation, then for the reasons outlined previously, this leads to the strongest possible incentive for journalists to air any intraparty criticism of the president. Such criticism is novel, conflictual, and authoritative and also may enhance balance (if balance is taken to go beyond simply including both parties and instead focuses on whether both sides of a controversy are represented).

A Two-Factor Model of News Content

The likelihood that the news contains a type of congressional statement can be viewed as a function of the product of the following two probabilities:[42]

1. The probability that a member will make the statement to a news organization.
2. The probability that a news organization will decide to broadcast the statement, if it has been made.

If partisans prefer praising their own party and attacking the other party, and avoid praising the other party or criticizing their own party, I can assume that partisans will frequently offer self-praise and cross-party attacks and seldom offer self-criticism or cross-party praise. Table 2.8 combines these preferences with those of news organizations and predicts which outcomes are more or less likely to occur. Beginning with presidential-party praise, although members of the presidential party

[41] In all cases and all else being equal, being in the majority party makes a partisan's statements more newsworthy.

[42] See Zaller (1997) for an accessible and intuitive discussion of a similar two-factor model predicting opinion change.

should be exceptionally willing to congratulate their chief executive, journalists should prefer almost any other story. This leads me to derive the following hypothesis:

> *Presidential-Party Praise Hypothesis*: Compared to all other types of messages, presidential-party praise is disproportionately unlikely to be selected by journalists.[43]

Conversely, if members of the presidential party choose to criticize their chief executive, the news media should be extremely eager to deliver that criticism to their viewers. Thus, the following hypothesis:

> *Presidential-Party Criticism Hypothesis*: Any criticism of the president by his party is disproportionately likely to be aired in the news.

Similarly, if the nonpresidential party chooses to praise the president, it can be reasonably sure of the following:

> *Nonpresidential-Party Praise Hypothesis*: Any praise of the president by the nonpresidential party is likely to be aired in the news.

Finally, attacks of the president by the nonpresidential party have the relatively unique property of being highly valued by both the nonpresidential party and the news media. This convergence of preferences implies that such messages should be extremely common in the news. Thus, I derive the following hypothesis:

> *Nonpresidential-Party Criticism Hypothesis*: Negative evaluations of the president by the nonpresidential party are the most common type of congressional message about the president.[44]

These hypotheses imply that the two parties face very different strategic environments as they attempt to get their message out to the public. The nonpresidential party possesses the ability to praise or criticize the president in the news, even when it lacks the institutional authority of a majority party. In contrast, the presidential party is largely silenced in

---

[43] "Disproportionate" does not imply a value judgment here (i.e., it does not translate to "too much") but rather reflects a comparison of actual news stories to some unseen, underlying population of "potential" news stories. See Groeling and Kernell (1998) and Groeling (2008) regarding the difficulties of empirically measuring such potential stories. Other sections of this chapter present tests to account for this unseen population of statements.

[44] Unlike the prior hypotheses, this hypothesis attempts to predict aggregate story outcomes. In doing so, it is predicated on the parties' relative likelihood to offer presidential praise or criticism. If the presidential party chooses to offer criticism of the president as often as the nonpresidential party, such messages would instead become most common.

its communication efforts unless it chooses to subject the president to volleys of "friendly fire." Moreover, as the additional hypotheses and tests presented in Chapter 5 will demonstrate, this sort of "friendly fire" by the presidential party is exceptionally credible – and damaging – in its effects on public opinion.

CONCLUSION

In this chapter, I presented a model of how journalists select which congressional responses to air in response to presidential initiatives. The basic model presented here is clearly a simplification of reality; however, it highlights the consequences of congressional reliance on the news as the primary means of communication with the public. If congressional parties controlled the distribution of their messages, they could present their own ideal message to the public.[45] Using this model, I demonstrate how the rules and incentives of the mass media can significantly alter the partisan tone and composition of presidential news. Significantly, journalists do not produce these changes through partisan "bias" but rather by following simple and widely accepted notions of what makes a "good" story.

The news media's influence is especially evident in cases in which the presidential party attempts to evaluate the president. When the party desires to present a message of unity and support for the president, it generally is unable to receive coverage. Conversely, if the presidential party disagrees with the president, it can criticize the president and virtually be guaranteed airtime. As Harry Jaffe, National Editor of *The Washingtonian*, observed, "[W]e reporters can only report what the Democrats do and what the Republicans do. I just think that there is going to be much more conflict within the Republican Party, and if the troops are not going to be lockstep with what Karl Rove wants them to do, that will make great reporting" (Garfield 2005). Assuming that members of the presidential party value the opportunity to appear on the news, the lure of near-guaranteed publicity creates an ever-present incentive to break with their team that can only exacerbate other pressures to defect (see Chapter 1).

---

[45] As will be discussed in the Conclusion chapter, for sizable periods of American history, partisan journalists could be counted on to serve precisely this function. I argue that, paradoxically, as the American press became more evenhanded toward the American parties in the latter half of the 20th century, it undercut their ability to communicate cohesively with their supporters and the general public.

The model's implications for the opposition party are less striking but still important. In most cases in which the presidential party chooses to support the president, journalists prefer to air *any* statement that the opposition chooses to make. In the extreme, the presidential party can face a rather bleak choice: seeing the opposition party oppose the president or opposing him itself.

The main implication of the model is that it is extremely difficult for the presidential party in Congress to present a "unified front" with the president in the news. The nonpresidential party, conversely, is relatively likely to have opportunities to express its ideal positions, even during unified government. This disconnect between political reality and media coverage should disquiet democratic theorists and scholars of journalism who believe that a well-informed public is necessary for the proper functioning of democracy (Bennett 1997, 2003; Dahl 1961; Patterson 2000, 2003). It may also prove troubling to scholars who praise the virtues of "low information rationality" (e.g., Lupia and McCubbins 1998; Popkin 1991), in that many of the information shortcuts and heuristic cues used to process the complexity of reality may already be systematically skewed.

In Chapter 3, I put these predictions to the test by examining patterns of partisan evaluations of the president on the evening news. Subsequent chapters expand the theory to account for news originating in Congress and to test for the predicted patterns, as well as to predict and empirically test the impact of these patterns on public opinion.

3

Breaking the "Eleventh Commandment"

Party Cohesion in Presidential News

> Since the liberals in the Washington press corps will always play up a
> Republican who fights other Republicans, there is a certain advantage in
> breaking with the team.
>
> – Newt Gingrich[1]

INTRODUCTION

In what became known as his "eleventh commandment," Ronald Reagan
famously warned his fellow Republicans, "Thou shall not speak ill of a
fellow Republican."[2] Unfortunately for politicians seeking such reticence
from their fellow partisans, based on the predictions of the model presented in Chapter 2, I conclude that journalistic standards of newsworthiness hobble the presidential party's attempts to do *anything but* speak
ill of the president in the news.

Conservative radio commentator Rush Limbaugh bitterly complained
about the news media's role in such violations of Reagan's commandment, saying, "You go against your own party...they'll love you in
Washington. They'll love you at *The New York Times* and *Washington
Post* if you talk that way" (Limbaugh 2005). Although Limbaugh, Newt
Gingrich, and others seem to attribute such outcomes to liberal malfea-
sance, Chapter 2 makes it clear that a model that explicitly assumes
that journalists balance their coverage of the two parties can account

---

[1] Lamb (1995).

[2] Norquist (1999), a Republican sympathetic to Reagan, calls the commandment "...a
little suspect. It was pronounced by a man who himself challenged a sitting Republican
president in 1976 and this newly coined commandment was issued when – conveniently –
Reagan was the front-runner for the 1980 nomination."

for them. Moreover, as this chapter shows empirically by examining stories from the unified Democratic governments under Carter and Clinton, the media's coverage of disputes within a party is certainly not only a Republican problem.

In this chapter, I empirically test the predictions and propositions advanced in Chapter 2, primarily through analyses of network evening news content spanning the past 25 years. The process starts with the introduction of the two sources of content analysis data used for my hypothesis tests. I then test my hypotheses against these data, finding considerable support for the notion that the presidential party in Congress is largely unable to praise the president in the news.

Next, I discuss the "unobserved population" problem inherent in such analyses of news content. To address this difficulty, I compare network news coverage to three different baselines: legislative support, public support, and the debate about NAFTA ratification. These three analyses bolster my confidence that the surprisingly high amount of presidential-party criticism discussed herein is largely the result of media preferences rather than a fair reflection of underlying support by the president's fellow partisans.

The Dependent Variable: Praise or Criticism of the President in the News

This chapter's primary dependent variable is praise or criticism of the president by congressional partisans in stories appearing on network evening news. Obtaining this measure, however, presents two major problems. First, television news content is transitory (i.e., unless it is recorded, it is lost to the ether), and unless prior transcription work has been done, it generally must be examined in real time; thus, such analysis is exceptionally costly. Second and more important, it is not immediately obvious what the unit of analysis should be for the variable of interest or how that variable should be measured.

Most evening news stories contain diverse elements. In fact, an important underlying assumption of my model in Chapter 2 is that journalists generally attempt to balance the content of political stories through the use of opposing viewpoints (i.e., the Balance Axiom). Hence, it is not unusual to find a single story containing various partisans offering sometimes-contradictory opinions about one or more targets or issues.

To make matters worse, content analysis of negativity in the news is notoriously difficult to analyze (Groeling and Kernell 1998; Groeling

2008).[3] Even if it is possible to satisfactorily determine whether individual units are positive or negative, it is not immediately clear how those units can be aggregated and studied systematically. Worse, such analyses generally face the problem of the unobserved population. As Epstein (1973, xii) noted, "... it is not possible to determine, simply by historical research or content analyses, systematic distortions in the images of events presented in the media without first independently establishing the actual course of the same events."

Solutions

While these problems indeed are daunting, I address them in this chapter through the careful use of two unique datasets, both of which conducted the sort of massive and expensive content analyses required for my analysis.[4] The first dataset, collected by the CMPA, codes every evaluation of or by a partisan figure on every network evening newscast for six complete years (i.e., 1981, 1992, 1993, 1994, 1995, and 2001). In collaboration with Harvard's Matthew A. Baum, I collected a second dataset for a research project examining rally events (Groeling and Baum 2006, hereafter referred to as the Baum and Groeling dataset) that codes every congressional evaluation of the president or his administration on ABC's *World News Tonight* or the *NBC Nightly News* within 30 days of a U.S. deployment of military force from 1979 to 2003. As discussed in the following sections, these complimentary datasets address the concerns listed previously. In addition, testing my predictions against data derived from two independent datasets provides greater confidence that the results presented are not the artifact of an idiosyncratic feature of a single dataset.

CMPA Dataset

As previously noted, the CMPA content analysis data, collected in association with a study sponsored by the Council for Excellence in Governance,

---

[3] Although computer-assisted content analysis has made tremendous strides in recent years, I was unable to find a resource that would allow reliable coding at the specific level of detail required for this analysis (i.e., clear coding of the specific source, target, valence, and issue area of individual statements of praise or criticism embedded in larger broadcasts containing multiple unrelated statements). I do use machine-assisted searches in the Chapter 4 discussion of the relative prominence of congressional parties and leaders on ABC's *World News Tonight*.

[4] I will address the unobserved-population issue separately later in this chapter.

TABLE 3.1. *Sample Content Analysis from CMPA Data: ABC* World News Tonight: *July 14, 1994*

Senator BOB GRAHAM, (D), Florida: "And the purpose is to restrict the President's range of options for an indefinite period of time, especially his option to use force."

JOHN COCHRAN: [voiceover] "Republicans said the last time American troops were in Haiti to establish order, they got stuck there for 19 years and failed to establish a peaceful nation. Now, Republicans argue that sending a congressional commission is better than sending troops again."

Senator JOHN KERRY, (D), Massachusetts: {**SOURCE**} "We have the very thug who was in charge of this operation applauding the Republicans {**TARGET**} for this particular amendment. They should be ashamed {**VALENCE=NEGATIVE**}."

---

coded every evaluation of or by a partisan figure on the three major evening newscasts for six complete years (Farnsworth and Lichter 2004). According to the CMPA codebook, an evaluation is a statement consisting of "words or phrases that convey an unambiguous assessment or judgment about an individual, an institution, or an action."[5] CMPA used the evaluation as its unit of analysis because:

> ... [a]lthough time-consuming and labor-intensive, this allowed us to analyze the building blocks of each story separately, rather than making summary judgments of entire stories. Instead of coding an entire story as "positive" or "negative" toward an individual or institution, we coded each evaluation within the story for its source, topic, object, and tone. A single story might contain several evaluations of various actors; our system captured each one individually. This procedure produces a very detailed picture of the news media's treatment of government (Farnsworth and Lichter 2004, 678).

Table 3.1 is an example of this coding in practice that examines a story from the July 14, 1994, edition of ABC's *World News Tonight*.

In this example, CMPA did not code Senator Bob Graham's comments into the dataset because the statement's valence is not completely clear. Similarly, the reporter's voiceover, which references Republican criticism of the policy, is excluded because those comments were paraphrased from unidentified individuals. Senator John Kerry's comments, however, met CMPA requirements by having a clear partisan source, target, and valence.

---

[5] "CMPA Coding Guidebook" (1997, 120).

It is important that these data exclude significant partisan communication and rhetoric. For example, a Republican senator's criticism of health-care reform was not included unless it was directed at a particular political actor or institution. A Democratic senator who anonymously leaked criticism of a fellow senator for her handling of protesters at a town hall meeting also was excluded because the statement did not come from a named source and was not presented in verbatim form. Similarly, the data do not include instances in which congressional Democrats advocated a position on tax cuts that stood in direct opposition to that of the president unless they explicitly criticized him in doing so.

As discussed previously, my choice of data clearly excludes a wide variety of influential commentary from other partisan or nonpartisan sources, such as journalists or partisan figures outside of the White House or Congress. It also ignores less overt or confrontational channels for communicating the views of partisan politicians. These omitted actors and messages undoubtedly form a substantial portion of the typical news-consumer's diet of partisan information, thereby placing limits on the broader applicability of the tests. However, I argue that these omissions should increase – not decrease – confidence in some of the more counter-intuitive predictions of the theory (e.g., high levels of reported criticism within the governing party) by selecting data that form a particularly "hard test," thereby representing an especially parsimonious and effective way to understand forces in the larger universe of partisan communication. These evaluations are among the clearest and most extreme type of partisan communication, in which the most important strategic politicians at the same level of government have chosen not to duck, weave, or hide behind anonymity but rather to "plant their flag" by overtly supporting or opposing another powerful political actor. Such evaluations inherently raise the potential repercussions for the speaker and audience beyond those which cannot be traced back to their source or whose source is largely outside the reach or notice of Washington politicians.

In other words, a Democratic senator in Washington who is unhappy with the Obama Administration's handling of health-care reform is probably warier about expressing that dissatisfaction on camera on the evening news than anonymously leaking the same comments to a trusted journalist.[6] Similarly, the ability of the president or members of Congress

---

[6] This is not to say that the Senator might not ultimately benefit from such an appearance; indeed, a central point of this book is that many partisans choose to engage in this sort of intraparty stone-throwing because they believe it ultimately will be to their advantage *despite* such costs.

to enforce message discipline on journalists, local political figures, party activists, anonymous sources, or other sources outside their own membership seems to be more tenuous than among their fellow partisans in Washington. If the parties truly have the ability to enforce such cohesion, it should be at its most effective in the cases selected here for analysis. Moreover, each statement can be reduced to a standard syntax – that is, source, valenced message, and target – that corresponds neatly to the typology of partisan messages introduced in Chapter 2.[7]

Baum and Groeling Data

The Baum and Groeling data, in turn, collect content analysis data for a large study on presidential "rally events."[8] In our studies, we analyzed the content of news programming surrounding 42 such events that represented "major uses of force" by the United States between 1979 and 2003.[9]

---

[7] The typology is presented in Table 2.1. To review, the four main message types are intraparty praise, intraparty criticism, cross-party praise, and cross-party criticism.

[8] Mueller (1970, 1973) lists six categories of rally events: sudden military interventions, major military developments in ongoing wars, major diplomatic developments, dramatic technological developments, meetings between the U.S. president and leaders of other major powers, and the start of each presidential term. He argues that for an event to be classified as a potential rally event, it should satisfy three criteria: (1) be international; (2) directly involve the United States in general and the president in particular; and (3) be "specific, dramatic, and sharply focused" (1973, 209). Oneal, Lian, and Joyner (1996, 265) further restrict their definition of rally events to "major uses of force during a crisis." This, they argue, ensures that they are "considering only cases that were truly consequential for the U.S. and salient to the public, necessary conditions for a rally...." Following Oneal, Lian, and Joyner, this analysis is restricted to major uses of force during foreign-policy crises (Baum and Groeling 2004; Groeling and Baum 2006).

[9] The initial list of events relied on Baum (2002), whose data encompass the period 1953–1998. Baum's data were derived from an updated version of Blechman and Kaplan's (1978) dataset on political uses of force (see also Fordham and Sarver 2001; Oneal, Lian, and Joyner 1996). Following Oneal, Lian, and Joyner (1996), we coded all uses of force measuring levels 1 to 3 on Blechman and Kaplan's (1978) scale as "major uses of force." Of these, also following Baum (2002), we excluded several events that appeared inconsistent with the previously mentioned definitions because they represented long-scheduled military exercises (e.g., "Team Spirit" in Korea in March 1990); a cancellation of a previously scheduled withdrawal of forces rather than a proactive and unscheduled force deployment (e.g., November 1991 in Korea); or clearly did not constitute major uses of force during a U.S. foreign-policy crisis (e.g., U.S. support for withdrawal of UN forces from Somalia in January–March 1995, which took place long after the U.S. withdrew forces from that nation). Finally, we updated Baum's data to add the years 1999–2003. A list of rally events from 1989 to 2003 (i.e., those not included in Oneal, Lian, and Joyner's 1996 study) is in Baum and Groeling (2004, Appendix B). This dataset also includes 101 presidential evaluations coded from just outside the 60-day windows as part of the pilot coding for the project.

With the aid of a small army of research assistants, we collected data on congressional comments about the president and the executive branch of government during the 30 days immediately preceding and following each event.[10] For each event, we first searched the Vanderbilt Television News Abstracts to locate every instance on the *CBS Evening News* or ABC's *World News Tonight* in which a senator or representative appeared in stories related to the president or the executive branch of government.[11] Next, the research assistants viewed videotaped recordings or read verbatim transcripts of each selected story, copied each member's statement, and coded the statement's valence (i.e., positive, negative, or neutral) along several issue dimensions (e.g., foreign policy, budget, taxation, and leadership). Figure 3.1 is a sample coding form.[12]

[10] Coders were UCLA and UCSD undergraduate political science and communication studies students. They attended an orientation for the coding scheme with one of the principal investigators or their two graduate student research assistants and then practiced their coding using a series of five online interactive examples and quizzes before beginning the coding.

[11] We located observations by searching Vanderbilt's Abstracts (rather than verbatim transcripts) for two reasons: (1) Vanderbilt maintains a consistent metric for citing appearances by members of Congress; and (2) verbatim transcripts were unavailable for substantial portions of their date range. Videotapes were acquired from Vanderbilt's Television News Archive and from UCLA's News and Public Affairs video archive. Transcripts were viewed on LexisNexis when available. Data for an additional network (i.e., NBC) were collected for two later iterations of the project (Groeling and Baum 2008; Groeling and Baum 2009) but are excluded herein as part of an agreement governing their publication.

[12] Each story was assigned to two different student coders, who independently coded the member statements. Graduate student research assistants then reviewed and arbitrated any disagreements in the initial coding, producing the final dataset. Inter-coder agreement on the main dependent variables (i.e., praise and criticism of the president) prior to arbitration was 95% and 88%, respectively, for CBS. The kappa scores for these variables were 0.44 and 0.51, respectively, which is characterized as "moderate" agreement (Altman 1991, 404). The inter-coder agreement for ABC was slightly lower, at 80%. We do not report a kappa score for the ABC coding because the procedures for that network required recording the arbitrated coding and coder disagreements but not the original individual paper coding for each student. Although we used the same coding form for both networks, the complicated logistics of the coding evolved over time. For example, in one large subset of ABC data, students hand-coded the stories onto paper, met to compare their coding, and submitted the results to the graduate student for further examination. In contrast, all of the CBS data and the remainder of the ABC data were submitted online, with students unaware of the identity of their anonymous coding partner. In addition, for the CBS coding, students were provided with an abstract and the specific list of congressional sources that Vanderbilt had identified as appearing in the relevant story; for the ABC coding, students were provided with only the story's abstract. In a small subset of cases in which tapes or transcripts were damaged or unavailable, the observations were dropped.

AssignCode	Beta05		Sen or Rep?	O Sen ● Rep O Unidentified
AssignUID			Name	Richard GEPHARDT
StoryID	C210		State?	MO
RecordNum	613		Party Affiliation (if given)	● Dem O Rep O Ind O Not Given
NAPATape	12168		Rank or Position in Legislature?	
Date	4/27/1987		Quoted?	● Yes O No
Time	05:32:00 pm			

Take me back to the main login page

	President Praise	President Crit	President Neu	Government Praise	Government Crit	Government Neu
Management of the U.S. Economy	□ Yes	□ Yes	□ Yes	□ Yes	□ Yes	□ Yes
International Trade/Finance	□ Yes	☒ Yes	□ Yes	□ Yes	□ Yes	□ Yes
Government Budget/Deficit/Spending/Taxation	□ Yes	☒ Yes	□ Yes	□ Yes	□ Yes	□ Yes
Foreign Policy/Military	□ Yes	□ Yes	□ Yes	□ Yes	□ Yes	□ Yes
Domestic Policy	□ Yes	□ Yes	□ Yes	□ Yes	□ Yes	□ Yes
Scandal/Personal Behavior	□ Yes	□ Yes	□ Yes	□ Yes	□ Yes	□ Yes
Personal characteristics/Leadership	□ Yes	□ Yes	□ Yes	□ Yes	□ Yes	□ Yes
Other Praise						
Other Criticism						

Quote (use back of paper if necessary)

The time bomb is really the Reagan policy on trade and the time bomb has already exploded. It's exploded with a $170 billion trade deficit.

PROBLEMS   Done Entering ● Yes O No

Headline : US-Japan Trade Relations / Nakasone Visit   Abstract

(Studio: Dan Rather) Report introduced. (DC: Bill Plante) Growing conflict between President Reagan and Congress over US-Japan trade relations and Congress's call for harsher sanctions against Japan prior to Prime Min. Yasuhiro Nakasone's upcoming Washington, DC visit examined; details given, scenes shown. [REAGAN - hopes sanctions on Japanese imports can be lifted soon; attacks proposed legislature currently in House] Gephardt Amendment President said referring to explained. [Representative Robert MICHEL - attacks amendment.] [Representative Richard GEPHARDT - criticizes Reagan's trade policy.] Nakasone said arriving on same day House votes on amendment.

FIGURE 3.1. Sample Baum and Groeling online coding form.

To be included in the analysis, the member's statements had to be presented in the broadcast as a direct quote of an identifiable member and the statement had to pertain to the president or executive branch of government. Therefore, each unit in the dataset consists of a summary of the content of a statement by a single member of Congress in a single story on the evening news. Although each statement might contain multiple instances of praise and/or criticism of the administration and/or president, the main measures collapse these into simple binary indicators of the presence or absence of praise or criticism along several dimensions. Similar to the CMPA data, these data are well suited to study the types of congressional messages identified in Table 2.1.

However, these data have several important differences from the CMPA data (see Table 3.2). The first salient difference between the

TABLE 3.2. *Comparison of CMPA and Baum and Groeling Content Analysis Data*

	CMPA	Baum and Groeling
Unit of Analysis	"Evaluation" (clear positive or negative evaluation by a specific source of specific target)	Entire statement by a member of Congress within a single evening news story
How would it code a member of Congress who criticized the president three different times in a single story?	Three separate negative evaluations (with source and target of each noted)	Entire statement coded as containing criticism of the president
How would it code the president if he criticized a member of Congress three different times in a single story?	Three separate negative evaluations (with source and target of each noted)	Statement not coded (the dataset only codes verbatim statements by members of Congress)
How would it code a member of Congress who spoke about the executive branch but did not praise or criticize any target?	Observation not included	Observation included with zero values for praise and criticism
Sample	All evening news broadcasts on ABC, CBS, and NBC for 1981, 1992, 1993, 1994, 1995, and 2001	Any verbatim quote by a member of Congress about the president or his administration in 61-day windows surrounding 42 U.S. deployments of military force on ABC *World News Tonight* or the *CBS Evening News*
Total Days in Sample	2,191 days	2,115 days[13]
Coding Procedure	Single-coded with subset audit	Double-coded with arbitration/review of all disputes
Total N, All Sources and Targets	28,878 evaluations	2,979 statements
N Congressional Praise or Criticism of the President	3,317 evaluations	846 statements

[13] Several of the rally events occurred at relatively close intervals such that their 61-day windows overlapped. About 7% of the coded evaluations (i.e., 202 of 2,880) occur fewer than 30 days before one rally *and* fewer than 30 days after another rally. Also, not every day in the sample has an evaluation; evaluations actually occurred on 1,165 separate days.

TABLE 3.3. *Institutional Control Covered by CMPA Data: 1981,*
1992–1995, and 2001

	Republican President	Democratic President
Republican legislative control	Early 2001	1995
Democratic legislative control	1992	1993, 1994
Shared legislative control	1981, Late 2001	None

Note: This table excludes the lame-duck period following an election but prior to the inauguration.

datasets was the unit of analysis. Like CMPA, the Baum and Groeling data break down news stories into constituent units rather than code them at the story level. However, the Baum and Groeling data use a slightly broader unit of analysis: statements. As Table 3.2 shows, this means that if a member of Congress were to criticize the president in a story for three different mistakes, CMPA would treat them as three separate negative evaluations, but Baum and Groeling would record only a single negative statement. However, the Baum and Groeling data provide more information regarding the full population of stories: If a member appeared on the news and spoke in a story related to the president or his administration, the quote was included, even if the member did not praise or criticize either target. The CMPA data, conversely, exclude any statements that do not include explicit positive or negative evaluations.[14]

As was discussed earlier, each dataset also has a different selection criterion. Although it is obviously preferable to have a single dataset that codes every evaluation on every evening newscast on every day from 1979 to the present, such a dataset would be prohibitively difficult and costly to assemble. The CMPA and Baum and Groeling datasets provide what is arguably the next best thing: two complementary datasets that offset one another's selection idiosyncrasies. The CMPA dataset provides depth, but not breadth: It samples every partisan evaluation in every network evening newscast, but only for six years. While those years cover tremendous variation in partisan control of government (Table 3.3), that actually raises the concern that the six years might be aberrations in recent history.

---

[14] To address this issue, in the Chapter 5 public-opinion analysis, the full CMPA includes evaluations in which members of Congress chose to evaluate figures *other* than the president in the included observations (albeit with a net valence toward the president of zero).

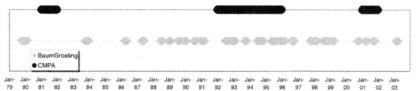

FIGURE 3.2. Days in CMPA versus Baum and Groeling datasets.

Albeit examining a narrower range of partisan figures on fewer networks, the Baum and Groeling data cover a similar number of days (i.e., 2,115 versus 2,191 for CMPA) but are spread over a much broader 25-year span.[15] Figure 3.2 graphically demonstrates this point, showing the days included in each dataset.

Table 3.4 summarizes the sources and targets of all partisan evaluations coded by CMPA. The data shown in this table highlight the media's reliance on the parties in Congress for their evaluations: More than half of the partisan evaluations originated there. Conversely, the most popular target seems to be the executive branch, with about two thirds of all evaluations directed at those figures.

The Baum and Groeling data included statements only by the congressional parties concerning the executive branch; therefore, they reveal less about the relative pecking order of sources. Table 3.5 shows a pronounced two-to-one advantage for the nonpresidential versus the presidential party in getting coverage of its evaluations of the president or his administration.

Now that I have introduced the data and their broad contours, I will apply them to the hypotheses derived in Chapter 2.

HYPOTHESIS TESTING

The Presidential-Party Praise Hypothesis predicted that *compared to all other types of messages, presidential-party praise is disproportionately unlikely to be selected by journalists.* In contrast, the Presidential-Party Criticism Hypothesis predicted that *any criticism of the president by his party is disproportionately likely to be aired in the news.*

For the nonpresidential party, I hypothesized that *any praise of the president by the nonpresidential party is likely to be aired in the news* (i.e.,

---

[15] Although the Baum and Groeling sample is not random, it was selected based on consistent criteria derived from prior unrelated research projects in the field of international relations.

TABLE 3.4. *Sources and Targets of Partisan Evaluations (CMPA Data)*

	Source of Evaluation (percent of column total)	Target of Evaluation (percent of column total)
President	2,383 (17%)	12,362 (48%)
Administration	2,242 (16%)	4,846 (19%)
Presidential Party in Congress	3,280 (24%)	2,023 (8%)
Nonpresidential Party in Congress	5,010 (36%)	5,420 (20%)
Other Partisans	909 (7%)	1,478 (6%)

Note: This includes evaluations from nongovernmental sources.

the Nonpresidential-Party Praise Hypothesis). However, given the non-presidential party's likely unwillingness to offer such praise, these messages are not likely to comprise much of the actual content of broadcasts. Unfortunately, it is unclear whether a failure to observe nonpresidential-party praise in the news reflects the absence of such statements or lack of interest on the part of journalists to broadcast them. As such, testing this hypothesis is deferred until subsequent sections where I have an independent idea about the likely unobserved population of praise versus criticism.

In contrast, attacks on the president by the nonpresidential party have the relatively unique property of being highly valued by both the non-presidential party and the news media, which implies that such messages should be extremely common in the news. This led me to hypothesize that *negative evaluations of the president by the nonpresidential party are the single most common type of congressional message about the president* (i.e., the Nonpresidential-Party Criticism Hypothesis).

As a first attempt at testing these hypotheses, I first examine exactly what members of Congress say about the president. Table 3.6 breaks

TABLE 3.5. *Sources and Targets of Congressional Statements (Baum and Groeling Data)*

	President is Target n (percent of total)	President & Administration are Target n (percent of total)	Administration is Target n (percent of total)
Presidential Party in Congress	215 (13%)	52 (3%)	280 (17%)
Nonpresidential Party in Congress	423 (25%)	156 (9%)	553 (33%)

TABLE 3.6. *Valence of Congressional Statements Targeting the President (Baum and Groeling Data)*

	Presidential Party			Nonpresidential Party	
N	Percent Critical	Percent Praise	N	Percent Critical	Percent Praise
267	60%	43%	578	88%	14%

Note: Sum >100% because some comments included both praise and criticism.

down the quantity and valence of congressional evaluations of the president in the Baum and Groeling data.

Table 3.6 provides strong support for both hypotheses. Although the high levels of negativity (i.e., 88% of all evaluations) in nonpresidential-party evaluations may plausibly reflect the actual level of support for the chief executive, the negativity from the president's own party (i.e., three of every five evaluations were negative) is difficult to explain as a fair sample. The Nonpresidential-Party Criticism Hypothesis also receives strong support: Nonpresidential-party criticism is featured in about twice as many statements as presidential-party praise and criticism *combined*.

Table 3.7 repeats this exercise for the CMPA data. Because these data are denser and cover fewer years, the tallies are further disaggregated by president.

As was the case with the Baum and Groeling data, Table 3.7 shows that under every president in the CMPA sample, the nonpresidential party numerically dominated the evaluations of the president and his administration, and such statements were overwhelmingly negative.[16] In addition, the results show similar discord within the presidential party, with about three fifths of all broadcast evaluations of the president by members of his own party being negative (consistent with the Presidential-Party Criticism Hypothesis). Only Reagan appears to have fared better, mustering a slightly favorable balance from his congressional party.

ANALYSIS

The preponderance of negative evaluations of the president by his own partisans discovered thus far is difficult to explain as a "fair" sample

---

[16] Clinton's first term in office is the only year in which the presidential party secured more airtime; when Clinton's two other years in office are averaged into the equation, the nonpresidential party leaps far ahead in total evaluations.

TABLE 3.7. *Valence of Presidential/Administrative Evaluations by Congressional Parties (CMPA Data; Excludes Lame-Duck Period)*

	Presidential Party		Nonpresidential Party	
	N	Percent Critical	N	Percent Critical
Reagan (1981)	141	45%	251	92%
H. W. Bush (1992)	111	60%	204	98%
Clinton (1993)	469	60%	460	75%
Clinton (1994)	471	68%	776	88%
Clinton (1995)	156	65%	778	86%
W. Bush (2001)	155	63%	351	89%

unless the presidential party actually disagrees with the president twice as often as it agrees with him. Although it seems unlikely that fellow party franchisees would strategically choose to savage the value of their party brand name through such attacks, it is possible that the media are accurately reflecting an underlying political split between the president and his party. In other words, it is difficult to definitively discern whether patterns of political statements in the news reflect the news media's selection criteria or the underlying population of political messages from the president's party.

Although these "potential" stories cannot be observed directly, there are strategies that allow additional insight about how the news media might filter the messages sent by members of Congress. In the next three sections, I use (1) measures of presidential support within the legislature, (2) presidential-approval data, and (3) a case study of the ratification of NAFTA to delineate the media's independent and limiting effect on partisan support and opposition of the president.

Inferring Rhetorical Support from Legislative Support

Members of Congress use a variety of communication strategies and media in their attempts to communicate with the public. Some scholars try to observe the full population of congressional attempts to gain press coverage; however, such efforts generally are limited to a single strategy or communications medium.[17] In addition, many of the public-relations tactics (e.g., one-on-one interviews or off-the-record briefings) are

---

[17] For example, Lipinski (2004) cataloged the direct mailings and press releases of members; Sellers and Schaffner (2007) examined Senate records of press conferences. On the executive side, collections of the papers of the president or collections of speeches are often used for the same analytical purpose.

observable only by the participating individuals. However, a member voting on the floor is easy to observe; although these votes may be strategic, at least the full range of behaviors can be viewed.

Using these votes to further test the hypotheses requires the assumption that members' supportive presidential statements to the media roughly correspond to their vote support for the president. This is a strong assumption, but it is made more palatable because these votes are so public. The news media are particularly vigilant regarding clear cases of hypocrisy – in large part because they are objective, negative, and easy to report. Similarly, opponents in upcoming elections would be delighted to be offered an opportunity to attack the member with a resulting "flip-flop" advertisement.

I therefore expect that if the media were presenting an unbiased sample, party support in the news should roughly correspond to its support of the president within the legislature. If my model is correct, however, I expect the presidential party in the legislature to appear far less supportive of the president in the media than in its voting (i.e., the Presidential-Praise Hypothesis). Given the relative freedom of positioning granted to the opposition party in the model (per the Nonpresidential-Party Praise and Nonpresidential-Party Criticism Hypotheses, both its praise and criticism are newsworthy), I expect in turn a much closer correspondence between votes and statements in the news.

To measure voting support for the president, I use *Congressional Quarterly's* index of presidential support scores, which tracks annual average partisan support or opposition to presidential initiatives.[18] Figure 3.3 contrasts support in the media with this measure of roll-call voting.[19]

Figure 3.3 shows a clear divide between legislative actions and support as reported by the media, particularly for the presidential party. The president's partisans in Congress actually support their leader's position

---

[18] *Congressional Quarterly* determines presidential positions on congressional votes by "examining the statements made by President Clinton or his authorized spokesmen. *Support* measures the percentage of the time members voted in accord with the position of the president. *Opposition* measures the percentage of the time members voted against the president's position.... Absences lowered parties' scores" (*Congressional Quarterly Almanac.* 1996, C-15). I would prefer to use House support scores for Representatives and Senate support scores for Senators, but most of my data do not distinguish between House and Senate partisans of the same party. In the analyses that follow, I therefore use the House support score, which also avoids the effect of Senate confirmation votes on presidential nominees.

[19] Because the Baum and Groeling data contain partial months that are irregularly spaced, I was unable to match votes to equivalent periods. As a result, I chose to rely on the more regularly spaced CMPA data for this analysis.

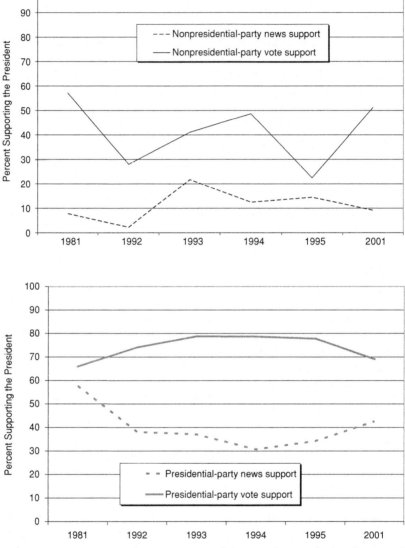

FIGURE 3.3. Congressional-party support of the president in the legislature and in the news (CMPA data).

about 75% of the time in their voting but only in about 40% of their evaluations in the national news. The absolute disparity is typically smaller for the nonpresidential party; however, it also generally offers about twice as much support in votes than in media statements.

TABLE 3.8. *Congressional Net Positive Evaluations of President (CMPA Data) as a Function of Presidential Support Scores in Roll-Call Votes*

	Monthly Percent Positive Evaluations of Incumbent by Presidential Party	Monthly Percent Positive Evaluations of Incumbent by Nonpresidential Party
	Coefficient (Standard Error)	Coefficient (Standard Error)
Intercept	−7.29	−40.29***
	(6.34)	(3.94)
Average Presidential Support Score	2.72	29.85***
	(7.51)	(9.51)
Transition	0.73	−8.55
	(6.29)	(10.23)
Presidential-Party Majority in at Least One Chamber	−3.89	−6.80
	(2.36)	(4.31)
Nonpresidential-Party Majority in at Least One Chamber	4.60*	15.83***
	(2.37)	(3.77)
	Adj. R^2 = 0.02	Adj. R^2 = 0.40

Note: * indicates $p < 0.05$; ** indicates $p < 0.01$; *** indicates $p < 0.001$.

To examine this result more carefully, I have disaggregated the annual percentages from Figure 3.3 into a monthly series. I then used ordinary least squares (OLS) regression to estimate the relationship between presidential support and the net volume of favorable messages (e.g., total positive minus total negative messages) directed at the president by members of Congress.

In Table 3.8, there is no significant relationship between the presidential party's support for the president in the legislature and its support for him in the news. The nonpresidential party's support for the president in the news, conversely, significantly and positively correlates with its support in the legislature (consistent with both the Nonpresidential-Party Praise and Nonpresidential-Party Criticism Hypotheses).

This analysis supports the notion that the public does not receive a fair sampling of the president's support from his party in the news (which is consistent with both the Presidential-Party Praise and Presidential-Party Criticism Hypotheses). However, these results are more suggestive than conclusive because of the strategic nature of voting and rhetoric. Presidents are strategic in allotting their scarce legislative resources and can be expected to choose their legislative battles carefully.[20] Statements in the press, conversely, may reflect payoffs to different constituencies or be less directly related to the legislative process.

Likewise, final votes on legislation comprise only a small piece of the newsworthy relations between the government branches. Unfortunately, the number of potential stories concerning the president and Congress approaches infinity, few of which can be precisely measured. If such stories were directly observable by individuals other than journalists, there would be little reason to employ journalists in the first place.

Although the potential stories are difficult to observe directly, there are situations in which one has prior beliefs about changes in what members of Congress might *want* to say about the president. A case in point is presidential popularity.

Inferring Presidential-Party Support from Presidential Popularity

As the most prominent politician in America, the president strongly influences the public's perception of his party. It is not surprising that the president's approval rating has been shown to be closely related to his congressional party's electoral fortunes (Campbell 1993; Kernell 1977; Tufte 1975) – a consequential point discussed in Chapter 6. When a president is popular, his party can bask in his reflected glow. However, if a president becomes unpopular, members of his party in Congress have a greater incentive to dissociate their brand name from his. Criticizing the president's position seems to be an effective means of achieving such distance, whereas praising the positions of a popular president helps associate a party more closely with him.[21]

In this section, I therefore assume that *the true proportion of supportive statements by the presidential party is directly related to the president's current approval rating.* Conversely, I assume that *the proportion of negative statements by the presidential party is inversely related to his*

---

[20] See, for example, Langdon (1994, 3619).

[21] Some argue that presidential popularity helps a president hold sway over the opposition party as well – or, at least, unpopular presidents might find themselves attacked more from both parties. As Neustadt argued, "Popularity may not produce a Washington response. But public disapproval heartens Washington's resistance" (1990, 76). However, while members of the opposing party might fear a popular president, they seem to have little incentive to build him up further with praise. Conversely, the opposition always seems to have an incentive to harm the presidential party.

approval. Based on these assumptions, I derive and test three different hypotheses regarding the relationship between presidential approval and evaluations of the president by his party in the news.

Null Hypothesis. The null prediction is that there is no relationship between presidential approval and his party's evaluations. In this scenario, the presidential party in the legislature should be expected to praise and criticize the president at relatively consistent levels, regardless of how popular he is.

Representative Sample Hypothesis. In this case, the media simply present a random or representative sample of all the evaluations of the president by his own party. Therefore, this hypothesis predicts that increases in presidential approval should produce more stories containing statements of support from his party, and decreases in presidential approval should produce an increase in stories containing criticism from his party.

Negative Bias Hypothesis. The third alternative, which follows directly from my theory, is that the media are eager to increase coverage of presidential-party criticism of the president but avoid presenting messages of presidential-party praise of the president. Therefore, decreases in presidential approval should produce an increase in stories containing criticism from his party, but increases in presidential approval should *not* produce more stories containing statements of support from his party.

Table 3.9 summarizes the three hypotheses.[22]

Testing these hypotheses requires an examination of the relationship between presidential approval and monthly aggregate presidential evaluations from the CMPA and Baum and Groeling datasets.[23] Table 3.10 presents the results of a regression in which the president's Gallup approval rating is used to predict his likelihood of being targeted with

---

[22] A fourth hypothesis is excluded from this scheme: *Increases in presidential approval significantly correlate with increases in support from his party in Congress, but decreases in approval do not significantly correlate with statements of criticism*. Although including this hypothesis would render Table 3.4 mutually exclusive and exhaustive, I am unaware of any theoretical justification to support this hypothesis except pro-administration bias. Because the empirical results also show no support for this hypothesis, I have excluded it here.

[23] The 61-day windows in the Baum and Groeling analysis do not follow a consistent monthly pattern – that is, they do not cleanly overlap with calendar months and therefore include all of some months but only portions of others. Therefore, I have included a control variable called "partial month" in the Baum and Groeling regressions in Tables 3.10 and 3.11, which takes a value of 1 if there are fewer than five total evaluations by either party in that month.

TABLE 3.9. *Summary of Hypothesized Changes in Network-News Coverage of the Presidential Party Given Changes in Presidential Popularity*

	Presidential Popularity Decreases *(Implies Increase in Critical Statements from Presidential Party)*	Presidential Popularity Increases *(Implies Increase in Supportive Statements from Presidential Party)*
Null Hypothesis	No relationship	No relationship
Representative Sample Hypothesis	Significant increase in criticism	Significant increase in support
Negative Bias Hypothesis	Significant increase in criticism	No relationship

TABLE 3.10. *Hypothesis Test #1: Decreases in Presidential Approval are Significantly Correlated with Increases in Criticism by His Party in the News (CMPA Data)*

	Coefficient (Standard Error)
Intercept	21.76 (7.33)**
Gallup approval	−0.49 (0.13)***
Transition	−0.39 (4.96)
Democratic president	9.41 (3.06)**
Presidential-party majority in at least one chamber	13.05 (2.86)***
Nonpresidential-party majority in at least one chamber	1.74 (2.93)
	Adj. $R^2 = 0.43$

	Baum and Groeling Data Coefficient (Standard Error)
Intercept	9.43 (2.71)***
Gallup approval	−0.13 (0.03)***
Transition	−0.68 (1.15)
Democratic president	1.26 (0.55)**
Presidential-party majority in at least one chamber	1.75 (0.66)**
Nonpresidential-party majority in at least one chamber	2.64 (1.01)**
Partial month	−1.88 (0.47)***
	Adj. $R^2 = 0.32$

Note: * indicates $p < 0.05$; ** indicates $p < 0.01$; *** indicates $p < 0.001$.

criticism by his fellow party members. The regression also controls for the presence or absence of a presidential transition period (beginning with the election and ending at inauguration) and the presence of a Democratic president, presidential-party majority, or nonpresidential-party majority in at least one chamber.[24]

The results from tests performed on both datasets in Table 3.10 are not consistent with the Null Hypothesis. In both the CMPA and the Baum and Groeling data, there is a significant relationship between decreases in presidential approval and increases in criticism by his party in the news. In the CMPA data, for example, for every two points the president drops in the polls, he should expect to be criticized by his party in the news one more time per month. In the Baum and Groeling data, the results suggest that for every nine points a president drops in the polls, another member of his party will appear on the news and criticize him. These results are consistent with both the Negative Bias and the Representative Sample Hypotheses.

Table 3.11 repeats this analysis – in this case, for supportive statements by the presidential party.[25]

Table 3.11 severely undercuts the Representative Sample Hypothesis by showing that presidential approval is *not* significantly associated with statements of praise by the president's party in Congress. For the Baum and Groeling data, increases in presidential approval have no effect on his party's praise in the media, while in the CMPA results, there is an insignificant *negative* coefficient. Together, Tables 3.10 and 3.11 provide strong support for the hypothesis that the media are far more willing to broadcast presidential criticism than praise by the presidential party in Congress.

In the following section, I present the final test for an independent-selection effect by the news media.[26] In this case, I examine a case where

---

[24] I control for a Democratic president for two reasons: (1) Clinton is president for half of the CMPA sample, in contrast to the three different Republican presidents across the other three years; and (2) Table 3.7 shows that evaluations of the president spiked during Clinton's three years in the CMPA sample. Clinton is included in the Baum and Groeling regressions for comparability.

[25] Tables 3.10 and 3.11 both generally show a significant relationship between being in the majority party and being able to evaluate the president, which is consistent with the Authority Axiom.

[26] In a separate project with my coauthor Matthew Baum (Groeling and Baum 2009), we address the unobserved-population issue by content-analyzing congressional evaluations on Sunday-morning interview shows and tracking which statements are selected for the

TABLE 3.11. *Hypothesis Test #2: Increases in Presidential Approval are Not Significantly Correlated with Increases in Praise by His Party in the News (CMPA Data)*

	Coefficient (Standard Error)
Intercept	7.60 (5.44)
Gallup approval	−0.18 (0.10)
Transition	−1.73 (3.68)
Democratic president	4.87 (2.72)*
Presidential-party majority in at least one chamber	6.27 (2.12)**
Nonpresidential-party majority in at least one chamber	2.51 (2.18)
	Adj. R^2 = 0.19

	Baum and Groeling Data Coefficient (Standard Error)
Intercept	3.50 (1.71)*
Gallup approval	0.00 (0.20)
Transition	−0.93 (0.73)
Democratic president	−0.46 (0.35)
Presidential-party majority in at least one chamber	−0.78 (0.42)
Nonpresidential-party majority in at least one chamber	−1.53 (0.64)*
Partial N	−1.56 (0.47)***
	Adj. R^2 = 0.25

Note: * indicates $p < 0.05$; ** indicates $p < 0.01$; *** indicates $p < 0.001$.

the news media may have expected the presidential party to increase its *criticism* of the president: the debate over ratification of NAFTA.

Changing Standards of Newsworthiness

As discussed in Chapter 2 and the previous section, the media receive a higher "novelty" payoff from presenting new or unexpected stories. Given the common party brand between a president and his fellow party franchisees in the legislature, the news media generally should expect the president's party to support the president, and the nonpresidential party to oppose him. However, as discussed in Chapters 1 and 6, even

evening news. These data also strongly support the conclusion that journalists exercise an independent influence over the partisan rhetoric selected for inclusion on the news.

relatively homogeneous parties can have intense internal disagreements about ideology and the party "brand name."

These observations invite the question of whether there are situations in which the media might expect such criticism of the president by his own party and thus discount its novelty. In other words, might there be cases in which the media expect the presidential party to oppose the president and thus prefer stories containing presidential-party support of the president? If so, a rise in presidential-party support in the news *despite* a drop in actual support in the legislature would provide strong evidence of the intervening influence of journalistic standards of newsworthiness.

To test this notion, I examine network-news coverage of the 1993 debate about NAFTA. The NAFTA trade agreement was largely the product of negotiations conducted under the first Bush Administration, but the treaty finally came up for a vote during the subsequent Clinton Administration. Even before Clinton and the Democrats came to power in 1993, core factions within the Democratic Party opposed the agreement, including organized labor and many congressional Democrats. In fact, the dissidents included two of the three highest-ranking Democratic members: Majority Leader Richard Gephardt (D-MO) and Majority Whip David Bonior (D-MI). As a result, it was initially unclear whether the Clinton Administration would pursue ratification or let the agreement die.[27]

Conversely, most Republicans were vocal in their support for NAFTA, as were business leaders and other core Republican constituencies. Although a faction of the Republicans led by Patrick Buchanan strongly opposed ratification, the Republican leadership in the House and Senate publicly proclaimed support very early in the process.[28]

Thus, the ratification debate over NAFTA seems to be a case in which journalists should have reversed their a priori expectations regarding the

---

[27] For example, Cokie Roberts (1993) of *This Week with David Brinkley* observed that "Labor unions have launched a vigorous campaign against NAFTA and their fierce opposition threatens to tear apart the Democratic Party. With core Democratic constituencies opposing the trade agreement, some of President Clinton's political advisers have urged him to let NAFTA die, to call it a bad deal negotiated by a Republican administration."

[28] For example, in his August 22, 1993, appearance on *This Week with David Brinkley*, Bob Dole said, "You're going to see in this case the Republican leaders in the Senate and the House and the Democratic president on one side." Newt Gingrich, in a Halloween appearance on *Face the Nation*, said that despite the closeness of the vote, he thought the Republicans could "win it on the Republican side. We're going to do everything we can to get every member who can possibly vote for it to do so. But, frankly, we need to keep the president focused on the Democratic side, where they have far fewer votes than we do" (Dole 1993).

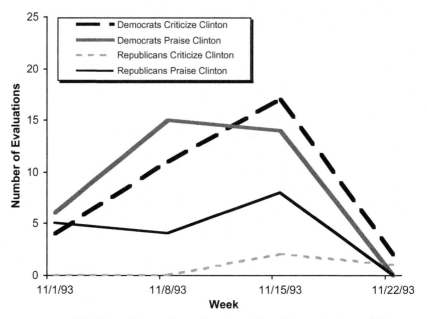

FIGURE 3.4. Weekly positive and negative economic policy evaluations of Clinton during NAFTA debate (CMPA data).

likely sources of support and criticism of the president. The paradoxical prediction is that *because the media expect more opposition from the presidential party, they should be more willing to broadcast support.*

Figure 3.4 presents the CMPA coding of partisan evaluations associated with NAFTA.[29]

As shown in the figure, support or opposition by congressional Democrats received considerably more coverage than equivalent Republican statements. For this period, Democrats made a total of 69 evaluations, as opposed to only 20 by Republicans. In contrast, Table 3.7 shows that for the remainder of the year, congressional Democrats and Republicans received about the same amount of coverage for their Clinton evaluations (i.e., 469 from Democrats versus 460 from Republicans). Also, in contrast to the overall results for 1993 shown previously in Table 3.7, it appears that support by Democrats is considered newsworthy, accounting for

[29] Summary data from CMPA do not preserve segment-level coding specifically related to NAFTA; instead, it is grouped with "Economic Policy Issues" according to the "CMPA Coding Guidebook" (1997, 94). Thus, use of this variable is limited to the month up to and including the vote, to avoid contamination by other similarly coded issues.

TABLE 3.12. *Support of the President on NAFTA, in Votes and on the News (Figures in Parentheses are Percentages of Column Total)*

	Congressional Democrats, Vote	Congressional Democrats, News	Congressional Republicans, Vote	Congressional Republicans, News
Support	102 (40%)	35 (51%)	132 (75%)	17 (85%)
Oppose	156 (60%)	34 (49%)	43 (25%)	3 (15%)

slightly more than half of their evaluations of Clinton. Table 3.12 further breaks down this analysis and compares the rhetoric of members on NAFTA with their actual votes.

As predicted, Table 3.12 shows that although Democrats appeared to be negative in their actual votes regarding NAFTA, media coverage appears to be disproportionately positive, producing a slight majority of evaluations in the news expressing support of Clinton on NAFTA. Also, unlike earlier results in which they criticized the president, congressional Republican evaluations of Clinton on NAFTA actually seem disproportionately positive.

Although it is possible that some of the discrepancy stems from last-minute vote-switching or horse-trading on the part of pro- or anti-NAFTA politicians, the contrast with other results presented in this chapter is stark: While the other cases illustrate situations in which the media disproportionately sampled criticism of the president by his own party, here – when opposition is expected – they appear to disproportionately sample praise. This result again highlights the selection power of journalists as well as the critical role of their expectations in determining story value.

CONCLUSION

Overall, the patterns of intraparty evaluations discussed here correspond quite well to the preferences of the journalists who have final control over which party messages are transmitted to the public. This introduces a profound irony of American politics – at least within the realm of partisan communication: Institutional power often begets communication weakness. Although controlling the presidency usually is seen as a boon to a legislative party's ambitions, the findings presented here indicate that controlling the presidency can undermine the ability of his party to collectively communicate a consistent brand name to the public.[30] The nonpresidential party, conversely, is actually given a relatively free hand in attempts to define its brand in its preferred manner, particularly in the case of divided government. Given the centrality of the president in political news, this finding has ominous implications about the potential political viability of unified government on the national stage. Chapter 6 presents a detailed discussion of these implications for unified and divided government and concludes that divided government actually presents a silver lining to both the president and the opposing majority party.

However, the analysis thus far has concentrated exclusively on Congress's role in presidential news. Although these stories represent the majority of congressional evaluations, congressional parties also are given opportunities to evaluate themselves and one another in the news. In the next chapter, I will use a variant of Chapter 2's model of partisan communication to examine stories initiated by congressional actors. Unfortunately for the presidential party, this extension of the model again demonstrates how the president can hinder his fellow franchisees' party-branding efforts, even in their attempts to initiate stories within their own branch of government.

---

[30] A potential objection to this result is that the parties might be systematically differing in the content of their criticism. For example, one party might be criticizing fellow party members for gross incompetence and corruption, and the other party might be criticizing fellow partisans for insufficient zeal in support of the party's agenda. Such problems are clearly an issue in any empirical examination that attempts to quantify qualities such as negativity (Groeling and Kernell 1998). However, I argue that in the subset of news examined herein, aggregate, partisan criticism is a distinctly interesting and clear analytical category that is inherently damaging within a party. As I argued in Chapter 1, such public disputes over the content of the brand necessarily undermine consistency of the brand: The failure to resolve disagreements behind the scenes and maintain collective responsibility is confusing to voters. Unlike simply staking out contrary positions, the criticism here must cross a high threshold: To be counted, these observations only include instances in which a member chose to explicitly criticize the positions or actions of another partisan.

4

Life in the Shadows

The President's Legislative Party as Newsmaker

> As for the Democratic Party [in Congress], the handwringing these last two weeks may prove to be of little value. Over the next two years, its future is likely to be determined more by the actions of President Clinton and the Republicans.
>
> – Elizabeth Arnold, NPR's *Morning Edition*, November 23, 1994

INTRODUCTION

In March 2005, House Majority Leader Tom DeLay (R-TX) was fighting for his political life. After a series of escalating ethics scandals and investigations into DeLay's alleged overseas junkets and ties to lobbyists, the powerful Republican leader appeared to be on the ropes politically. Congressional Democrats eagerly seized on the charges against DeLay to paint a picture of congressional Republicans as arrogant, corrupt, and incompetent – themes that would serve them well in the 2006 midterm elections. For their part, congressional Republicans appeared deeply worried by DeLay's problems but steadfastly refused to criticize him publicly.[1] House Majority Whip Roy Blunt (R-MO) said DeLay "has always had, and continues to have, the strong support" of his fellow Republicans, adding, "His leadership and dedication to maintaining and growing our numbers are a significant reason for our Republican majority" (Allen 2005).

---

[1] Many Republican staffers and lobbyists criticized DeLay off the record, and eventually Representative Christopher Shays (R-CT) received considerable media attention when he called for DeLay to step down, as I will discuss. DeLay resigned as Majority Leader in September 2005 after being indicted on campaign money-laundering charges and resigned his House seat the following June.

It was in this setting that a *New York Times* editorial page staff member sent an e-mail to former Republican congressional leader Robert Livingston (D-IL) asking if Livingston could write "a short op-ed on DeLay's political future" (Novak 2005). Livingston was famous in Washington for his shocking resignation as Speaker of the House and from Congress following his admission of marital infidelities coinciding with President Clinton's impeachment; Livingston called on Clinton to follow his example by also resigning (*Allpolitics*, Jonathan Karl, and the Associated Press 1998). When one of Livingston's aides called back *The New York Times* to indicate Livingston's willingness to write an op-ed supporting DeLay, the offer was rebuffed. *The Times*, the staffer explained, was "seeking those who would go on the record or state for the good of the party he (DeLay) should step aside" (Novak 2005).

A short time later, Representative Chris Shays did, in fact, call for DeLay to step down as House Majority Leader. In an interview with the Associated Press (AP), Shays complained that "Tom's conduct is hurting the Republican Party, is hurting this Republican majority and it is hurting any Republican who is up for reelection.... My party is going to have to decide whether we are going to continue to make excuses for Tom to the detriment of Republicans seeking election" (Kesten 2005). In addition to their wide dissemination through the AP, Shays's comments received tremendous media attention during the subsequent week, including more than 100 television stories and major write-ups in dozens of newspapers, such as *The New York Times* and *The Washington Post*.[2]

In this chapter, I contend that it is unsurprising that dissent within the governing congressional party was considered far more newsworthy than support. In the previous chapters, I examined the difficulties that the parties confront in controlling their communication through the news media, highlighting the obstacles faced by members of the presidential party in Congress as they attempt to build a common brand name with the executive branch. In this chapter, I turn to stories on Congress's home turf: news messages by and about members of Congress.

I find that although legislative members of the presidential party apparently treat one another slightly better than they treat their president in the news, they still fail to present a consistent brand name to the public.

---

[2] Results are from LexisNexis searches for terms (Shays, DeLay, resign* or ethics or scandal) in the Major Papers database (40 results) and All Transcripts database (109 results) for the week April 10–17, 2005. The transcripts database includes substantial numbers of hits from local news abstracts, repeated showings on CNN, and so forth.

The nonpresidential party's branding efforts, conversely, actually benefit from the presence of a "hostile" president, even while in the minority. Building on the theory of news values in Chapter 2, I argue that the president systematically harms his congressional comrades by satisfying the media's demand for viewpoints from his party and by inflating the stature and newsworthiness of the nonpresidential party.

First, I situate this inquiry in the broader research on congressional news. Next, I examine the conditions that might be expected to enhance rhetorical unity within the congressional parties, including ideological and pragmatic connections between partisans and the influence of party communication institutions. I then explore how institutional control of Congress and/or the presidency can affect the ability of a legislative party to communicate with the public through the news media. This discussion highlights the role of the president in usurping the ability of his legislative party to initiate news coverage, as well as the media's role in privileging the communication of the nonpresidential party. Finally, I test the model by applying its predictions to actual news content.

LITERATURE ON CONGRESSIONAL NEWS

Since the 1960s, political scientists have been concerned about the allure of television and other mass media for members of Congress. In particular, political scientists feared that a new breed of media-seeking "show horses" might shirk legislative duties, leaving such duties to other "work horses" (Matthews 1960). Some suggest that the distinction between such types of members is now less relevant (Ranney 1983); however, scholars remain curious about the relative newsworthiness of members of Congress.

In the examination of congressional news-making, some authors focus on the actions or efforts that members make to gain traction in the news media.[3] Others look for specific characteristics that enhance individuals' newsworthiness (Hess 1986; Sinclair 1989; Squire 1988). Although factors such as home-state size (Squire 1988; Weaver and Wilhoit 1974), ideological extremity (Kuklinski and Sigelman 1992), and issue alignment

---

[3] See Cook (1986), Sellers and Schaffner (2007), and especially Lipinski (2004) and Sellers (2005). Sellers, in particular, is advancing a research program that parallels this chapter. However, his research focuses more on the factors leading to successful media coordination by congressional parties, whereas I am more interested in the systemic factors that can boost or hamper that coordination. For attempts to study this at the aggregate level, see also Bartels (1996) and Edwards and Wood (1999).

(Rutkus 1991) often appear to aid members' media efforts, a consistent finding is that those in leadership and authority positions receive disproportionate coverage (Cook 1986; Hess 1986, 1991; Kedrowski 1996; Sinclair 1989).

Another common finding of the congressional communication literature concerns the pervasive failure of most members' publicity efforts. Cook (1989, 60), for example, observes that in 1986, more than half of the House members were never mentioned on the evening news. Hess (1986, 16) similarly concludes that about a third of the Senate appeared one time or less on those same programs. Even when examining local news, Hess (1991, 105) found that "most members of Congress . . . rarely get seen. . . . " Hess went so far as to criticize congressional members and reporters for not coming to terms with the scant coverage:

[Members and reporters] tend to overestimate the extent of television coverage and hence its importance in the legislative and electoral processes. . . . Reality to reporters is what they can see, to politicians what they can touch. And Capitol Hill is always crammed with cameras, lights, sound equipment, tape recorders, news conferences, handouts, stakeouts. . . . This also contributes to the myth of television's power as they react to its presence rather than to its output. . . . Scholars, however, have been less likely to fall into the journalists' trap. A number of studies have noted the modest television coverage of congressional campaigns. (Hess 1991, 105–6)[4]

A persistent weakness in Hess's and other related research is the emphasis on the individual member of Congress as the unit of analysis. This shortcoming was perhaps exacerbated by the Democratic Party's four-decade monopoly of the congressional majorities.[5] Although understandable, concerns about the potential negative effects of candidate-centered elections or individual show horses have distracted some scholars from a useful and important unit of analysis: the party and members' collective stake in their party's brand name.[6]

Metaphorically, much of the previous research appears to conclude that a football team's kicker is losing the game because he sits on the sideline more than the quarterback. As discussed herein, leadership

[4] Hess cites Kingdon (1984), Westlye (1991), and Wormser (1982) as examples.
[5] In fact, some of the more interesting work on partisan communication stems from authors interested in the use of "outside" strategies to push legislation. See Connelly and Pitney (1994), Jones (1970), Rohde (1991), Schattschneider (1960), and Sinclair (1989, 1997). Cook (1989, 129–31) notes a party leadership role in setting the political agenda, observing that such a finding was "not expected."
[6] Work by Evans and Oleszek (1999, 2001), Lipinski (1999, 2004, n.d.), Sellers (2005), and Vinson (2005) exemplifies a new variant of the literature that examines congressional communication from the perspective of the parties.

"dominance" in the news should be regarded as assisting rank-and-file efforts to foster their common party brand name rather than undermining or competing with their efforts. Here, I explicitly build on the model of partisan communication developed in previous chapters and argue that congressional communication is systematically influenced not only by party affiliation but also by the institutional setting that each congressional party confronts. Specifically, I argue that a party's attempts to gain coverage in the free news media are aided by achieving majority status within the legislature and (paradoxically) by having a president of the opposing party in office.

BUILDING THE BRAND NAME

As I discussed in Chapter 1, parties are like business franchises, whose members have an incentive to present clear and consistent messages to the public because of their shared "brand names." However, Chapter 1 also described the temptation for party members to customize the message of the party for their own gain or to seek publicity at the expense of their fellow partisans. This temptation is even stronger in the case of the president and his legislative party, for whom the institutional and political features of the American presidential system provide strong incentives to pursue different party brands. As suggested by the evidence presented in Chapters 2 and 3, party members seeking to advance their own political fortunes by turning on their fellow partisans across branches of government virtually can be assured of reaping tremendous personal publicity – but only to the detriment of their fellow party franchisees.[7]

---

[7] Some argue that the intraparty criticism highlighted in Chapter 3 may reflect – in part or in whole – attempts by partisans to enforce "good" branding by publicly criticizing fellow partisans who have departed from the agreed-on party brand. In fact, the 1991 Republican revolt against Bush's abandonment of his "No New Taxes" pledge, the 2007 revolt by Republicans against George W. Bush on immigration reform, and the 2008–2009 criticism of Bush's emergency interventions in the economy can be viewed as exactly this type of cross-branch criticism for poor party brand management. However, I argue that in successful party brand management, such disputes should be kept behind the scenes and negotiated, rather than erupt in public combat. When they do break out in public, they are inherently confusing for the brand and demoralizing for rank-and-file partisans, who will have difficulty determining which of their fellow partisans to believe on the issue (see Chapter 5). George W. Bush, for example, saw his approval among Republicans drop from 75% in April 2007 to 62% two months later – apparently because of the uproar among Republicans over immigration (NBC News/WSJ polls cited in Kuhn and Martin 2007). I will return to this theme later in Chapter 6, which discusses why presidents may derive benefits from having their party lose control of Congress and how a congressional majority also may see its electoral fortunes benefit from its party's loss of the presidency.

However, the presidential party's repeated failure to present a clear and consistent brand name across branches of government may not reflect or predict behavior toward fellow partisans in their *own* branch of government. In other words, although the news media still may have similar preferences regarding the partisan stories they want to show, the partisans themselves might have reason to behave differently. Within the legislature, the parties' closer pragmatic and ideological bonds should provide members with a greater incentive to create institutions or delegate powers to leaders to enforce a common party brand name than that which applies across branches. Moreover, the legislative institutions established to maintain party discipline in voting conceivably could be adapted to address communication issues.[8]

The following sections explore the incentives and institutions on which the congressional parties might rely to increase their party cohesion in the news media.

Pursuit of Majority Control

First, each member of Congress prefers to have a majority of ideologically similar members in place to bless his or her legislative proposals. Therefore, members of congressional parties have an incentive to pursue majority control of the chamber for their party. Such reasoning also applies to the desire to have a president of one's own party available to sign the bill into law.

However, achieving majority-party status within the legislature has advantages beyond simply maximizing coalition size. Members of the majority party can exercise even greater control over legislation through committee leadership positions, favorable bill rulings, larger staff resources, and other perquisites of majority status. In dollars and cents, Cox and Magar (1999) argue that majority status also can provide substantial financial dividends to members. They estimate that members of the majority party in the House can expect an additional $36,000 in Political Action Committee (PAC) contributions than comparable members of the minority party. Similarly, a majority senator can expect to receive almost $75,000 more in contributions than comparable minority peers.[9]

---

[8] However, such discipline would be exceptionally difficult to apply across branches of government.

[9] The figures presented are in 1994 inflation-adjusted dollars. Cox and Magar's (1999) analysis controlled for factors such as committee assignments and voting record.

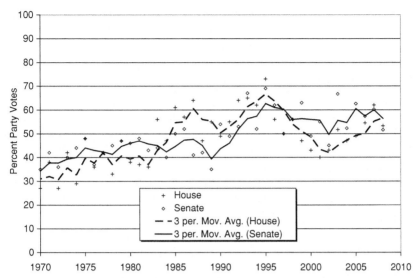

FIGURE 4.1. Party voting in the House and Senate, 1970–2008. (Source: *Congressional Quarterly Weekly* (2008), "Party Unity History," 15 December: 3338.)

Thus, in their quest to reach or maintain majority status in the legislature, members have an interest in fostering the election chances of their fellow party mates and a clear disincentive to take actions that would harm them. The zero-sum party competition for majority status therefore provides each party with an incentive to harm the reelection chances of members of the opposing party.[10]

Ideological Bonds

Studies of congressional voting highlight a substantial increase in the ideological cohesion of the congressional parties during the last four decades. As the "conservative coalition" of Republicans and Southern Democrats declined in numbers and influence and the Northeast became more Democratic, majorities of one party increasingly are pitted against majorities of the other party in their voting (Bond and Fleisher 2000). Figure 4.1 illustrates that "party voting" reached a historical apex in the mid-1990s and rebounded again in recent years.

[10] In Chapter 6, I explicitly argue that this is not necessarily the case across institutions, as exemplified by the 1996 "conspiracy of incumbents."

While the ideological gap between parties has expanded in recent years, ideological distances within parties appear to have diminished. Figure 4.2 illustrates that, at least as measured by roll-call votes, party unity in the House reached exceptionally high levels in recent years. If majorities of one party today oppose majorities of the other party, they should expect to receive the support of 85% to 95% of their fellow partisans.

Of course, although shifting ideology likely played a large part in this impressive voting cohesion, members of Congress also had incentives to vote with their fellow partisans. The conditional party government school of thought argues that members of Congress are more willing to delegate enforcement authority to congressional party institutions when the parties are ideologically homogeneous and distinct from one another.[11] Scholars generally examine such institutions in the context of voting unity in the legislative parties. However, in the next section I describe institutions that have been established to foster communication coherence within each legislative party.

Legislative Party Communication Institutions

Parties have long recognized the importance of voting cohesion and created institutions such as caucuses and whips to foster such unity. Because cohesive voting and communication both involve structuring the incentives of members, it is plausible that some of the institutions created for voting discipline and coordination may be adaptable for communication. Although communication-related discipline might be expected to take place outside the public eye, anecdotal evidence suggests that party caucuses will sanction members who too visibly "thumb their noses" at the party in the press.

One example – albeit one that blurs the distinction between party unity in votes and in the news – was Senator Zell Miller's (D-GA) endorsement of President George W. Bush's tax-cut bill in 2001, which provoked lobbying by Senator Tom Daschle and other members of the Democratic leadership to reverse his stance (Novak 2001). Miller also faced scorn from his party for his keynote speech at the 2004 Republican National Convention that attacked John Kerry and endorsed George W. Bush for president. A *New York Times* preview of the speech begins, "Zig Zag Zell, his critics call him. Zellout. A traitor. An elephant in donkey's

---

[11] See Abramson, Aldrich, and Rohde (1996); Aldrich (1995); and Rohde (1991).

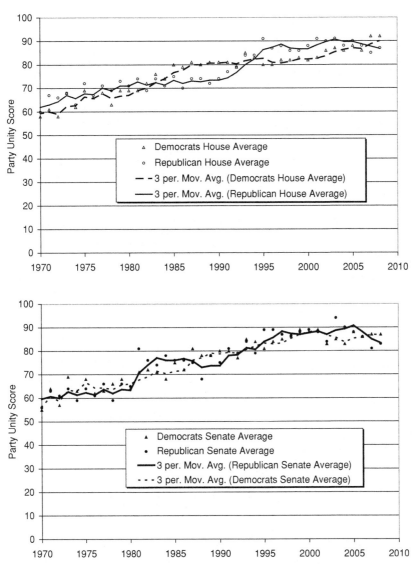

FIGURE 4.2. Average House party-unity score, by party: 1970–2008 and average Senate party-unity score, by party: 1970–2008. (Source: *Congressional Quarterly Weekly* (2008), "Party Unity History," 15 December: 3338.)

clothing" (Stolberg 2004).[12] As will be discussed in Chapter 5, Democratic electoral and committee sanctions against Connecticut Senator Joe Lieberman for his vocal support of both the Iraq War and the presidential candidacy of his friend John McCain provide another clear example of such punishment.

In addition to traditional institutions such as caucuses and whips, congressional parties recently have established completely new institutions specifically designed to foster coordinated communication through the news. While much of the prior research into congressional media strategies focuses on the efforts and resources of individual members, parties increasingly delegate power and authority to their leaders to coordinate these individual activities.[13]

For House Democrats, the House Democratic Policy Committee was recently the entity responsible for "production and communication of the party message," although Speaker of the House Nancy Pelosi (D-CA) has worked to centralize Democratic message and communication strategy in her office.[14] The revamped House Democratic Steering and Policy Committee is co-chaired by Representatives Rosa Delauro (D-CT) and George Miller (D-CA) and consumes substantial staff resources.[15]

On the Republican side, party communications efforts are coordinated in the House by the Republican Conference, chaired in the 110th Congress by Representative Adam Putnam (R-FL). The Conference also has a large staff, with 12 staffers devoted to "writing, outreach, coordination, and technical assistance." In addition, before the Republicans lost their majority, the Speaker's office employed another six staffers devoted to party communication.[16]

According to Lipinski (1999), in addition to establishing an agenda for its party, the party communications leadership facilitates unified communication across individual members of Congress through three types

---

[12] See Chapter 5 for a discussion of the likely persuasive impact of Miller's action.

[13] For an overview of literature on the press offices of individual members, see Cook (1989). For an overview of the increasing role that communication skills play in leadership selection, see Foerstel (2000), Kedrowski (1996), and Lipinski (n.d.). Both Evans (2001, 218–21) and Sellers (2005) provide excellent discussions of legislative party message institutions and strategies.

[14] Billings (2003), cited in Lipinski (n.d.).

[15] Lipinski (n.d.) indicated nine communications staff members between the offices of the Majority Leader and the Democratic Steering and Policy Committee, and that the number increases substantially when all staff members who aid message communication are included.

[16] Lipinski (1999, 6).

of activities: leadership communication, special events and outreach, and individual message coordination.[17] By "leadership communication," Lipinski means the various media activities that leaders pursue in an attempt to gain publicity: television appearances, press releases, briefings, town meetings, floor speeches, and so forth.[18] "Special events," in turn, refer to media-friendly events designed to communicate the party brand. According to Lipinski, such events cater to the media through tactics such as featuring newsworthy individuals like the president or celebrities; assembling large, supportive crowds; providing good "visuals"; and other techniques. As was discussed in Chapter 1, the Republicans' Governing Team Day and Contract with America signing ceremonies are good examples of such events. Other events include the Democrats' 2000 "Haunted News Conference," which one jaded journalist previewed as follows:

Organized to draw attention to what Democrats call "GOP-killed legislation" in the 106th Congress, the conference will also feature Thomas Daschle (S.D.) – Democratic Leader from the greatest deliberative haunted house in the world: the United States Senate. I have probably been haunting the spooky halls of the Capitol just a tad too long to be able to inform you with confidence – hours before the event – what you will see and hear if you stop by: Scary music. Grim Reapers. And tombstones. Lots of tombstones – each with a particular RIP "killed" piece of legislation inscribed on the front. Gun control. HMO reform. School construction. You get the drift. I certainly hope Gephardt and Daschle dress for the occasion.[19]

Finally and perhaps most important, the leadership is entrusted with the task of coordinating the communication of individual members. According to Lipinski (1999), the leadership of both parties meet weekly with individual members' press secretaries to provide suggestions for getting more local press coverage and "apprise them of the current party

---

[17] Lipinski (1999, 11). I paraphrased and reordered Lipinski's list.

[18] The literature's finding regarding the leadership's dominance of congressional news is consistent with Lipinski's description here.

[19] In the same column, Mills (2000) praises "Congressional Props 'R' Us" for their "hi-tech, computer-graphic version of a billboard showing a clothesline with drying laundry," which was intended to illustrate the point that the Republicans had hung the American people "out to dry." Mills reported he "was so enamored by the effort that went into the billboard picture of the clothesline, I had a hard time following what they were actually saying. I think these Hill computer folks are running the entire show these days. I couldn't help but wonder just how much taxpayer money went into creating the billboard wall with the laundry....I have no idea if this nation is being governed correctly or not, but I've got to report to you folks that you should be very proud of all the charts and pictures that both sides use to trash the other." (See www.democrats.senate.gov/resource_center_floor_charts.htm for examples of these charts.)

message and the events being held to promote the message."[20] In addition, the group briefs staff, conference, and caucus meetings on "the party's message and how it is going to be promoted."[21] To shape responses to Republican initiatives and statements, congressional Democrats have also formed "Rapid Response" teams to provide quick and coordinated attacks.[22]

For rank-and-file members, both parties often supply simple, consistent briefing materials or talking points (Figure 4.3) that coordinate the party's brand-related messages, even when members are outside Washington. The Democrats, for example, have provided Democratic members with a packet called the "Weekender," which contains the following:

> ... not only materials explaining the party message on various current issues but also how to get press coverage in the district [including]... statistics... samples of op-ed pieces for local papers, samples of press releases... samples of letters which can be sent to local editorial boards, ideas for mailings to constituents, and suggestions for local events that are packaged to get maximum media attention.[23]

Prior to the July 4, 2006, congressional recess, for example, each party sent its members home to their districts with carefully selected talking points "to speak from as they hold public forums and meet with their constituents over the next week [so members could] eloquently promote their party's agenda and vision, while at the same time casting doubt on their opponents' goals" (Preston 2006). For Republicans, members were told to highlight an improving economy, the implementation of the Medicare prescription drug plan, the war on terror, and GOP efforts to address the energy crisis. Democrats, in turn, were told to highlight Republican failures to pass immigration reform, lobbying reform, a minimum wage

---

[20] Lipinski (1999, 11).

[21] Lipinski (1999, 11).

[22] Foerstel (2001, 818). This strategy relates to the Message Group or Theme Team efforts on the part of the Congressional parties, although the latter activities are targeted primarily at one-minute Special Orders floor speeches intended for C-SPAN consumption. See Maltzman and Sigelman (1996) and Schneider (2001) for discussions of these speeches.

[23] Lipinski (1999, 13). The Republicans apparently publish a similar packet called the "Boarding Pass," although Lipinski contended that their packet is generally less comprehensive. When preparing for contentious town hall meetings in the summer of 2009, Democrats provided "seven-inch-long pocket cards for their members to carry like political shields. The cards listed popular parts of the legislation to be emphasized at town hall meetings, including banning insurance companies from denying coverage to people with preexisting conditions and prohibiting them from dropping or declining to renew coverage for people who become sick" (Kane, Pershing, and Bacon 2009).

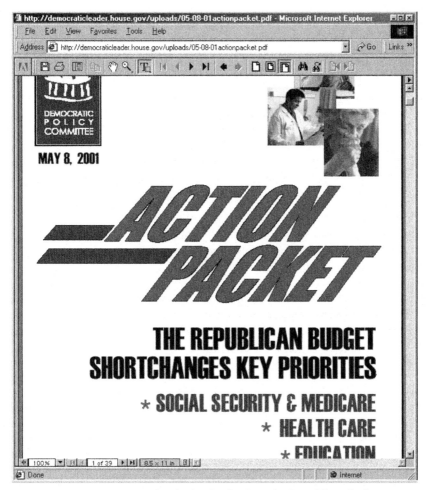

FIGURE 4.3. 2001 Democratic "Action Packet" on the Republican budget.

increase, or a "comprehensive budget" and to promote the Democratic "New Direction for America" legislative agenda (Preston 2006).

These packets recently have become increasingly detailed and thorough. In fact, then-Minority Leader Pelosi was actually criticized by many Democrats for going overboard with a massive 78-page briefing packet in 2003 (Cusack and Nichols 2003). The packet – described as "didactic," "patronizing," and "laughable" by some unidentified Democrats – was intended to help guide members' communication efforts on several issues over the long August recess. One of the most derided sections of the document provided detailed daily instructions for how members should prepare a telegenic "birthday party" for Medicare, including the following (Cusack and Nichols 2003):

- Monday: "Order your cake! Order a sheet cake with 'Happy Birthday Medicare' written on it. . . . Buy additional party supplies. Be creative. Buy a 'Happy Birthday' tablecloth for the center table. Purchase disposable plates and utensils if the facility will not provide them. You may also wish to purchase additional party favors – horns and whistles can be very useful to 'boo' the Republican agenda."
- Tuesday: "Review supply check list. Confirm cake/food orders and make sure supply checklist is complete. Provide writing utensils and paper for seniors to complete letters to the editor."
- Day of party: "Arrive early. . . . Set up tables. Spread a 'Happy Birthday' tablecloth on the center table, where cake will be placed. All other tables should have pens/pencils, writing paper, and copies of the sample letter to the editor."[24]

Many of these techniques have been in use for years in one form or another, although they have not always been so comprehensive. In 1992, for example, the House Republicans used a group called CommStrat (i.e., Communication Strategy) to coordinate the legislative party's message. According to Maraniss and Weisskopf (1996):

Every morning at eight, the press secretaries of CommStrat would participate in a conference call to discuss their message for the day. They would go over what the party office would say in its faxes, what the press secretaries would emphasize in their chats with reporters, what House members on a special Theme Team were planning for the one-minute speeches and longer special orders that begin and end the day on the floor, and what the House Republican Conference was doing to provide cover for members back in their home districts. It was all part of what Gingrich called the "unified approach" to communications, which gave him tighter control of the message.[25]

Increasingly, congressional parties have tried to exert greater message control over their members in election cycles. Under the leadership

---

[24] Republicans responded to the leaked briefing packet with scorn. Speaker Hastert's spokesperson noted that although Republicans provided their members with "broad thematics, [their] members don't need detailed instructions because they understand the issues. . . . The reason why [Pelosi] needs to script her caucus is because she's marching them over the cliff" (Cusack and Nichols 2003).

[25] Maraniss and Weisskopf (1996, 133, 138) later added that Gingrich "wanted to centralize communications in an office that would force-feed the message to members, monitor its delivery, and help shield it from enemy attack in the home districts."

of Representative Rahm Emanuel (D-IL) and Senator Charles Schumer (D-NY), Democrats in the 2006 election went so far as to link party financial support to conditions imposed by the central party. Schumer told donors, "We'll give [Democratic candidates] money, but [they] have to hire a campaign manager, a finance director and a communications director who we approve. . . . They have to toe the line" (Nagourney 2006).

Emanuel, in particular, took an exceptionally active role in monitoring (and occasionally punishing) the communication efforts of his fellow Democrats. According to Nagourney (2006), Emanuel contacted 40 Democratic candidates "every weekend, demanding to know what they have done for him lately" and was "paternal and approving when his candidates meet his standards for raising money or zinging an opponent [and] withering when they do not. Mr. Emanuel is legendary in Washington for ceasing communications with those who have displeased him (which presumably is preferable to the time he sent a dead fish to a Democratic pollster whose work he found lacking)." Emanuel's efforts did not cease following the Democrats' dramatic 2006 victory, as Representative Paul Hodges (D-NH) indicated, "He has been helpful and a pain-in-the-you-know-what, to my great benefit . . . he's an advocate for making sure folks in the district know what you're doing. . . . Of course, he keeps a close watch on doing what we need to do to get reelected" (quoted in Kaplan 2007). Representative Steve Kagen (D-WI) experienced that pain firsthand when he caused a stir by boasting to a group of antiwar activists that he had rebuked President Bush's top political adviser, Karl Rove, during a White House reception. After the administration denied the story, Emanuel reportedly "threw a fit. Kagen's staff was hauled into the Democratic Caucus's office for lessons on how to handle the media, Democratic sources said" (Kaplan 2007). Following the 2008 election, the Obama Administration's selection of Emanuel as White House Chief of Staff was interpreted as a sign that the new administration was planning to take a similarly aggressive tack toward message coordination with its congressional majority.[26]

And of course, as discussed in Chapter 1, Gingrich's famous Contract with America was primarily intended to help shape Republican communication efforts and branding rather than serve as a wish list of preferred

---

[26] Emanuel was called the "Democrats' Newt Gingrich" by Bruce Reed, a colleague in the Clinton White House: "He understands how much ideas matter, he always knows his message, he takes no prisoners and he only plays to win" (quoted in Green 2005).

legislation. Although such tactics may seem extreme, the desire to produce a coherent message through television news dictated that both legislative parties had to devote more energy to "staying on message." As former Representative Lee Hamilton (D-IN) observed:

> ... the other thing that developed shortly after TV arrived was a concerted effort by the two parties to develop a message that was tailored to the broadcast media and for the TV watcher. This involved keeping it simple and repeating the same poll-tested phrases on a particular subject over and over again. The most important virtue in a floor speech became one of "staying on message."
>
> ... At the same time, many members, who prided themselves on their individualism and independence, found it somewhat difficult to be told what to say and how to say it. They resented the theme message. But they were advised that going off message might give the media an opening to focus on something other than the party's preferred slant on the matter.[27]

Members of Congress have good reasons to fear providing such an "opening" for members of the press. As previous chapters show, the preferences of the news media play a critical role in determining which actions or statements actually reach citizens through the news. Despite increasing voting cohesion and sophisticated coordination of the parties' message efforts, it is unclear how much of this unity is actually presented to the public through the media. The next section addresses this question.

MESSAGE SUCCESS AND FAILURE IN THE LEGISLATIVE PARTIES

As one might expect given the findings from the discussion of presidential news in Chapters 2 and 3, both legislative parties face difficulties in getting the news media to air uniformly positive messages about themselves. However, members of the presidential party in Congress face several additional hurdles in their attempts to present themselves to the public. In particular, I contend that the president harms the communication attempts of his party by fulfilling the media's appetite for presidential-party news and by increasing the stature and prominence of the nonpresidential party.[28]

---

[27] Hamilton (1999) further observed that he believed that television had "diminished the quality of the debate and the quality of the legislative record." He added that he did "not offer these observations as wholly critical of TV in Congress because I think in several ways television helped the parties to forge greater unity and think more about what kind of message they wanted to communicate to the people. It may not always have been a policy-forcing mechanism, but it certainly was a message-forming influence."

[28] Again, as Chapters 2 and 3 show, the presidential party in Congress generally can be assured of coverage if it chooses to define its brand in defiance of or opposition to the president.

Congressional Stories

In Chapter 2, I argued that two factors determine which partisan messages will be broadcast: the probability that a party will offer a message and the probability that a news organization will decide to broadcast the message, if offered. Chapter 2 applies my predictions from this model to the dominant type of political news: stories about the president. In this chapter, I will be examining when and how congressional parties can succeed in getting messages about themselves (or the other party) into broadcasts.

Choosing Stories for a Broadcast

Both congressional parties face a major obstacle in trying to gain coverage of their endeavors: scarcity of network news time. While the president is generally assured coverage on the evening news (see Chapter 2), the congressional parties are often left fighting for "scraps" of news time in a broadcast that already contains a news story about the president. In this section, I argue that the institutional setting can affect a congressional party's newsworthiness through its majority status and role as a balancing counterweight to the president.

As I discussed in Chapter 2, the news media tend to feature greater coverage of actors who possess higher degrees of authority over the levers of government (i.e., the Authority Axiom). The media's strong valuation of institutional power produces some straightforward predictions: Those with institutional power are more likely to appear on the news. Given the institutional power associated with congressional majorities (Cox and McCubbins 1993), the *Majority Hypothesis* contends that *all else being equal, the majority party should appear in more congressional stories than the minority party in Congress.*

However, it is important to recognize that the majority party's power has limits, particularly in the Senate. For example, in 1993, Democrats controlled the presidency as well as majorities in the House and Senate. Nonetheless, they soon found that the Republicans in the Senate were able to use filibusters and other delaying tactics to prove decisive in some legislation. Even when "out of power," the Senate Republicans had substantial influence over the legislative process through their control of a "veto gate." Similarly, in 2005, Democrats in the Senate – despite being in the minority – were able to block or delay many controversial Bush nominees to the court and to credibly challenge changes to Social Security. This is consistent with the record of the last 15 years, in which the majority party prevailed in 83% of party unity votes in the House

TABLE 4.1. *Newsworthiness of Congressional Parties*

	Unified Government	Divided Government
Presidential Substitution Hypothesis	Boost nonpresidential party	Boost nonpresidential party
Majority Party Hypothesis	Boost presidential party	Boost nonpresidential party

but only 71% in the Senate. The 2008 contrast across chambers was especially sharp, with the Democratic majority in the House prevailing in more than 93% of party unity votes, but less than 54% in the Senate.[29]

In the case of divided government, conversely, the president's legislative parties are seldom pivotal. Even in situations in which the presidential party can gather enough votes to scuttle initiatives, the president likely would have killed the legislation anyway, rendering the efforts of the party far less consequential.

The "redundancy" of the presidential party's authority in the legislative process points to another potential source of importance: the uniqueness of a legislative party's power. The nonpresidential party members in Congress generally represent the most important group of actors of their party in government.[30] A member of the presidential party in Congress, by contrast, is basically *never* the most important actor representing his or her party. Given this, the *Presidential Substitution Hypothesis* predicts that, *all else being equal, the presidential party should appear in fewer congressional stories than the nonpresidential party in Congress.*

Together, the hypotheses imply that it will be especially difficult for the presidential party in Congress to receive coverage of its activities in divided government, while the majority party should prosper. In unified government, conversely, the two hypotheses push in opposite directions, presumably leading to some rough equivalence of coverage between the majority and minority parties (Table 4.1). In the following sections, I

---

[29] Data are derived from the Victories in Party Unity Votes table in "Party Unity Background." *Congressional Quarterly Weekly* (15 December 2008: 3337).

[30] Presidential candidates, governors, and party officials sometimes vie for party "leadership." Ferraro (2001) also identified Al Gore, Senator Joseph Lieberman (D-CT), Senator Hillary Rodham Clinton (D-NY), Terry McAuliffe, Senator John Edwards (D-NC), Senator Evan Bayh (D-IN), and Senator John Kerry (D-MA) as possible competitors to be the standard-bearer for the Democratic Party. As I discuss in the conclusion to this chapter, Kerry obviously took on that role as his party's nominee for president in 2004. However, after his 2004 election loss and lapses during the 2006 midterm elections (including his "stuck in Iraq" gaffe), he was largely pushed out of the role. Following the 2006 midterm, senators Barack Obama (D-IL) and Hillary Rodham Clinton (D-NY) seized the spotlight, along with Speaker Nancy Pelosi (D-CA) and Majority Leader Harry Reid (D-NV).

test these hypotheses by examining the initiation of and responses to congressional news.

CONGRESS-INITIATED STORIES IN THE NEWS

In this section, I again use the CMPA content analysis data of evening news stories to test the predictions of the Majority and Presidential Substitution hypotheses.[31] In so doing, I determine whether a legislative party's ability to initiate and respond to stories varies with control of Congress and the presidency.

Who Can Initiate Congressional Stories?

As discussed in Chapter 2, analysts are generally unable to observe directly "potential" stories that are not broadcast by news organizations.[32] In addition, the content data collected by CMPA examined in Chapter 3 are not coded regarding whether a particular partisan actor is the "subject" of an entire story. However, the data are coded for the target of individual evaluations within stories.[33] Although clearly not a perfect measure, the inclusion of such an evaluation within a particular story implies that the actor being evaluated was the focus of some attention in that story. In other words, for a story to be edited to include an evaluation of a congressional Republican, it had to be at least somewhat concerned with the individual or his or her actions as a subject.

Table 4.2 displays the targets of congressional evaluations. As expected from the discussion of the relative attractiveness of the president as story subject in Chapter 2, he is the dominant target of these evaluations and accounts for nearly two of every three evaluations.[34] The nonpresidential

---

[31] The Baum and Groeling content analysis dataset used in Chapter 3 cannot be applied here because it only records congressional evaluations of presidential and administration targets.

[32] See Groeling and Kernell (1998) and Groeling (2008) for discussions of this problem in the context of news content analysis. For innovative examples of congressional research that attempt to tackle this difficult issue, see Lipinski (2004), Sellers (2005), and Sellers and Schaffner (2007).

[33] See Chapter 3 for a discussion of the coding methodology used in the CMPA data.

[34] The Baum and Groeling coding in Chapter 3 showed a more even distribution of evaluations across the president and his administration. This is likely the result of the case selection for that data, which draws heavily from periods when the country was undertaking military action abroad. In addition, the Baum and Groeling coding rules allowed evaluations of "U.S. Policy" to count toward the administration's total. For this reason, key comparisons across the datasets rely on personal evaluations of the president, which are more consistent in their coding.

TABLE 4.2. *Partisan Targets of Congressional Evaluations Coded by CMPA: 1981, 1992–1995, and 2001*

Target of Evaluation	Count (Percent)
President	3,317 (45%)[35]
Administration	986 (13%)
Presidential Party in Congress	949 (13%)
Nonpresidential Party in Congress	2,181 (29%)

party also maintains a respectable presence, with 29% of all evaluations directed at it. The presidential party in Congress, however, apparently is ignored by most evaluators, receiving only 13% of the congressional evaluations. Although the president's dominance as a story subject is expected, it is important to note the prominence of the nonpresidential party in Congress, consistent with the Presidential Substitution Hypothesis. In Table 4.3, these results are disaggregated for each congressional party in unified and divided government to test the predictions shown in Table 4.1.

Table 4.3 shows that in unified government the nonpresidential party and the presidential party are fairly even in total evaluations: 55% were targeted at the nonpresidential party (which benefited from the presidential-substitution bonus) and 45% were targeted at the presidential party (which benefited from its majority status). In divided government, however, both factors benefit the nonpresidential party, which should result in a large advantage over the presidential party. Table 4.3 shows results that strongly support this inference, with the nonpresidential-party evaluations ballooning to more than four of every five evaluations.[36]

---

[35] The total does not include 41 evaluations of the president-elect or out-of-office presidents.

[36] One interpretation of these results is that they are an artifact of the 1995 Republican majority's novelty after four decades in the minority. Although the total number of congressional evaluations spiked in 1995 for both parties, the parties' relative prominence in 1995 is similar to that of instances of divided government. In 1995, the Republicans were the target of 83% of congressional evaluations. In the only other CMPA purely divided government year (i.e., 1992), the nonpresidential Democrats received 71% of evaluations. In 1981 (in which Republicans still controlled the Senate), Democrats received 64% of evaluations. In 2001, prior to the return to divided government, Democrats received 53% of congressional evaluations; following the resumption of divided government (but still facing a Republican majority in the House), Democrats increased their share of evaluations to 60%.

TABLE 4.3. *Congressional Targets of Congressional Evaluations, Unified and Divided Government*

	Unified Government	Divided Government
Presidential Party in Congress	45%	19%
Nonpresidential Party in Congress	55%	81%
(n)	1,354	1,776

Who Can Initiate Congressional Self-Praise?

Another measure of the parties' abilities to initiate stories is the evaluations in which they praise their own legislative party. As discussed in Chapter 2, both parties should be eager to consistently offer self-praise in news stories: The obstacle in this quest is the news media's relatively low opinion regarding the newsworthiness of such self-praise. Thus, I again expect the relative prevalence of such self-praise to mirror the parties' relative newsworthiness, as captured in Table 4.1. Table 4.4 tests these predictions by presenting instances of CMPA-coded self-praise for each congressional party under unified and divided government.

If nothing else, Table 4.4 shows worse news for the presidential party than did Table 4.3. In unified government, almost two thirds of self-congratulatory evaluations come from the nonpresidential party. Moving to divided government almost completely mutes the presidential party in its attempts at self-praise: Consistent with my predictions, it is exceptionally difficult for the presidential party to gain coverage of self-praise when faced with an opposing majority and a president of its own party. Conversely, the majority party in divided government is afforded substantial opportunities for self-promotion.

TABLE 4.4. *Party Shares of Congressional Self-Praise, Unified and Divided Government*

	Unified Government	Divided Government
Presidential Party in Congress	39%	9%
Nonpresidential Party in Congress	61%	91%
(n)	547	641

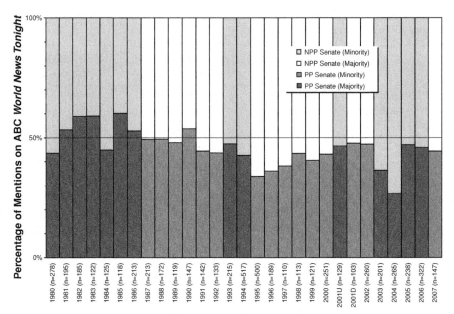

FIGURE 4.4. ABC *World News Tonight* coverage of the presidential party versus the nonpresidential party in the Senate, 1980–June 2007.

Verbatim Transcript Search

Overall, the CMPA data produce substantial support for the notion that the nonpresidential party in Congress is privileged in its communication attempts, especially in the case of divided government. However, the CMPA dataset covers only six years of recent American politics and is restricted to situations in which members are the source or target of a positive or negative partisan evaluation. To supplement these results, I have compared the prominence of the two legislative parties in the news for an additional 21 years, using verbatim transcripts of ABC's *World News Tonight*. Figure 4.4 presents the results of a search for stories that mentioned each legislative party in the Senate from 1980 through the first half of 2007.[37]

---

[37] The searches, conducted using the Lexis-Nexis archive of ABC News transcripts, were as follows:

For mentions of Democrats in the Senate: (senat! or sen.) w/10 (democrat!) and show (world news tonight or gibson).

For Senate Republicans: (senat! or sen.) w/10 (republica!) and show (world news tonight or gibson).

Figure 4.4 shows again the pronounced dominance of the non-presidential-party majority as a subject of Senate news coverage, which is consistent with the Presidential Substitution Hypotheses. The nonpresidential party received a majority of mentions in all but 1 of the 15 years in which it was in the majority and in all but 5 of the 14 years in which it was in the minority.[38] The Majority Hypothesis receives somewhat less support, in that when the presidential party moves from majority to minority control, its share of the ABC coverage sometimes rises (i.e., 1993 and early 2001) but also drops (i.e., 2003 and 2007). However, with the exception of post-Jeffords 2001, the presidential-party movement from majority to minority control (i.e., 1987 and 1995) seems to deflate the relative coverage, which is consistent with the Majority Hypothesis.

Figure 4.5 repeats this search for the House.[39] The results shown in the figure also provide substantial support for the Presidential Substitution Hypothesis: In all but 1 of its 19 years in the minority and all but 3 of its 10 years in the majority, the presidential party received less coverage than the nonpresidential party.[40] Although the presidential party had only two transitions from minority to majority status (i.e., 1993 and 2001), both changes resulted in greater coverage, which is consistent with the Majority Hypothesis. Similarly, the three presidential-party changes from majority to minority status (i.e., 1981, 1995, and 2006) show drops in coverage, although the decrease in 1981 is minimal.

For House Democrats: (rep. or representativ! or congres! or capitol hill) w/10 (democrat!) and show (world news tonight or gibson).

For House Republicans: (rep. or representativ! or congres! or capitol hill) w/10 (republica!) and show (world news tonight or gibson).

The search terms did not include the names of individual members of Congress and thus may understate each party's total coverage in the news. In 1996 and 2004, the results include mentions of presidential nominees Bob Dole and John Kerry if they included mentions of their title as a senator (83 of the results mentioned Dole in 1996 and 197 mentioned Kerry in 2004).

[38] Note that 2001 has separate values for both unified and divided government, corresponding to Senator James Jeffords's (I-VT) switch to caucusing with the Democrats. The exceptional newsworthiness of the Republican majority in 1980–1986 might have been a function of its novelty: It was the first Republican majority in either chamber since the 1950s.

[39] Unlike Senate Republicans, House Republicans did not lose control of their chamber in 2001. Nonetheless, the 2001 results are broken out separately for pre- and post-Jeffords to test for differences in coverage coinciding with the return to divided government.

[40] Two outlying years, 1981 and 1982, appear to coincide with Reagan's exceptionally successful first two years in office, in which a conservative coalition of Republicans and Democratic defectors was able to push significant legislation through over the objection of other Democrats.

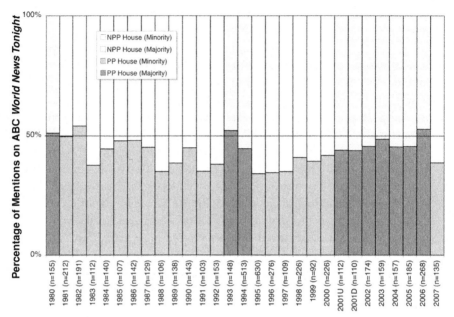

FIGURE 4.5. ABC *World News Tonight* coverage of the presidential party versus the nonpresidential party in the House, 1980–June 2007.

In summary, both the detailed CMPA analysis and a broader search of television-news transcripts appear to confirm that the president undermines the newsworthiness of his legislative party. While Chapter 3 indicates that both parties are exceptionally negative in their evaluations in presidential news, in the following section I examine what congressional sources say about one another in the news about Congress.

Who Responds to Congressional News?

This section examines what happens when partisans compete to be included in news stories initiated within Congress. Like the Chapter 2 model of presidential news, different actors can evaluate congressional news; unlike the Chapter 2 model, the president is now a potential source for such responses.

Given the news media's preference for stories with greater balance and novelty, the party initiating the story will find it difficult for its self-praise to appear in the story. Conversely, the novelty of intraparty disputes greatly increases the likelihood of coverage of such an event, although this clearly has an adverse effect on the communication of a cohesive

TABLE 4.5. *Sources and Valence of Congressional Evaluations*

Source, Unified Government	Pct. Critical of Presidential Cong. Party	N (Percent of All Unified Government)	Pct. Critical of Nonpresidential Cong. Party	N (Percent of All Unified Government)
Presidential Party in Congress	38%	318 (20%)	78%	375 (24%)
Nonpresidential Party in Congress	94%	286 (18%)	33%	375 (24%)
President	38%	69 (4%)	71%	147 (9%)
Source, Divided Government	Pct. Critical of Presidential Cong. Party	N (Percent of All Divided Government)	Pct. Critical of Nonpresidential Cong. Party	N (Percent of All Divided Government)
Presidential Party in Congress	54%	91 (4%)	95%	667 (29%)
Nonpresidential Party in Congress	95%	254 (11%)	27%	764 (33%)
President	36%	14 (1%)	93%	504 (22%)

brand to the public. In addition, by virtue of his greater authority, the president will dominate equivalent statements by his party. Thus, if the president and his legislative party both oppose a nonpresidential party's statement, the president's statement is more likely to be selected.

A critical difference in this situation is that by initiating the story, the congressional party gains a chance for self-praise. However, as demonstrated in the previous section, the presidential party in Congress has difficulty getting coverage when its members praise themselves, especially in the case of divided government. Table 4.5 is a summary of the legislative parties' relative success at presenting positive messages about themselves in the news.

As expected, the table reveals that despite their increasingly unified voting behavior within the legislature and efforts to stay "on-message," legislative parties still spend significant time criticizing their fellow members. In unified government, both the presidential and nonpresidential parties are frequently evaluated, although the nonpresidential party is a target about 50% more often. While the majority presidential party criticizes its fellow partisans within the chamber about two fifths of the time, it spends a similar amount of time evaluating (and primarily criticizing) its opponents. The nonpresidential party, conversely, criticizes itself about one third of the time and attacks the presidential party approximately

19 of every 20 evaluations. For his part, the president is a relatively infrequent evaluator of Congress, providing only about 13% of the evaluations. Within these statements, most are negative evaluations directed at the nonpresidential party.

Moving to divided government drastically remaps the patterns of evaluations. The nonpresidential party, which is already the subject of most congressional evaluations in unified government, dwarfs the presidential party as the target of 84% of all congressional evaluations. The evaluations of the nonpresidential party, in turn, are far more polarized along party lines, with near-unanimous criticism by the president and his party and substantially more positive self-evaluations by the nonpresidential party.

The presidential party receives roughly the same tenor of evaluations from the president and nonpresidential party as before, but at reduced volumes. Its self-evaluations are significantly more critical (i.e., 54% negative versus 38% in unified government); however, the massive absolute and proportional drop in their total comments means that the actual number of critical comments also decreased by about half.

Throughout the process, the president is seldom seen evaluating his own legislative party. Perhaps fearing that a shift in his focus to Congress will "step on" his preferred message of the day, the president says little about his congressional party. However, he commands a large portion of nonpresidential-party evaluations, particularly in divided government.

CONCLUSION

In the last few decades, the presidential party in the legislature has had relatively little control over its image in the news media. Although both parties increasingly have adopted more sophisticated and media-friendly tactics in an attempt to break out of their media-imposed obscurity, their efforts often seem to succeed or fail based on factors largely outside of their control.

Partisans have had the party leadership take on an expanded role in representing their party in the news media in an attempt to increase control over their image in the news media. Figure 4.6 graphically illustrates the difficulty that the presidential party faces in getting coverage, even for members of its leadership.[41]

---

[41] A chart of the Senate majority/minority leaders shows similar results, except for the years including Bob Dole, who was a presidential aspirant twice in the date range.

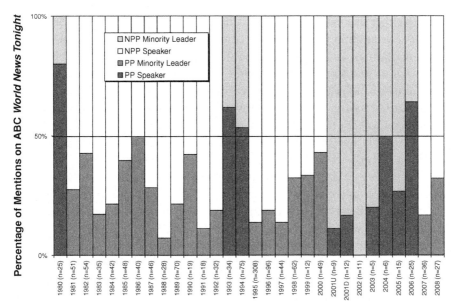

FIGURE 4.6. ABC *World News Tonight* coverage of the leaders of the presidential party versus the nonpresidential party in the House, 1980–2006.

Figure 4.6 is depressing for any congressional leader from the presidential party who hopes to emulate the president's ability to "go public." Across the years of divided government, the nonpresidential-party House Speaker received more than three times as much coverage as the presidential party's minority leader (i.e., 855 stories versus 263).[42] In every year of divided government except 1986, the Speaker received more coverage than the minority leader; in 1986, the minority leader had only a one-story advantage.

Conversely, during the years that the presidential party controlled the House gavel, its Speaker actually received slightly *less* coverage than the nonpresidential-party minority leader (i.e., 108 stories versus 109). In this case, the outlying years of relatively high coverage appear to have

---

[42] As with Figures 4.5 and 4.6, the LexisNexis searches for 1990–1993 returned results from the broadcast rather than story level. Excluding 1995 – a clear outlier in coverage due to massive coverage of Newt Gingrich and his "Republican Revolution" (see Chapter 1) – drops the ratio to 589:221, which is a 73:27 ratio. The search terms used were as follows:

(rep. or representativ! or congres! or capitol hill) w/30 (last name of leader!) and show (world news)

If there was a change in the leader in the course of the year, the tallies include hits for both leaders for the entire year of the handover.

been either the first year of presidential administrations (except, curiously, 2001) or election years in which control of the chamber was thought to be at risk (i.e., 1994, 2004, and 2006). In particular, the 2004 numbers – a total of five stories mention either Hastert or Pelosi in the first nine months of the year – were so low that I performed additional searches in transcripts for the *CBS Evening News* and NBC *Nightly News*.[43] NBC returned a total of five stories (two for Hastert); CBS yielded nine stories, only one of which mentioned Hastert. In contrast, searches for "John Kerry" across the same broadcast dates returned 289, 366, and 341 stories for ABC, NBC, and CBS, respectively.

These results reinforce a point first made in Chapter 2: Most congressional news is actually presidential news. If members of Congress (particularly members of the presidential party) want to increase their chances of appearing on the evening news, they probably will have to involve the president. As discussed in Chapter 3, for statements by the presidential party to be considered newsworthy, that "involvement" generally has to be in the form of criticism.

In the next chapter, I examine the public opinion consequences of the patterns of coverage identified here and in Chapter 3. The analyses show that if the presidential party indulges in criticism of the president, the results are exceptionally damaging to his standing with the public, particularly among both independents and members of his own party.

---

[43] The LexisNexis coverage of ABC extends considerably farther back than its transcripts for NBC or CBS, so it was impossible to duplicate all the searches across the 24-year span shown in Figures 4.4 through 4.6.

5

When Politicians Attack

The Political Implications of Partisan Conflict in the Media

> We can't have this infighting between conservatives and moderates and maintain our majority.
>
> – House Majority Whip Tom DeLay (R-TX)[1]

INTRODUCTION

Party nominating conventions no longer receive the highly-rated gavel-to-gavel coverage that characterized them in the "golden age" of television.[2] However, even as the party conventions have lost much of their grip on public and media attention, convention keynote speeches still catch the public eye. Because of the prominence and prestige attached to such speeches, party officials traditionally use the spotlight to advertise the party's core values and especially to showcase up-and-coming political stars (Coleman, Cantor, and Neale 2000). For example, in 1988, relatively unknown Texas State Treasurer Ann Richards vaulted from obscurity to the Texas governor's mansion after criticizing George H.W. Bush in her keynote as having been born "with a silver foot in his mouth." Even more auspiciously, in 2004 Democrats used the keynote to boost the senatorial campaign of a then-unknown Senate candidate named Barack Obama.[3] Following Obama's speech, Republican Party

---

[1] Quoted in Eilperin (2000).

[2] In the 1952 presidential race, for example, more than 55 hours of each party's convention were covered live by at least one of the three television networks. The typical American household watched more than 10 hours of *each* convention (Stanley and Niemi 2000, Table 4.13).

[3] The speech immediately catapulted Obama into the public spotlight. For example, even the conservative *Washington Times* praised Obama's performance in an editorial, saying

officials considered a range of speakers for their convention's keynote and announced that their choice was Zell Miller, a relatively obscure Democratic senator from Georgia.

If the traditional functions of the keynote speeches are to highlight party values and raise the stock of promising new candidates, why would Republicans choose to feature a Democrat who was on the verge of retirement – a speaker who had, in fact, given the *Democratic* keynote in 1992 for then-Governor Bill Clinton? Why not emulate the Democrats and give a boost to a deserving up-and-coming Republican candidate? I contend that Republicans had two important motivations for selecting Miller: His speech was especially likely to be considered newsworthy (see Chapter 2), and perhaps more important, his praise of the Republican president and criticism of the Democratic nominee were more likely to be considered credible by most Americans than a comparable speech given by a Republican. As Bush himself later said in a campaign appearance in West Virginia, "See, my message is for everybody. . . . I think old Zell Miller set a pretty good tempo for Democrats all across the country. He made it clear it's all right to come and support the Bush ticket."

In this chapter, I examine the credibility of exactly these types of partisan messages. I focus on how this credibility is systematically predictable by examining the content of those messages, as well as the identities of the speaker and audience. I derive several testable hypotheses regarding the likely credibility of different types of partisan messages for different viewers and then test the predictions using data on presidential approval and evening news content. The results confirm that Bush and his fellow Republicans were probably correct to assume that a ringing endorsement across party lines would aid their cause.

CHEAP TALK?

In this chapter, I again rely on the following four basic categories of partisan messages, first introduced in Chapter 2:

- statements that attack the other party (i.e., cross-party attacks)
- statements that support one's own party (i.e., intraparty praise)
- statements that support the other party (i.e., cross-party praise)
- statements that attack one's own party (i.e., intraparty attacks)

As discussed in Chapters 1 and 2, parties prefer to provide the public with messages that are consistent, that increase their own standing, and

he "hit all the right chords, wowed the audience without resorting to Bush-bashing and fulfilled his promise as a rising star in the Democratic Party" (*Washington Times* 2004).

that diminish the opposing party's standing. Thus, the parties generally prefer to broadcast messages from the first two categories (i.e., cross-party attacks and intraparty praise) and avoid presenting messages from the last two categories (i.e., cross-party praise and intraparty attacks).

These preferences stem in part from a basic intuition regarding which types of messages help or harm politicians. However, partisan messages are not "injected" into the public; rather, they are processed and can be accepted or rejected based on their credibility (Asch 1952; Druckman 2001; Kuklinski and Hurley 1996; Sniderman, Brody, and Tetlock 1991; Zaller 1992). Modern scholars are not the first to conclude that speakers' characteristics might influence the persuasiveness of their communication. As Aristotle observed in *On Rhetoric*, "Persuasion is achieved by the speaker's personal character when the speech is so spoken as to make us think him credible. We believe good men more fully and more readily than others: this is true generally whatever the question is, and absolutely true where exact certainty is impossible and opinions are divided."[4]

Modern experimental scholars, in turn, have contributed greatly in determining exactly which characteristics of a speaker convey credibility and in what context. In a series of experiments in the 1950s, Carl Hovland verified that students were more persuaded by messages from sources regarded as trustworthy or experts (Hovland, Janis, and Kelly 1953; Hovland and Weiss 1951–1952).[5]

Therefore, I argue that in order to determine the effect of partisan messages on viewers, not only should the content of the message be considered but also the credibility of the message and its speaker. Furthermore, although there are unpredictable elements that might influence the credibility of various individual messages, I argue that there are systematic characteristics of messages that enhance or reduce their credibility in the aggregate.

One source of credibility for a message is the listener's belief that the speaker and listener have common interests (Crawford and Sobel 1982). In an example of this reasoning in partisan practice, political columnist Paul Gigot noted that:

If only Republicans are calling for people to resign, it's not going to happen. When Bob Torricelli said on one of the Sunday shows that he thought Janet Reno should think about resigning, he went back to the Democratic Caucus on Tuesday

---

[4] Translation by W. Rhys Roberts (www.ac-nice.fr/philo/textes/Aristotle-Works/22-Rhetoric.pdf).

[5] Extending on this and other research, Druckman (1999) used an experiment to demonstrate that source credibility is also necessary to influence public opinion through framing.

and I'm told he had a very rough time of it. They said you can't do that, you can't open this up to Republicans' attack: that just validates the Republican themes. (Gigot 1999)

Similarly, parties often try to deprive their opponents of "political cover" by ensuring that no member speaks or votes in favor of controversial proposals, as noted in the Chapter 1 discussion of the congressional Democrats' remarkably unanimous and cohesive drive to withhold support for President George W. Bush's 2005 attempt to reform Social Security.

Putting this notion into partisan terms, *statements by a listener's own party should be regarded as more credible than those of the opposing party, all else being equal* (i.e., the *Partisan Credibility Axiom*).[6] In extreme cases, it is possible that partisan figures might have such low credibility with viewers who are members of the opposing party that their messages are taken as a disendorsement, leading such viewers to reach the opposite conclusion from the speaker's intention.

It is important to note that such credibility is based solely on the characteristics of the speaker and viewer of the messages and is independent of content. However, another important source of credibility derives from the interaction of source and message – that is, whether a message is costly to the speaker (Spence 1973). Many experiments have found that messages that impose costs on their speakers (Koeske and Crano 1968; Lupia and McCubbins 1998; Walster, Aronson, and Abrahams 1966) or that are unexpected for other reasons (Dutton 1973; Eagly 1981; Eagly, Wood, and Chaiken 1978; Levine and Valle 1975) are more persuasive than so-called cheap talk or expected messages, even when delivered by the same speaker.[7] Thus, in the context of partisan messages, *messages by partisan speakers that appear to hurt their own party or help the other party are regarded as being more credible than messages that help their*

---

[6] This does not imply that voters will regard their own party's statements as unvarnished truth, but rather that they will be less willing to believe the same statement coming from a member of the opposite party. This hypothesis also is consistent with observations of partisan perceptual screens, such as those discussed by Zaller (1992).

[7] The intuition behind this principle is embodied in the legal concept of "statements against interest," which are recognized as factors that may allow into evidence statements that would otherwise be excluded as hearsay. In many cases in the literature, there is confusion or conflation of disconfirming information (which deals with priors about source positions) and discrepant information (which simply represents information that disagrees with one's own prior opinions). See Kaplowitz et al. (1991) for a discussion of this confusion and an experiment that explicitly separates the effects of disconfirming and discrepant information.

TABLE 5.1. *Party and Costly Credibility by Party of Speaker and Viewer*

	Viewer is Presidential Partisan		Viewer is Independent		Viewer is Nonpresidential Partisan	
	Costly Credibility	Party Credibility	Costly Credibility	Party Credibility	Costly Credibility	Party Credibility
Presidential-Party Praise	Low	High	Low	Low	Low	Low
Presidential-Party Criticism	*High*	High	*High*	*Low*	*High*	*Low*
Nonpresidential-Party Praise	*High*	*Low*	*High*	*Low*	*High*	High
Nonpresidential-Party Criticism	Low	Low	Low	Low	Low	High

Note: All credibility values assume that the messages are targeted at a member of the presidential party. Italicized messages indicate that the message is costly for the speaker.

own party or hurt the other party (i.e., the *Costly Credibility Axiom*). Moreover, such messages should gain credibility *regardless of the listener's party affiliation.*

Table 5.1 summarizes the relative credibility of different political messages about the presidential party based on their partisan and costly credibility. Messages that harm the speaker's party are italicized.

Table 5.1 shows a central paradox for parties as they try to control their brand name with the public: The messages a party least desires to communicate actually tend to be very believable, which is consistent with the Costly Credibility Axiom. Similarly, the messages of "politics as usual" (i.e., attacking the other party and praising one's own) should represent a particularly unpersuasive form of "preaching to the choir." In such cases, only fellow partisans should find such messages especially persuasive. In contrast, both bipartisanship and internal disputes appear to have the ability to move people regardless of their party affiliation.

Based on Table 5.1, I derive the following three hypotheses about the relative credibility of different messages from the congressional parties, when those messages are targeted at the presidential party:

- *Independent Viewer Credibility Hypothesis*: Independent viewers should be most swayed by presidential-party criticism and *nonpresidential-party praise. They should be least swayed by presidential-party praise and nonpresidential-party criticism.*

- *Presidential-Party Viewer Credibility Hypothesis*: Because it combines both partisan and costly credibility, *presidential-party criticism should be the most damaging type of message for presidential-party viewers.* Conversely, because it lacks both costly and partisan credibility, those same viewers *should be unpersuaded by nonpresidential-party criticism.*

- *Nonpresidential-Party Viewer Credibility Hypothesis*: Because it combines both partisan and costly credibility, *nonpresidential-party praise should be the most persuasive type of message for nonpresidential-party viewers.* Because it lacks both partisan and costly credibility, those same viewers *should be unpersuaded by presidential-party praise.*

In the following sections, I test these hypotheses against both experimental and national survey data. First, I present a series of multivariate OLS regressions using the CMPA and Baum and Groeling content analysis data introduced in Chapter 3 to examine the impact of various partisan messages on subsequent Gallup approval ratings. Then, to maximize confidence in the causal relationships observed in these aggregate data, I report the results of two experiments– one that I conducted and another that enlisted my frequent coauthor, Matthew Baum (Baum and Groeling 2008) – that test the impact of different partisan messages on public opinion. The results show strong support for the hypothesized variations in credibility across message types.

HYPOTHESIS TEST #1: AGGREGATE ANALYSIS, BAUM AND GROELING DATA

In this section, I test the differential impact of congressional evaluations on presidential approval using the Baum and Groeling content analysis dataset.

Dependent Variables

In this analysis, I test a base and a more-controlled model for three different partisan subgroups: independents, viewers from the presidential party, and viewers from the nonpresidential party. My dependent variable in each case is the presidential approval of each subgroup in the subsequent Gallup presidential approval poll.

Control Variables

In the base models, I only control for current approval at the time (t) of the evaluation (i.e., Approval$_t$). In the fully-controlled models, I also control for the number of days between approval polls; changes in consumer sentiment; inflation; presidential and midterm election years, and the presence of congressional majorities in the presidential and nonpresidential parties.[8] I also include dummy variables controlling for presidential administrations (George W. Bush is the excluded category) as well as the major military conflicts included in this dataset – the invasions of Grenada and Panama, the start of the Gulf War and subsequent ground invasion, the 9/11 attacks and invasion of Afghanistan, and the Iraq War.

Explanatory Variables

The main explanatory variables in these multivariate OLS regressions are the types of messages identified previously: praise and criticism of the president by the presidential and nonpresidential parties in Congress. For partisan viewers, I simply include each message type directly in the models.[9] Because the Independent Viewer Credibility Hypothesis assumes that Partisan Credibility does not apply to independents, I created two index variables for these viewers that separate partisan messages into those with and without costly credibility. The Costly Evaluations variable scores nonpresidential-party praise as +1 and presidential-party criticism as −1; the Cheap Evaluations variable scores presidential-party praise as +1 and nonpresidential-party criticism as −1.

Base-Model Results

Columns 1 through 3 in Table 5.2 present results of my first test, which examines the relationship between high- and low-credibility evaluations and presidential approval by independents. The Independent Viewers

---

[8] This separation of divided government into single- and dual-chamber opposition-party control follows the discussion in Chapter 4 about the president's tendency to diminish coverage of his party, even while it is in the majority. It is obvious that there are no cases in which both control variables are zero, but there are two substantial periods (i.e., 1981–1986 and early 2001) included in these data in which each party controlled a chamber.

[9] Because the Baum and Groeling data use statements as the units, the four message categories are not mutually exclusive for a given evaluation; therefore, no category needs to be excluded from the regression for the model to run.

TABLE 5.2. *Statement-Level OLS Analyses of Effects of Congressional Evaluations of President on Presidential-Approval Ratings (Baum and Groeling Data)*

	Base Models			Controlled Models		
	Independents	Presidential Party	Nonpresidential Party	Independents	Presidential Party	Nonpresidential Party
Prior Presidential Approval	0.84 (0.012)***	0.821 (0.011)***	0.949 (0.008)***	0.682 (0.014)***	0.593 (0.015)***	0.677 (0.012)***
Costly Evaluations	1.8 (0.462)***	—	—	1.155 (0.413)**	—	—
Cheap Evaluations	0.601 (0.301)*	—	—	0.285 (0.268)	—	—
PP Criticism	—	-1.51 (0.419)***	-1.143 (0.55)*	—	-0.837 (0.382)*	-0.733 (0.48)⌢⌢
PP Praise	—	0.762 (0.493)⌢⌢	0.718 (0.65)	—	1.215 (0.443)**	0.897 (0.556)⌢⌢
NPP Criticism	—	0.195 (0.252)	-0.828 (0.332)**	—	0.231 (0.227)	-0.316 (0.285)
NPP Praise	—	0.948 (0.57)⌢	2.549 (0.754)***	—	0.829 (0.513)	2.036 (0.644)**
Days between Polls	—	—	—	-0.093 (0.012)***	-0.093 (0.009)***	0.013 (0.011)
Grenada Invasion	—	—	—	-5.352 (0.87)***	0.473 (0.634)	-0.858 (0.795)
Panama Invasion	—	—	—	2.559 (0.941)**	4.646 (0.679)***	2.401 (0.855)**
Gulf War Air War	—	—	—	4.782 (0.779)***	3.266 (0.565)***	7.835 (0.723)***
Gulf War Ground War	—	—	—	-0.013 (1.017)	-0.658 (0.736)***	2.574 (0.938)**
9/11-Afghanistan War	—	—	—	11.714 (1.513)***	1.291 (1.095)***	18.281 (1.427)***
Iraq War	—	—	—	10.879 (2.846)***	3.41 (2.071)⌢	4.455 (2.596)⌢
ΔConsumer Sentiment$_t$	—	—	—	-0.095 (0.029)***	0.005 (0.021)	-0.192 (0.027)***
Inflation	—	—	—	-0.17 (0.811)	-0.779 (0.591)	-0.851 (0.74)
Presidential Election Year	—	—	—	-1.023 (0.338)***	-0.681 (0.236)***	-4.014 (0.316)***
Midterm Election Year	—	—	—	0.897 (0.36)**	0.099 (0.261)	0.815 (0.332)**
NPP Majority	—	—	—	5.28 (0.621)***	2.452 (0.458)***	0.934 (0.569)⌢
PP Majority	—	—	—	8.27 (0.694)***	6.332 (0.523)***	4.042 (0.628)***
Carter	—	—	—	8.028 (1.204)***	-5.961 (1)***	9.581 (1.105)***
Reagan	—	—	—	4.714 (0.803)***	-2.839 (0.616)***	1.029 (0.726)⌢⌢
Bush 41	—	—	—	10.898 (0.838)***	-0.831 (0.638)	7.063 (0.758)***
Clinton	—	—	—	5.31 (0.736)***	-3.003 (0.561)***	-1.611 (0.674)***
Constant	9.565 (0.637)***	15.139 (0.875)***	2.942 (0.295)***	5.104 (1.183)***	31.933 (1.418)***	6.849 (0.943)***
Adj. R^2 (N)	0.654 (2868)	0.673 (2,879)	0.831 (2,879)	0.734 (2,868)	0.740 (2,879)	0.878 (2,879)

Notes: PP is presidential party; NPP is nonpresidential party. ⌢⌢$p \leq 0.15$, ⌢$p \leq 0.10$, $*p \leq 0.05$, $**p \leq 0.01$, $***p \leq 0.001$.

Hypothesis predicts that independent viewers should be most swayed by presidential-party criticism and nonpresidential-party praise and least swayed by presidential-party praise and nonpresidential-party criticism.

The independent base model corresponds exactly to this prediction, with the Costly Evaluations coefficient showing greater significance (i.e., $p \leq 0.001$ versus 0.05) and magnitude (i.e., 1.8 versus 0.6) than the Cheap Evaluations coefficient.

The second base model tests the Presidential-Party Viewer Credibility Hypothesis, which predicts the largest effects from presidential-party criticism (which combines Costly and Partisan Credibility for these viewers); the smallest impact for nonpresidential-party criticism (because it lacks both Costly and Partisan Credibility); and moderate impact for praise from the nonpresidential and presidential parties (because these lack Partisan and Costly Credibility, respectively). As Table 5.2 shows, the base presidential-party model precisely fits these predictions. Presidential-party criticism is the largest and most significant category of rhetoric, as predicted. In contrast, the type of rhetoric predicted to have the smallest persuasive impact (i.e., nonpresidential-party criticism) is not only the least statistically significant, but it also has a direct (not an inverse) relationship with presidential approval. This indicates that the more nonpresidential-party criticism offered, the more the presidential-party viewers rally to the president (albeit insignificantly). Finally, both presidential- and nonpresidential-party praise fall between the two extremes, with moderately positive, marginally significant impacts on public opinion.

For the non-presidential party, on the other hand, my hypothesis predicts that nonpresidential-party praise should be most beneficial and presidential-party praise should be least persuasive. Again, the base model strongly supports the predictions, with nonpresidential-party praise producing the largest and most significant coefficient; presidential-party praise producing the smallest coefficient and significance; and both presidential- and nonpresidential-party criticism falling in between in both magnitude and significance.

Fully Specified Model Results

Although the base model certainly supports the predictions derived from my model, attributing all changes in presidential approval to these rhetorical factors ignores many other "real-world" causes that may be independently influencing presidential approval. While some may argue that elite rhetoric is a primary path through which the public is made aware of the existence and significance of such events, I nonetheless attempt in this section to "throw the kitchen sink" into the model to see how such changes in specification alter the observed relationships. The last three models in Table 5.2 present the results of this analysis.

Beginning with independent viewers, controlling for disparate foreign, domestic, economic, and situational variables actually strengthens support for the predictions, with Costly Evaluations increasing in both coefficient size and significance and Cheap Evaluations decreasing to complete insignificance.

Presidential-party viewers perform similarly to the base model, with presidential-party criticism again producing the most damaging impact on presidential approval, with a large and significant coefficient, and nonpresidential-party criticism showing an insignificant "boomerang" result. Nonpresidential-party praise falls in between. Somewhat surprisingly, the largest and most significant result is the positive impact of presidential-party praise, which is even larger and more significant than in the base model.

The nonpresidential-party viewers also are similar to the base model, with nonpresidential-party praise providing the largest and most significant effects. In fact, although the remaining three types of rhetoric have the same sign as in the base model, none reaches conventional levels of statistical significance.

Analysis

A consistent finding across all three models in Table 5.2 is that the messages predicted to be most influential were, in fact, strongly associated with public-opinion change in the expected direction. Similarly, in every case, the variables expected to be least persuasive were, in fact, statistically insignificant.

To bolster confidence in these results, I repeat this analysis using aggregate data provided by CMPA (see Chapter 3). Although these data are similar to the Baum and Groeling data, they cover a different period (specifically, a period with fewer foreign-policy crises) and were coded by a completely separate organization using different coding parameters. Thus, the CMPA data provide an excellent validity check for the findings.

HYPOTHESIS TEST #2: AGGREGATE ANALYSIS, CMPA DATA

This section repeats the prior section's statistical tests by examining CMPA-coded data. As with the Baum and Groeling data, I begin with simple base models and then move to fully specified models. The models presented here are identical except for the omission of controls for events or conditions that do not apply to the CMPA data.[10]

Base-Model Results

The first three columns of Table 5.3 present the base-model results for independents, presidential-party viewers, and nonpresidential-party viewers, respectively. The results closely parallel my predictions, as well as the results of the Baum and Groeling data presented previously. For independents, the results again show the index of Costly Evaluations strongly outweighing the index of Cheap Evaluations. The differences here are even starker than in the base-model Baum and Groeling data, with Cheap Evaluations entirely losing significance. Moreover, the Cheap Evaluations have a negative coefficient, implying that the relationship with public opinion in these evaluations may have reversed such that criticism from the nonpresidential party may actually help the president (or, conversely, that praise from the presidential party may hurt him).

This suspicion is borne out in the partisan results, in which three of the four coefficients for cheap evaluations are actually "reversed" from their apparent intent: Presidential-party praise seems to hurt the president's approval (albeit insignificantly for presidential-party viewers), while nonpresidential-party-criticism seems to help significantly his standing with his own party. Except for the (insignificant) presidential-party praise result for his own party, this boomerang effect of cheap partisan evaluations on the other party is consistent with both the Presidential- and the Nonpresidential-Party Viewer Credibility Hypotheses. Both the large, significant, negative impact of presidential-party criticism on viewers from the president's own party and the large, positive (but only marginally significant) impact of nonpresidential-party praise on the other party's viewers are also consistent with these hypotheses.

---

[10] Because CMPA only coded evaluations from 1981, 1992–1995, and 2001, many date-based controls fall outside of the sample. These variables include Carter, who appears only as a lame duck and is therefore excluded from the analysis; all "rally events" except 9/11 and the Afghanistan War; and all presidential elections. The CMPA data tested here include observations for any instance in which a member of Congress made a partisan evaluation; however, only evaluations of the president himself are included as nonzero values in the rhetorical dummy variables. This specification is intended to model instances in which the member of Congress had sufficient access to the news media to make a partisan evaluation in the news. This also enables the inclusion of all four mutually exclusive types of presidential evaluations in the model by providing a reasonable "zero" category in which no evaluation of the president was given.

TABLE 5.3. *Statement-Level OLS Analyses of Effects of Presidential Party and Nonpresidential Party Congressional Evaluations of President on Presidential-Approval Ratings (CMPA Data)*

	Base Models			Controlled Models		
	Independents	Presidential Party	Nonpresidential Party	Independents	Presidential Party	Nonpresidential Party
Prior Presidential Approval	0.645 (0.008)***	0.719 (0.008)***	0.884 (0.006)***	0.36 (0.011)***	0.326 (0.012)***	0.636 (0.011)
Costly Evaluations	1.537 (0.195)***	—	—	1.303 (0.172)***	—	—
Cheap Evaluations	-0.145 (0.136)	—	—	-0.358 (0.119)**	—	—
PP Criticism	—	-0.642 (0.183)***	-0.041 (0.176)	—	-0.237 (0.159)^	0.24 (0.166)~
PP Praise	—	-0.32 (0.232)	-0.562 (0.224)*	—	0.078 (0.199)	-0.129 (0.208)
NPP Criticism	—	0.302 (0.127)*	-0.119 (0.123)	—	0.422 (0.109)***	0.074 (0.115)
NPP Praise	—	0.333 (0.292)	0.439 (0.282)^	—	0.894 (0.248)***	0.714 (0.259)**
Days between Polls	—	—	—	-0.182 (0.008)***	-0.128 (0.006)***	-0.082 (0.006)***
9/11-Afghanistan War	—	—	—	19.411 (0.796)***	6.615 (0.53)***	15.701 (0.753)***
Δ Consumer Sentiment$_t$	—	—	—	-0.35 (0.019)***	0.137 (0.014)***	0.127 (0.014)***
Inflation	—	—	—	-7.956 (0.493)***	-4.873 (0.36)***	1.246 (0.378)***
Midterm Election Year	—	—	—	1.621 (0.185)***	1.19 (0.138)***	0.712 (0.143)***
PP Majority	—	—	—	-4.504 (0.474)***	-6.124 (0.351)***	0.546 (0.364)~
NPP Majority	—	—	—	-2.154 (0.439)***	-2.783 (0.321)***	1.774 (0.336)***
Reagan	—	—	—	12.158 (0.549)***	4.182 (0.393)***	2.205 (0.434)***
Bush 41	—	—	—	-8.435 (0.465)***	-10.629 (0.391)***	-1.927 (0.343)***
Clinton	—	—	—	-5.119 (0.321)***	-10.936 (0.292)***	-3.741 (0.257)***
Constant	16.408 (0.398)	22.227 (0.635)***	2.678 (0.143)***	41.308 (0.979)***	68.992 (1.242)***	10.398 (0.648)***
Adj. R^2 (N)	0.430 (8,050)	0.492 (8,066)	0.747 (8,066)	0.566 (8,050)	0.643 (8,066)	0.792 (8,066)

Notes: PP is presidential party; NPP is nonpresidential party. ~ $p \leq 0.15$, ^ $p \leq 0.10$, * $p \leq 0.05$, ** $p \leq 0.01$, *** $p \leq 0.001$.

Fully Specified Model Results

The last three columns of Table 5.3 present fully controlled results that test the impact of CMPA-coded rhetoric on independents, presidential partisans, and nonpresidential partisans. Beginning with independents, Costly Evaluations continue to be strongly and significantly associated with independent approval in the predicted direction. Cheap rhetoric achieves statistical significance – but in the opposite direction, thus providing even stronger support for the predictions of the Independent-Viewer Credibility Hypothesis. For partisans, presidential-party praise is now insignificant for both parties (but has switched to a positive coefficient for presidential partisans) and the nonpresidential-party criticism boomerang positive effect for presidential-party viewers increased and is now even more significant here than in the base model. Costly nonpresidential-party praise also increased in magnitude and significance compared to the base model (somewhat surprising for the presidential party but as predicted for the nonpresidential party). Presidential-party criticism actually has a minor positive impact on the nonpresidential party (another boomerang effect of rhetoric from the other party) and the expected – but smaller than predicted – negative impact on presidential partisans. In the latter case, the presidential-party criticism is the only rhetorical variable with a negative coefficient, which suggests that the control variables account for more of the decrease in approval than in the uncontrolled base model.

Analysis

The monthly level CMPA data present strong support for the hypotheses. Again, independent viewers provide exceptional support for the Independent Viewer Credibility Hypothesis, with the relative coefficient size and significance of Costly versus Cheap Evaluations corresponding exactly to the predictions in all four cells. The predictions for partisan viewers also receive strong validation. As predicted, for presidential partisans, presidential-party criticism was the most damaging type of rhetoric; for nonpresidential partisans, praise from their party was the most beneficial to the president. Also consistent with the hypotheses, Cheap Evaluations from the other party had either insignificant or significantly inverse relationships on approval for presidential- or nonpresidential-party viewers. That is, praise from presidential-party evaluators hurt his standing with nonpresidential-party viewers (significantly in the base model), while nonpresidential-party criticism was associated with significant *increases* in approval by his fellow partisans in both models. Evaluations with purely partisan credibility were less influential than in the Baum and Groeling data, with both presidential-party praise and nonpresidential-party criticism failing to achieve statistical significance with fellow partisans. Costly cross-party evaluations were insignificant in the base model but significant (marginally in the case of presidential-party criticism; highly in the case of nonpresidential-party praise) among viewers from the other party in the fully specified models.

OVERALL AGGREGATE RESULTS DISCUSSION

Overall, the aggregate public-opinion tests presented here provide strong support for my hypotheses. In testing the Independent-Viewer Credibility Hypothesis, I have found that Costly Evaluations have a stronger and more significant correlation with approval than Cheap Evaluations in all four tests. Moreover, the Cheap Evaluations have negative coefficients in both CMPA models, further indicating that independent voters are unswayed by such rhetoric. As predicted, testing my Presidential-Party Viewer Credibility Hypothesis reveals that presidential-party criticism is the most damaging type of rhetoric in all four models. Conversely, criticism from the nonpresidential party, which was predicted to be the least credible type of evaluation for presidential-party viewers, actually helps the president's approval (significantly in the CMPA data). For nonpresidential-party viewers, my hypothesis predicts that praise from the nonpresidential party will be most beneficial for presidential approval; across all four models, that is precisely what I find, with the positive coefficient on such praise being at least twice as large as any other positive coefficients across all four regressions. Furthermore, this rhetoric has the most statistically significant relationship in every model except the CMPA base model, in which the negative impact of presidential-party praise is more significant. Finally, my Nonpresidential-Party Viewers Hypothesis also predicted that praise from presidential-party sources will be the least credible for these viewers, and the data support that conclusion. In both CMPA models, I find an inverse relationship – statistically significant in the base model – for these positive evaluations, indicating that they do not help and may actually harm the president's standing with those viewers. For the rally-event–centered Baum and Groeling data, both coefficients are positive on such rhetoric, with marginal significance (i.e., $p \leq 0.15$) in the fully specified model. However, the magnitude of the positive effects for these evaluations – even in the marginally significant fully specified model – is no more than half the size of the credible nonpresidential-party praise.

Of course, a potential objection to these results is that the causal direction in the relationship could be reversed. In other words, the changing patterns of evaluations might reflect rather than cause the change in presidential popularity. Because this is a valid concern, it was addressed in the regressions in three ways. First, the current popularity of the president at the time of the evaluation is already factored into the equation in every regression model. Second, unknown future approval presumably cannot cause present actions.[11] Third, if future approval affected present statements, why would it significantly impact only a subset of messages from both parties? In other words, if a future increase in presidential approval caused politicians to increase their support for the president, why is the increase in approval systematically associated with only subsets of these statements and viewers? In the case of independent viewers, why would it be more associated with credible versus noncredible evaluations? For presidential-party viewers, why would it improbably cause increases in *criticism* from the other party? The theory presented herein provides a firmer foundation for predicting such disparate effects.

In a related vein, attributing these changes in presidential approval to changes in evening-news content also appears to risk falling prey to a "media determinism" fallacy, especially when viewership for such programming has been in decline.[12] Because these statements tend to track the flow of agreement and disagreement within the legislature – at least, in the case of the nonpresidential party (see Chapter 3) – it is legitimate to question whether an outside political reality may be the ultimate cause.

---

[11] Of course, in some cases, future presidential approval can be accurately forecasted. In the case of rally events such as the 9/11 attacks, it was probably clear to most politicians that the public would rally around George W. Bush, at least somewhat. However, in most cases, it seems unlikely that a member of Congress could predict a president's future popularity with enough certainty to affect present actions.

[12] When the Pew Research Center surveyed Americans about where they got most of their national and international news in December 2008, it found that 70% still reported relying mainly on television – double that of newspapers and 30% more than Internet sources. However, the percentage for television represented a 12-point drop from the 2002 82% result. Moreover, among viewers younger than age 30, television was locked in a tie with the Internet, with 59% citing it as a main source of news.

In response, it should be noted that although fewer Americans obtain their news from television news, the newsworthiness assumptions of the model by no means are restricted to these programs. Rather, as discussed in Chapter 2, they seem to reflect broadly held views in the journalism community (but see the Conclusion chapter for a discussion on how this is changing in the 21st century). Even if politicians attempt to bypass the evening news to communicate to their constituents, they may face the same journalistic preferences in other media. Similarly, although factors such as wars, recessions, and other real-world events clearly affect public opinion about the president, the media in general (and congressional sources in particular) have an important role in mediating public understanding of the causes and responsibility of these broader events (Brody 1989; Iyengar 1991; Mutz 1992).

However, it must be said that the best method to address such issues of causality conclusively is to conduct an experiment. In the following section, I do precisely that.

EXPERIMENTS

Experiments are recognized as tools for social inquiry that maximize causal inference in research (Iyengar and Kinder 1987, 12). Rather than relying on naturally occurring events, experiments attempt to provide answers to causal questions by *intruding* on nature (Cook and Campbell 1979; Kinder and Palfrey 1993). In this case, I will be controlling the subjects' exposure to a particular type of message in the news (i.e., criticism of the president). Although such messages occur with great abundance in the natural setting (see the previous section), determining exactly which messages a survey respondent has seen "in the wild" is extremely difficult.[13]

In addition, by creating conditions and then randomly assigning subjects among them, experimenters mitigate against alternate explanations of the type I discussed previously. As Kinder and Palfrey note, by creating settings for research, researchers aim to "exclude various nuisance factors that might otherwise interfere with the causal relation of interest" (1993, 7).

---

[13] Most surveys that include questions of media consumption do so at a very broad level of aggregation. Even if respondents report viewing a particular broadcast or newspaper, it is difficult to infer that they consumed *all* of the content in that outlet. Conversely, respondents also may consume news without being able to report its source.

My aggregate survey analysis of presidential popularity was potentially vulnerable to exactly these sorts of "nuisances." Although experiments have inferential difficulties of their own (e.g., external validity and construct validity), I contend that the combination of these methods' strengths produces a more persuasive analysis than either method does alone.[14]

EXPERIMENT #1: COSTLY CREDIBILITY FOR INDEPENDENT VIEWERS

In this experiment, I exposed participants to criticism of the president from either the presidential or nonpresidential party in Congress. As discussed previously, such evaluations should be costly when coming from the president's own party and cheap when coming from across the aisle. The treatments were embedded in a document mimicking the format of the Yahoo! News Reuters Text News Summary and separately criticized a presidential Medicare initiative and a nuclear-weapons treaty. All six story summaries appearing on the page were adapted from actual wire-service stories. Care was taken to find treatment conditions in which at least some Republicans and Democrats had taken the positions described.[15]

The experiment's participants were a convenient population of undergraduate students. They were recruited to participate in "a study on political communication, attitudes, and the Internet" via in-class announcements and online discussion announcements. Participants were offered an inducement of $20, distributed by lottery.[16]

To minimize "demand" effects, in which participants choose to respond in a way they believe the experimenter wishes (Orne 1962), I embedded the news treatments in a survey probing a plausible line of inquiry regarding Internet news sources, including several other questions about web usage and Internet news.[17] Random assignment for the study was

---

[14] See Iyengar and Kinder (1987) for an eloquent defense of "methodological pluralism."

[15] The line that Clinton was "more interested in having Medicare as a political issue" than in solving Medicare's financial problems, for example, was taken from a statement by Senator John Breaux (D-LA) (Lipman 1999).

[16] Participants also were told that the survey would take about 10 minutes to complete and that only those students who were older than 18 could participate. The recruitment messages, survey, and consent forms were submitted to and approved by the appropriate university agencies. Subjects were recruited at UCSD in 1999–2000.

[17] The other web-related questions included: "3. About what percent of your news and information comes from surfing the web?; 4. In general, what do you like best about

TABLE 5.4. *Experimental Test #1: Costly Credibility*

	Percentage of Independents and "Leaners" Approving of President's Job Performance
Cheap (Nonpresidential Party) Criticism	70%
Costly (Presidential Party) Criticism	46%
N (significance)	55 (0.07)^

Note: ^ $p \leq$ 0.10.

done with an online script that obscured the fact that participants were taking part in an experiment rather than a survey.

Of the 87 participants who took the survey online, more than half majored in political science (45 respondents), with significant representation among biology majors (10 respondents), other social sciences (10 respondents), and undeclared or other majors (22 respondents). There were 25 self-described partisan Democrats or Republicans, 7 who provided no party information, and 55 who self-described as independents or as "leaning" toward one of the parties. Because the 25 stronger partisans were unlikely to be moved by such a mild treatment (i.e., only five words were changed across the two treatments), they and the 7 respondents who did not provide party information were excluded from this analysis.

As shown in Table 5.4, the results of this experiment demonstrate strong support for the impact of costly credibility. When the source of presidential criticism shifts to his own party, approval by moderate participants decreases 24 percentage points – an impressive drop. Because of the small number of respondents, however, the decrease is only marginally significant (i.e., $p \leq$ 0.07, two-tailed test) – but it meets conventional levels of significance (i.e., $p \leq$ 0.035) in a one-tailed test.

Although the results of this experiment support my predictions, I require a full range of partisan rhetoric and participants to truly test all of the credibility predictions.

surfing the web?; 5. In general, what do you like least about surfing the web?; 6. How many minutes do you spend online on a typical day?; 7. Indicate whether you agree or disagree with the following statements about online news: a. Online news sources are more reliable and complete than local television news; b. Online news sources are more reliable and complete than national television news, c. Online news sources are the best news sources to consult for news about the world." The credibility of this line of research was enhanced further by my contemporaneous ongoing research into computer-mediated communication, in which many students already had participated. See Groeling (1999).

EXPERIMENT #2: ALL MESSAGES, ALL PARTISAN GROUPS

In this experiment (see Baum and Groeling 2008 for the full results), my colleague Matthew Baum and I exposed participants to a series of distinct partisan messages embedded in video and web text versions of edited news stories attributed to either CNN or the Fox News Channel. These online experiments were designed to explore the effects of intraparty or interparty attacks on or praise of George W. Bush (i.e., two evaluation types times two evaluation sources) attributed to either Fox or CNN (two networks), for a total of eight possible treatments (although the latter network category is irrelevant to this analysis).[18] The treatments consisted of a streaming video regarding the National Security Agency (NSA) domestic-spying scandal, followed by a static web text report on the Iraq War.[19]

The 1,610 participants were drawn from communication studies (55%) and political science (45%) courses and were offered extra credit for participating. Of the total, 21% self-identified as Republicans (including leaners) and 54% self-identified as Democrats (including leaners). Independents and third-party identifiers accounted for the remaining 25% of the participants, and for brevity, they are excluded from this analysis because their results are similar to those reported in the prior

---

[18] Given the complexity of this comparison and the limited number of participants, we adopted a randomized comparative experimental structure, rather than incorporating an additional control group that would be unexposed to any treatment. For similar reasons, we interpreted our statistical results through a combination of ordinal logit analyses and simulations intended to help readers more easily interpret and visualize the impact of the treatment conditions across respondent and treatment groups.

[19] Our video treatments used actual news footage re-assembled into new packages designed to maximize realism. Due to a paucity of actual Democratic praise of President Bush in these issues, we were forced to misattribute positive remarks by Senator Charles Grassley (R-IA) to Senator Herb Kohl (D-WI) and to take other remarks by actual Democrats out of context. We selected Grassley and Kohl because of their relatively low name recognition. For instance, according to one survey, 62% of Americans outside of Iowa had never heard of Grassley (Beaumont 2005). Presumably, only a subset of the remaining 38% would recognize his face or voice. In a separate pilot study, only 11% and 21% of the Democratic and Republican participants, respectively, were willing to rate Grassley on a thermometer scale; the corresponding percentages for Kohl were 21% and 23%, respectively. The remaining rhetoric types were readily available. Still, by using real-world comments, the conclusions we are able to draw from our rhetorical comparisons are more tentative than would be the case with greater control. This tradeoff did not apply to the static web pages, in which statements attributed to members of Congress were constant within the praise and criticism categories, and only the identities were changed to reflect the known stances of existing members.

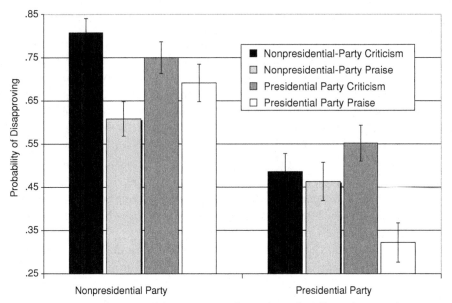

Probability of Disapproving

■ Nonpresidential-Party Criticism
☐ Nonpresidential-Party Praise
■ Presidential Party Criticism
☐ Presidential Party Praise

Nonpresidential Party   Presidential Party

FIGURE 5.1. Probability of disapproving of president's handling of national security, as message source and valence vary. Bars show standard errors (Baum and Groeling 2008 experiment).

experiment.[20] We employed national security approval as the dependent variable rather than overall presidential approval because the treatment conditions targeted foreign-policy issues, and because Democratic approval of Bush was so low at the time of the study. The analysis examines the impact of *four* different types of rhetoric on *three* different types of partisan viewers' decisions to approve or disapprove on a *five*-point scale. Therefore, we used statistical simulation software (King, Tomz, and Wittenberg 2000) to transform the key coefficients into probabilities of approving of President Bush's handling of national security and to chart the effects of moving from one type of treatment message to the next in the results shown in Figure 5.1.[21]

[20] Participants were recruited from UCLA courses from spring 2006 through winter 2007. The recruitment messages, survey, and consent forms were submitted to and approved by the appropriate university agencies. See Baum and Groeling (2008) for more details about the participants and the structure of the experiment. To view the treatment text and videos, see www.sscnet.ucla.edu/comm/groeling/warstories.

[21] In addition, our statistical model controlled for ideology, campaign interest, whether subjects were enrolled in a communication-studies or political-science course, ethnicity, a 10-point index of political knowledge, age, and their assessments of the ideological orientations of Fox and CNN on a liberal-to-conservative scale (from a pretest).

Figure 5.1 shows that for nonpresidential-party participants, praise from their fellow partisans is most beneficial to the president (as predicted), significantly decreasing the probability that they will disapprove of the president. Their probability of disapproving is highest, in turn, when they view their fellow partisans criticizing the president. The swing for rhetoric from fellow partisans significantly outweighs that produced by presidential-party sources.

The results for presidential-party participants are almost a mirror image of those for the nonpresidential party. Here, it is presidential-party sources that seem to hold the most sway over viewers, with presidential-party praise significantly driving down disapproval among presidential-party participants, while criticism from those same sources is the most damaging. Rhetoric originating with the other party, conversely, again falls in between and produces far smaller marginal effects.

OVERALL EXPERIMENTAL RESULTS DISCUSSION

The results of these two experiments again provide strong support for the Credibility Hypothesis. The first experimental results show significant public-opinion impact from Costly (versus Cheap) Evaluations among independents, while the Baum and Groeling (2008) results show that – as predicted – praise from nonpresidential-party sources was most beneficial and criticism from presidential-party sources was most harmful among those sources' fellow partisans. Also consistent with my Partisan Credibility Hypothesis, each party's rhetoric has significantly more impact on their members' probability of disapproving of the president than the other party's rhetoric.

CONCLUSION

This chapter shows that politicians are generally correct to carefully control their statements to the media and the public. Although in many cases politicians' messages are lost in the modern media maelstrom, even relatively subtle partisan messages can have significant effects on public opinion, particularly on relatively low-salience issues in which public opinion has not yet solidified. This is especially true in the case of disputes within parties, which have the potential to be credible and highly damaging for that party's standing with the public. Similarly, when party members like Zell Miller choose to support politicians across the aisle, their actions should be especially consequential.

It is therefore not surprising that four years later, both parties returned to the same strategy in their conventions by tapping prominent cross-party supporters to make major speeches. In the case of the Democrats, they featured a speech by Susan Eisenhower, granddaughter of the famous Republican president Dwight D. Eisenhower, on the day of Barack Obama's address to the 2008 Democratic National Convention. Senator John McCain and his fellow Republicans played up the endorsement and support of Senator Joe Lieberman – the 2000 Democratic vice presidential candidate and a strong supporter of the Iraq War – not only at the convention but also throughout the campaign. In fact, Lieberman's support of Republicans made him a pariah within the Democratic Party, which denied him its nomination for his Senate seat in 2006 and led Democrats to try to sanction him by stripping him of one or more of his committee chairs following the 2008 election (Kane 2008).

In the following chapter, I consider the implications of breakdowns in party-message discipline at a higher level of analysis than is highlighted in this and previous chapters. Specifically, I consider whether – especially in the case of the presidential party – politicians are better off pursuing unified party control of the levers of government and whether such control undermines party unity in their efforts to build a consistent brand name with the public.

6

With Enemies Like These

The Silver Lining of Divided Government

What we need is harmonious, consistent, responsible party government, instead of a wide dispersion of function and responsibility; and we can get it only by connecting the President as closely as may be with his party in Congress.

– Woodrow Wilson[1]

Keep your friends close, and your enemies even closer.
– Michael Corleone, *The Godfather: Part II*

INTRODUCTION: BEWARE OF CHARGING RINOS

In January 2001, Republicans were perceived as being in an excellent strategic position as they took over the reins of power. Despite losing the popular vote for the presidency and having to endure a protracted vote dispute in Florida, Republicans had emerged with the presidency, a tiny majority in the House, and – by virtue of Vice President Dick Cheney's tiebreaking vote – nominal control of the evenly divided Senate. Despite his party's razor-thin control of the legislative branch, by most accounts, President George W. Bush came out of the gates quickly and benefited from substantial early successes in governing.[2] Democrats, in particular,

---

[1] Woodrow Wilson. "Mr. Cleveland's Cabinet," in *Public Papers*, I: 221-2; quoted in Ranney (1954).

[2] Although many of these early favorable reviews came from journalists and current members of the government, one of the most surprising evaluations came from his predecessor, Bill Clinton. According to anonymous sources cited by *The New York Times*, Clinton called Bush a "formidable politician and far shrewder than many Democrats credit him with being." Clinton further spoke "admiringly" of the discipline of the Bush White

seemed to resent the comparatively smooth sailing that Bush and the Republicans enjoyed early in their unified government. According to critics within the Democratic Party at the time, congressional Democrats "essentially rolled over and are letting Bush have his way. They don't believe Democrats have a real strategy for taking the guy on."[3] However, Democrats soon received support from an unexpected source: Bush's fellow Republicans.

Despite Bush's early victories, there were many indications that Republicans would face increasing difficulties in maintaining their party discipline in unified government, particularly in the Senate. One predictable fault line divided conservative and moderate Republicans. As one journalist noted, "For all the euphoria of having one of their own in the White House, congressional Republicans face a trying few months as the conservative and moderate wings weigh their personal priorities against the agenda set by Bush" (Taylor 2001b, 269).

Many Republicans, especially conservatives in the House, soon criticized Bush's willingness to give ground so readily to Democrats on the party's core issues, preferring to defend their established conservative brand rather than compromising.[4] As a former GOP representative observed, "People in Congress end up having to subvert their agenda to the agenda the administration has picked, and that's sometimes very difficult, particularly if the administration is doing something which is not entirely philosophically compatible with large segments of the [GOP] conference."[5] This philosophical incompatibility was particularly acute with regard to issues such as Bush's tax cut, which pitted members who

---

House. However, Clinton also criticized Bush in a number of areas, particularly Bush's promise to "change the tone in Washington." According to these sources, Clinton felt that "of course, the tone would change now that Republicans in Congress were no longer going after the president with subpoenas. It's easy when your party's in power" (Berke 2001, A18).

[3] Carter Eskew, Gore's chief political strategist, quoted in Berke (2001). In a widely reported three-page memo to congressional Democrats titled "Nice Guys Finish Last," entertainer Barbra Streisand reiterated these themes (Reuters News Service 2001, A-6).

[4] For example, Representative Peter Hoekstra (R-MI) contrasted Bush's handling of education versus his stance on the tax bill. "Where on the tax plan just about all of Bush's elements have made it through relatively intact, the education bills in the Senate and the House don't even come close to resembling Bush's plan anymore. This is one where the political interests of the president diverge from the policy interests of the House" (Stevenson 2001).

[5] Former Representative Robert S. Walker (R-PA), (1977–1997). Ibid.

preferred low taxes and small government against those who valued balanced budgets and fiscal responsibility.

Many moderate Republicans, particularly those from Northeastern states carried by Al Gore, demonstrated a willingness and ability to defect from party positions on the budget and a variety of other issues. These "Republicans in Name Only" (RINOs, as they were derisively labeled) previously had been "shunted to the sidelines" but rose to new prominence in unified government (Milligan 2001, A2). These maverick Republicans had a significant impact, especially in the Senate, by challenging party leaders on Bush's proposed tax cut and economic plan, as well as other issues, such as campaign finance reform.

At the time, Senator Lincoln Chafee (R-RI) explained his opposition by pointing to the conflict between the "pressure to be a good, loyal Republican" and his personal platform, which favored reducing the national debt instead of passing Bush's tax cut (Taylor 2001a, 212).[6] Senator Susan Collins (R-ME) indicated that she was "concerned that people in the Northeast may look at the trend and conclude that the Republican Party is not for them, even if they are very comfortable with the brand of Republicanism I represent" (Edsall and Broder 2001, A1).

However, the most striking dissent came from Senator James Jeffords of Vermont, who – after several months of highly visible sparring with Bush and his fellow Republicans – called a press conference and announced that he literally was defecting from the Republican Party. Jeffords explained his decision by arguing that in contrast to his experience in the majority under a president of the other party, with a Republican president, the "various wings" of his party in Congress had lost their "freedom to argue and influence and ultimately to shape the party's agenda" (Jeffords 2001).

Jeffords's decision shifted majority control of the Senate to the Democratic Party and touched off a frenzy of press coverage. A consensus developed among journalists and analysts that Jeffords's action represented a "seismic shift" in American politics. Almost all of the stories described the defection as a disaster for Republicans, and particularly for George W. Bush. According to one especially extravagant scribe, "The Jeffords earthquake registered a 10 on the Senate seismograph. It shattered George W. Bush's monolithic grip on the gears of government, caused the roof

---

[6] As discussed in Chapter 1, Chafee's 2006 defeat indicates that he was correct to fear toeing the Republican line too closely.

to fall in on the GOP leaders, and left them wandering in the rubble of recriminations" (McGrory 2001, B1).[7] David Broder largely agreed, arguing that Bush had been transformed from "an aspiring Ronald Reagan, calling the tune for Congress, into a politician who risks becoming a fair replica of the often-frustrated president his father was" (2001a, A01). Various sources concluded that Bush suddenly faced a much more daunting leadership challenge and likely would confront new and severe obstacles to his legislative agenda.

When Republicans made the rounds arguing that Jeffords' decision had not fundamentally altered their strategic calculus, they were roundly mocked.[8] Broder (2001b) characterized the White House reaction as shell-shocked denial: "The first White House reaction to any political disaster is predictable. Like the corner man of the fighter who has been knocked down three times in one round, the president and his people chorus: 'He never laid a glove on you'."

However, a more careful reading of Bush's situation should have given pause to such dour interpretations. In this chapter I argue that the Republicans were already in a difficult situation before Jeffords' switch, and that the switch to divided government actually may have aided Bush. I also argue that the same logic applies to other modern instances of unified government, including the new administration of Barack Obama.

For political scientists, it seems intuitive that parties would seek to maximize their power through occupation of as many levers of government as possible. However, with few exceptions, the literature has not considered the possibility that strategic party members might have reasons to tolerate – or even occasionally prefer – sharing power across branches.[9]

---

[7] In retrospect, McGrory is obviously indulging in a certain amount of hyperbole here, overstating the power of Bush's position prior to the switch, as well as the depths of his difficulties after the switch. However, she does represent the popular wisdom in the press at the time, albeit in extreme form.

[8] Allen (2001, A14) reviewed the White House response thusly: "White House Chief of Staff Andrew H. Card Jr. said Thursday on PBS's *The NewsHour with Jim Lehrer* that with the Senate's 50–50 split, 'We had to deal very gingerly with the Senate, anyway.' Karen P. Hughes, Bush's counselor, said on ABC's *Nightline* that the historic shift will 'make some difference in terms of the calendar' for legislation. Karl C. Rove, Bush's senior adviser, said on CNN's *Larry King Live* that 'I don't think it will change the agenda. It will change the timing and the phasing of it.' Democratic researchers collected similar quotations from newspapers and proclaimed a 'White House bunker,' suggesting that the aides were in denial, isolated from political reality."

[9] A notable exception consists of scholars pointing out the president's corrosive effect on his congressional party's electoral fortunes. See Brady et al. (1996), Jacobson (1990), and Rae (1998).

Divided party control of government is undoubtedly unpleasant for the minority party in Congress, In contrast, in this chapter I argue that divided control of government can present a "silver lining" for the president and the opposing congressional majority by increasing the value of their communication with the public and allowing them comparable levels of legislative success while shifting responsibility for failure. Although the presidential party in Congress can suffer substantial indirect and direct costs from divided government, it has the least power to change the strategic situation and affect policy through its own legislative or rhetorical efforts, which contributes to the stability of the situation.

In developing this argument, I begin by briefly discussing the recent history of divided government. I then examine the scholarly literature on party government, with particular attention given to the debate regarding the legislative productivity of unified versus divided government. This literature suggests that the Republicans under Bush might not have lost much legislative traction as a result of the return to divided government. Although Senate Democrats gained greater abilities to push their own legislation and agenda, prior research suggests they possessed similar powers to block Republican initiatives even in unified government. Moreover, the Democratic majority in the Senate meant they would now share responsibility – and blame – for government actions and performance.[10]

I then return to the main focus of this book: partisan communication. The conclusion is that the return to divided government uncircled the Republican "firing squad" and reined in the most damaging type of message about the presidential party: intraparty criticism. By presenting a credible common foe, the Senate Democrats helped the Republicans refocus their rhetoric, decreasing such intraparty criticism and sharpening cross-party attacks. I then present a case study of the 1996 presidential

---

[10] I am not contending that the Republican and Democratic Parties are identical and interchangeable entities. In fact, Chapter 1's discussion of the Republican Party's message control tactics highlights the early lead that Republicans achieved in these efforts. Instead, I am arguing that both cohesive and incohesive parties should find it easier to present unified communication in divided government than in unified government, and that the public should find it easier to observe and punish poor performance in the governing party in unified government. Although busy voters are seldom well versed in the details of politics (Delli Carpini and Keeter 1996), such as which party holds majorities in each legislative body, unified control of government again makes command of these details substantially easier. In addition, even if a voter had been only loosely following the conduct of government prior to an election, in a contested election candidates from the out-of-power party have a strong incentive to highlight the governing party's responsibility for any undesired outcomes while in office.

election, in which Bill Clinton and the Republican-controlled Congress shaped their respective party "brand names" at the cost of their out-of-power peers. Finally, I conclude with a discussion of the current administration of Barack Obama, which likely will face similar trials as it tries to govern with Democratic majorities in the House and Senate.

POLITICAL SCIENCE AND PARTY GOVERNMENT

As I discussed in Chapter 1, despite the notably antipartisan leanings of the Framers, ratification of the U.S. Constitution was followed almost immediately by the foundation of organized political parties. Although their original aim sought to help existing members pursue common agendas within Congress, parties quickly began to attempt to alter the composition of the legislature. Prior to the Third Congress, Republicans established a partisan newspaper (i.e., *The National Gazette*) and "committees of correspondence" to aid party communication and attempt to achieve a majority in the House. The parties were actively involved in the presidential election of 1796, and by 1800 presidential elections were explicitly and publicly partisan affairs (Aldrich 1995).

From the beginning of political science as an academic discipline, scholars have argued that parties are essential in bridging the constitutional gulf between branches of government. Woodrow Wilson viewed single-party control as necessary to overcome the debilitating separation of powers written into the U.S. Constitution. Wilson also believed that a party could provide the common direction and machinery that would allow "the several active parts of the government [to be] closely united in organization for a common purpose" (Wilson 1911, 211–12). He said that without parties, "It would hardly have been possible for the voters of the country to be united in truly national judgments upon national questions" (Wilson 1908, 217). For Wilson, the president was the lynchpin of the new partisan system. He argued that Americans increasingly looked to the president to be the "unifying force in our complex system, the leader both of his party and of the nation" (1908, 60).

By the 1960s, the consensus among political scientists appeared to be that party government (and generally, by implication, unified party government) was essential for the proper functioning of American government (Sundquist 1988, 617–18). This consensus was exemplified in an influential report written in 1950 by the American Political Science Association (APSA) Committee on Political Parties: "Toward a More Responsible Two-Party System," which called the major political parties "indispensable instruments of government" and made several proposals for how they could be made more effective (APSA 1950). Although APSA's views were by no means unanimously shared, the "party government" school of thought did hold considerable sway in political science in the remainder of the 20th century (Sundquist 1992, Chapter 4).

Party government was premised on what Sundquist described as "one essential condition": There would be "a majority party in control of both branches of government" (1988, 625). Indeed, some politicians were so averse to the very concept of divided government that following the Republicans' crushing victory in the 1946 midterm election, Democratic Senator J. William Fulbright proposed that President Truman resign and name a Republican successor.[11]

DIVIDED CONTROL OF GOVERNMENT AND PUBLIC SUPPORT

In the modern era, however, unified party control of government has proven to be the exception rather than the rule. Prior to the 1950s, American elections generally gave a single party control of both the presidency and Congress.[12] Since then, however, about two thirds of elections at the national level have produced divided government. Unlike most previous occurrences of divided government – in which a midterm switch to divided government presaged a swing in party control at the next general election – both midterm and presidential elections now frequently produce divided government (Table 6.1).

Historically, presidential parties have picked up congressional seats during presidential election years only to see some of those gains evaporate in the following midterm election. However, as shown in Table 6.2, in recent years this pattern of "surge and decline" tends to be "one step forward, two steps back" for the presidential party. Even counting the Democrats' decisive victory in 2008, since the Jimmy Carter era the average surge for the presidential party in the House has been around seven

---

[11] Fulbright apparently believed that the gridlock produced by divided government was a national security threat in the age of nuclear weapons. Because the vice presidency was vacant, Fulbright's plan was for Truman to name a Republican Secretary of State and then resign. For a discussion of Fulbright's plan and Truman's reaction, see Cox and Kernell, 1991.

[12] Of the first 72 Congresses (i.e., 1789–1933), only 21 produced some form of divided control of government. Of these, nearly half occurred between 1861 and 1897, and most occurred at midterm as a leading indicator of a switch in partisan control of government (Stewart 1991, Table 9.1).

TABLE 6.1. *Unified and Divided Government*

Presidential	1897–1898	1953–1954
Midterm	1899–1900	**1955–1956**
Presidential	1901–1902	1957–1958
Midterm	1903–1904	**1959–1960**
Presidential	1905–1906	1961–1962
Midterm	1907–1908	1963–1964
Presidential	1909–1910	1965–1966
Midterm	**1911–1912**	1967–1968
Presidential	1913–1914	**1969–1970**
Midterm	1915–1916	**1971–1972**
Presidential	1917–1918	**1973–1974**
Midterm	**1919–1920**	**1975–1976**
Presidential	1921–1922	1977–1978
Midterm	1923–1924	*1979–1980*
Presidential	1925–1926	**1981–1982**
Midterm	1927–1928	**1983–1984**
Presidential	1929–1930	**1985–1986**
Midterm	**1931–1932**	**1987–1988**
Presidential	1933–1934	**1989–1990**
Midterm	1935–1936	**1991–1992**
Presidential	1937–1938	1993–1994
Midterm	1939–1940	**1995–1996**
Presidential	1941–1942	**1997–1998**
Midterm	1943–1944	**1999–2000**
Presidential	1945–1946	2001–2002
Midterm	**1947–1948**	2003–2004
Presidential	1949–1950	2005–2006
Midterm	1951–1952	**2006–2007**
Presidential		2008–2009

Note: Years with Divided Government are in bold
Source: Stanley and Niemi (1998, Table 1.9; updated by author). As discussed in the introduction to this chapter, Senator James Jeffords's defection from the Republican Party in 2001 marked a return to divided government after several months of unified government.

seats, while the average decline in the subsequent midterm has been more than twice that number. The Senate tells a similar story, with midterm seat losses averaging around twice as many presidential-year gains.

George W. Bush and Bill Clinton are the only two presidents to buck this trend in the last three decades. The midterm surge for Clinton in 1998 helped him to successfully ride out the Monica Lewinsky impeachment scandal. Bush also appeared to benefit: Immediately following the 2002

TABLE 6.2. *Recent Presidential-Party Electoral Gains and Losses*

	Presidential Election Year		Midterm Election Year	
	House	Senate	House	Senate
Carter	1	0	−11	−3
Reagan 1	33	12	−26	0
Reagan 2	14	−2	−5	−8
H. W. Bush	−3	−1	−8	−1
Clinton 1	−10	0	−53	−7
Clinton 2	9	−2	5	0
W. Bush 1	−2	−4	6	1
W. Bush 2	3	4	−30	−6
Obama	21	9		
Average	7.333	1.778	−15.250	−3.000

Sources: Stanley and Niemi (1998, Table 1.9) and Rothenberg (1998). Republicans actually picked up two Democratic Senate seats in George W. Bush's first midterm but lost a seat (and their majority) with the defection of Senator Jim Jeffords prior to the midterm. Obama's presidential election year Senate tally includes Democrat Al Franken, who was ultimately victorious in his Minnesota Senate bid. It does not include the defection of Pennsylvania Senator Arlen Specter from the Republican Party to the Democratic Party because he did not run for reelection in 2008. It also does not include the victory of Senator Scott Brown (R-MA), who won a special election to fill the late Senator Ted Kennedy's (D-MA) seat.

election, congressional Republican leaders increasingly delegated leadership of the party agenda to Bush rather than fighting to control it. In effect, Republicans conceded control of the party brand and decided to follow Bush's opinions, passions, and interests, at least initially. Although this aided Bush by muting many potentially damaging critics during the 2004 presidential race, the congressional Republicans' disastrous showing in Bush's second term (i.e., losing 51 House seats and at least 14 Senate seats in the next two elections) demonstrated the clear risk of tying themselves too closely to the president.[13]

The electoral impacts of divided government are not restricted to the legislature, of course. In addition to the increased freedom to maneuver politically I discuss in the following section, research shows that presidents in divided government enjoy significantly higher approval levels

[13] In an interview conducted shortly before he left office, Bush admitted he cared less about his party's electoral fortunes than his own policy preferences regarding Iraq: "During the darkest days of Iraq, people came to me and said, 'You're creating incredible political difficulties for us. And I said, 'Oh, really? What do you suggest I do?' And some suggested retreat, pull out of Iraq. But I had faith....I didn't compromise that principle for the sake of trying to, you know, bail out my political party" (Sammon 2009).

in their governing. This is true not only in the context of foreign-policy "rally" events (Groeling and Baum 2008) but also more generally in their standing with the public (Nicholson, Segura, and Woods 2002).

However, even if the president and the majority party in Congress fare better in the eyes of the public when they divide control, it is possible that they would prefer not to do so in order to better pursue their policy agendas. The following section reviews this perspective – particularly whether the legislative outputs of divided government can help those in power govern successfully.

A PRACTICAL PREFERENCE FOR DIVIDED GOVERNMENT?

The appeal of party government for scholars is straightforward. Cutting through the clutter of governmental institutions, unified government focuses accountability on the governing party. It also helps clarify and diametrically oppose the interests of the major parties. This zero-sum struggle between the parties ideally provides a clear choice for voters: If they like the current performance of government, they can reward the governing party; if they do not like it, they can vote for the opposition party.[14] Rather than exhaustively studying the candidates' issue positions and weighing their relative merits, voters can simply reward successful governments and punish the failures.

It seems intuitive that a party that gains control of the levers of government will be more able to act collectively to produce successful outcomes. In fact, Downs's (1957) classic definition of parties views them as teams "seeking to control the governing apparatus by gaining office.... "[15] Party ambition is generally assumed to be overarching. As one political scientist observed, "No major party has ever said, 'We want only the presidency,' or only the Senate or the House. They have always said, 'give us total responsibility'" (Sundquist 1988, 616).

However, in some ways the greatest strength of unified government is also its greatest weakness, at least for members of the governing party: total responsibility. In discussing the scholarly debate over the 1950 APSA Report, Sundquist argues, "The debate was joined on whether party

---

[14] Key (1966, 61) was perhaps the most famous advocate of this perspective, arguing that "shifting voters graphically reflect the electorate in its great, and perhaps principal, role as an appraiser of past events, past performance, and past actions. It judges retrospectively." See also Fiorina (1981).

[15] Downs (1957, 25) also specifies that the offices should be gained through a "duly constituted election."

government should or could be made more responsible, not whether it should exist at all.... Nobody argued that the ideal system was the one that was to be ushered in a few years later: coalition government in which no party is or can be held responsible" (1988, 619).

From the standpoint of elected officials, however, the appeal of total responsibility is far less clear. Although partisans undoubtedly want to receive all the credit for rousing successes, they most certainly do not want to be held entirely responsible for any disasters occurring on their watch – even those that are arguably outside their control.[16] Unfortunately, as I discuss next, pursuing the total responsibility implied by unified control of government is a dangerous gamble for parties for several reasons.

First, many studies show that unified government does *not* ensure more successful legislating than divided government. In fact, when the presidential party does not control at least three fifths of the Senate, it is in the unfortunate position of having accountability without commensurate ability.[17]

Second, although the president and his fellow partisans share a common brand name (see Chapter 1), they are being judged by different subsets of voters who potentially hold them to incompatible or even mutually exclusive standards of success. For example, presidents tend to have the most responsibility for providing or maintaining collective goods such as low tax rates, a strong economy, balanced budgets, low inflation, a strong defense, or smaller government, while members of Congress are famously rewarded for lavishing "pork" on the voters in their district (Jacobson 1990). These differences, as well as more prosaic issues of ego and personal ambition, can lead to serious – and damaging – disputes across institutions for control of the party agenda.

---

[16] Indeed, some argue that it was a natural disaster – Hurricane Katrina – and the poor governmental response to it that proved to be the turning point in the Bush Administration's influence on American public opinion. Matthew Dowd, Bush's pollster and chief strategist for his successful 2004 reelection bid, called Katrina a "tipping point" for Bush that broke the president's "bond with the public." Dowd, who has since publicly distanced himself from Bush, continued: "Once that bond was broken, [Bush] no longer had the capacity to talk to the American public" (quoted in Murphy and Purdum 2009). Dan Bartlett, White House communications director and later counselor to the president, concurred, saying simply that "Politically, it was the final nail in the coffin" (quoted in Murphy and Purdum 2009).

[17] However, the minority party's continual opposition of the majority can sometimes expose party members to dangerous charges of "obstructionism," as Former Democratic Senate Minority Leader Tom Daschle (D-SD) found out in his 2004 reelection defeat. This is another reason why such members of the minority party may desire to pair their obstructionism with a "positive agenda" (see Chapter 1).

Finally, even if a party were to achieve some measure of legislative success in unified government, the filtered information that the public receives through the news media regarding the party's words and actions would likely be skewed toward discord and failure.[18] I explore each of these three positions in the following section.

Does Unified Government Enhance Legislative Success?

As might be expected, given their strong endorsement of unified government, political scientists have expressed concerns about the potentially harmful effects of divided government on the legislative output of government (Cutler 1988; Sundquist 1988). However, even advocates of party government explicitly argue that divided government does not lead to a "standstill" (Schattschneider 1942, 89–93). Furthermore, the president increasingly has been able to pursue his legislative agenda by "going public" – a strategy less dependent on underlying support within Congress than traditional cross-branch bargaining (Kernell 1997).[19]

Other developments in the literature on divided government have given scholars even more hope about the parties' abilities to govern while sharing power. Mayhew's *Divided We Govern* (1991) ignited the scholarly debate on the effects of divided government, arguing that significant

---

[18] Politicians and parties conceivably can repair damage done to their brand in the news by compensating with greater quantities of controlled messages in "paid" media (e.g., paid advertisements). However, poor brand discipline in the free media can undermine these repair attempts in at least three important ways. First, party-aiding messages at odds with the prior brand delivered in the free media will face considerable credibility problems; the damaging messages have costly credibility (see Chapter 5) and are delivered through a neutral news media, while the "repair" paid ads should be far less credible in both their content and medium. Second, any attempts to shift from a prior damaging brand will be actively opposed by opportunistic opponents, who have an incentive to point out both the contradictions between the two brands and the low credibility of the messages attempting to repair the brand. Third, there is no guarantee that a party that was unable to cohesively manage its brand name across "franchisees" of the brand (see Chapter 1) will be any more likely to do so across those same franchisees in an election, especially in the face of complicating factors, such as contested primary fights in the party and the increasing modern role of unaffiliated interest groups (e.g., so-called 527 organizations), which are actually legally prohibited from coordinating their message-planning with the parties or candidates. Significantly, the 2008 Obama campaign made an explicit early call for donors to give money directly to his campaign rather than to such outside groups, which was interpreted as a means of further tightening control over the campaign's message (Smith 2008).

[19] In fact, the conflictual nature of "going public" implies that it is much more difficult to apply against one's allies than one's enemies. In contrast to a "bargaining" style of leadership, going public applies the stick but provides no carrot.

legislation was just as likely to occur during either type of government, especially when controlling for public support for activism and early administration momentum. Several authors have reevaluated Mayhew's claim, primarily taking issue with his measures of significant legislation. Some results bolstered Mayhew's findings of no significant difference (Cameron, Howell, and Adler 1997; Jones 1994; Krehbiel 1996; Quirk and Nesmith 1995); other analysts have found statistically significant differences, especially when controlling for party unity, the presence of legislative supermajorities, and presidential influence (Chiou and Rothenberg 2003; Coleman 1999; Edwards, Barrett, and Peake 1997; Kelly 1993). Although this debate is by no means settled, current evidence appears to support the notion that an ideologically unified ruling party that holds a supermajority in the Senate can be more productive legislatively, especially when bolstered by public and presidential support for activist legislation.

However, governments meeting these requirements for legislative success have been very uncommon in the modern party setting, individually or in combination. The presence of supermajorities, public support for change, and ideological cohesiveness within parties are nontrivial elements for success. For example, even before Jeffords switched parties in 2001, the Republican unified government seemed to fail these requirements on all three grounds: the razor-thin majorities were nowhere near filibuster-proof; the public was relatively supportive of the status quo[20]; and, as Jeffords's defection amply illustrated, the support of moderates within the Republican majority was often shaky at best.[21] The only recent government to meet all three requirements is the Obama Administration, which was swept into office during a period of economic crisis and political turmoil in January 2009 after explicitly running on a platform of "change" and (intermittently) achieving a Senate supermajority.[22] Unfortunately for Democrats, after an impressive series of early legislative

---

[20] See James Stimson (www.unc.edu/~jstimson/time.html) for a measure of public support for activist government. Such support was exceptionally high in 2008. Data for 2009 were unavailable at the time of this writing but presumably reflected a decline in such support.

[21] By the time of Jeffords's defection, many moderate Republicans – particularly those from Northeastern states carried by Al Gore – already had demonstrated a willingness and ability to defect from their party on a variety of issues. These RINOs previously had been "shunted to the sidelines" but rose to new prominence in unified government (Milligan 2001, A2).

[22] The Democratic supermajority in the Senate was achieved after a party switch by formerly Republican Senator Arlen Specter of Pennsylvania in April 2009 and a mid-2009

victories, the public's overall support for an activist agenda appeared to wane quickly such that by September 2009, more than half of Americans reported that they thought the government was doing "too many things that should be left to businesses and individuals" (Newport 2009).[23]

The Senate minority generally poses substantial problems for the presidential party as it attempts to act responsibly in unified government. As a senior aide to then-Majority Leader Bill Frist complained, "Obstructionism is woven into the fabric of things [in the Senate]. The leadership deals with it on a day-to-day, even a minute-to-minute basis" (Evans and Lipinski 2005, 2). The rules of the Senate allow for extended, unrestricted debate on most legislation and all nominations considered by the body unless a supermajority (currently 60 votes) decides to invoke cloture

ruling by the Minnesota Supreme Court that upheld Senator Al Franken's (D-MN) election. The Democrats lost their supermajority only a month after achieving it due to the death of Senator Edward Kennedy (D-MA) in August 2009. Democrats again achieved a supermajority after Massachusetts Democrats reversed a 2004 law that prevented Governor Deval Patrick (D) from naming an interim successor (Ironically, the law was put in place to prevent then-Governor Mitt Romney [R] from naming a successor to Senator John Kerry [D], had he been elected president, but it was delayed by the Republican minority in the State Senate through procedural delays, despite its control of only 12.5% of the seats in the body) (Viser and Ryan 2009). The interim successor, Paul Kirk, helped Senate Democrats achieve the supermajority necessary to pass a version of health care reform in late 2009 without a single Republican vote. Brown's victory (which occurred as this book went to press) again deprived Senate Democrats of their supermajority and threatened the ultimate passage of health care reform. However, one unexpected benefit of Brown's victory for the Democrats was to raise public awareness of the existence and impact of the filibuster in the Senate. According to a poll taken shortly after the special election, 70% of respondents thought it was "good for the country" that Democrats "cannot pass bills without cooperation from at least one Republican Senator" (CNN 2010). Similarly, news coverage of the Democrats' supermajority (or lack thereof) jumped tremendously following the election. A Lexis Nexis search of Major U.S. and world publications showed more stories mentioning the word "supermajority" in the first three months of 2010 than in all of 2009 combined (260 versus 197). As a result, I expect that Brown's victory might actually have made the Republicans more accountable for failures than they would otherwise be, and also a more legitimate target for criticism than if they lacked the ability to block legislation.

[23] In a survey, 57% said government was doing too much, compared to only 38% who said it was not doing enough. The wording of the question was "Some people think the government is trying to do too many things that should be left to individuals or businesses. Others think that the government should do more to solve our country's problems. Which comes closer to your own view?" The same survey showed that 45% of respondents believed there was generally too much government regulation of business and industry (compared to only 27% who thought it was about right and 24% who thought it was too little). The percentage answering "too much" in September 2009 was the highest of any Gallup survey since it began asking the question just before the 1994 midterm election (Newport 2009).

and restrict debate.[24] As an indicator of how difficult this barrier can be to surmount – even in relatively favorable legislative circumstances – one need only witness how Senate Democrats contemplated using a legislative loophole (i.e., the "reconciliation" tactic) in 2009 to overcome Republican resistance to health-care–reform legislation. Because there are statutory limits on debate for budget resolutions requiring only a majority vote to proceed to a vote (i.e., "reconciliation" budget items), Democrats considered dividing their proposed reforms into two parts. The first bill was designed to attract filibuster-proof bipartisan support by targeting largely nonbudgetary reforms, including a mandate that Americans have health insurance or pay a fine, a prohibition on insurers rejecting customers based on preexisting conditions, and a cap on out-of-pocket expenses. The second bill, which would then proceed through the majority-rule budget-reconciliation process, would include many costly provisions that Republicans opposed, including federal insurance subsidies, expansion of Medicaid, and especially the higher taxes required to pay for these items (Weisman and Bendavid 2009). The tactic was considered risky because it "would present a variety of serious procedural and substantive obstacles that could result in a piecemeal health bill... [and] because the mere mention of reconciliation touches partisan nerves" (Hulse 2009b).

Although the final outcome of the legislation is far from certain at the time of this writing, Democrats seem to have failed in their attempted courtship of the same RINOs discussed at the beginning of this chapter. By bringing at least one Republican on board in the Senate, Democrats hoped to defeat a filibuster and avoid having to use the reconciliation option. Moreover, the presence of at least one Republican in the final vote for the legislation would diminish – however minutely – any appearance of illegitimacy that might stem from the perception that Democrats were forcing a major change in domestic policy without any bipartisan support using a dubious legislative tool (and setting the precedent for such tactics to be used against them in the future).[25]

---

[24] Evans and Lipinski (2005, fn6) noted that there are statutory limits on debate for budget resolutions, budget reconciliation bills, many trade items, and other items that limit obstructionism on these actions. As this book went to press, the Democrats apparently decided to use reconciliation to try passing health care reform, despite losing their supermajority in the Senate.

[25] See Harwood (2009) for an extensive discussion of the Obama White House's aggressive courting of Senator Olympia Snowe (R-ME) on health-care reform and other issues, which began even before Obama took office in January 2009. In an interview with

Thus, we see that even in the current Obama Administration, which seemed a near-best case of unified government, members of the opposition party control an important veto gate (Chiou and Rothenberg 2003; Krehbiel 1998). Perhaps more important, the public has been generally unaware of the power of Senate minorities to block legislation.[26] Therefore, unified government without a supermajority in the Senate represents the worst of both worlds for the presidential party: responsibility without ability. The unified government appears to be accountable for the actions (or inactions) of government but is actually substantially blocked by the nonpresidential party in the Senate. As Sinclair (2002, 135) observes:

The Senate majority leader lacks the control over the flow of legislation to and on the floor that the House Speaker possesses. Extended debate and the Senate's permissive amending rules mean that the Senate majority leader cannot keep off the floor issues his members would rather avoid or pass legislation they want with a simple majority.

Thus, even while in the minority, the opposition can and does seize some measure of agenda control. Sinclair (2002, 135) points to the Democratic minority's push for minimum-wage increases, tobacco regulation, gun control, managed-care reform, and campaign-finance reform between 1996 and 2001. Democrats succeeded in forcing floor debates on all of these issues (which Republicans desperately wanted to avoid) and, in some cases, succeeded in gaining enough support from defecting Republicans to actually pass the legislation.[27]

Harwood, she claimed that the "time has come" to act on health care, vouched for Obama's policy moderation, and disavowed her fellow Republicans' main criticism of the Democratic proposals. In discussing her stance, she indicated that she would be willing to support the "right policy" even if no other Republican were willing to join her in voting for it, and she explicitly criticized the Republican shift toward a more consistently conservative ideology, saying, "I haven't changed as a Republican. I think more that my party has changed." Snowe was previously one of only three Republicans voting for the Democrats' $787 billion stimulus package, which infuriated fellow Republicans but played well in her home state of Maine (Harwood 2009). Eventually, Snowe voted for the Senate Finance Committee's version of health care reform but did not vote for the final Senate bill.

[26] However, as noted earlier in the discussion of Senator Scott Brown's (R-MA) surprising special election victory (which occurred as this book entered production), the Democrat's on-again, off-again supermajority status has received massive news coverage. Presumably, this coverage has helped the general public better understand and appreciate the limitations of unified party control without a Senate supermajority.

[27] Many of these successes were clearly aided by President Clinton, who helped shift public attention to the issues. However, the notable victory on campaign-finance reform occurred under George W. Bush's unified government in 2001.

Fighting Over the Steering Wheel

In addition to cross-party disputes, some scholars of American politics have noted systematic differences in intraparty agendas between the presidency and Congress as well as within Congress. For example, Burns (1963) argues that the New Deal fractured Republicans and Democrats at the national level, dividing them into distinct wings for the executive and legislative branches of the parties.[28] Others have observed a similar tendency, noting that Democratic presidents in the late 20th century tended to be liberal and national in their approach to governing, facing off against congressional Democrats who were more conservative and concerned with local affairs. For Republicans, the split was perceived to be between a moderate, internationalist president opposed by more conservative, rural Republicans in the congressional delegation (White and Mileur 2002, 22).

As I noted in the introduction to this chapter and in Chapter 1, disputes over the party agenda can arise even within a governing party with a relatively cohesive ideology. The president and his congressional party follow a different electoral schedule and face different constituencies in their various districts. As Sinclair (2002, 136) observed, "Given these different electorates, the best strategies for the candidates of a party may well differ." As discussed previously, many of the disputes between Bush and his Republican opponents in Congress in 2001 consisted of exactly this type of dispute over the party's branding strategy. Senator Collins (R-ME) and her fellow moderate Republicans had reason to be concerned that they might suffer from appearing too supportive of Bush: His failure in 2004 to carry any state in the Northeast except New Hampshire certainly indicated that his brand of Republicanism did not fit well with the needs of local Republicans. Also, as discussed in Chapters 1 and 4, linking oneself to a polarizing president can be a risky proposition, as congressional Democrats and Republicans discovered in 1994 and 2006–2008, respectively.[29]

Although this book is being written early in the Obama Administration, already there are signs that congressional Democrats – who had

---

[28] Burns's formulation consists of a parochial legislature largely insulated from national opinion facing off against a more activist and centrist president. Milkis (1993) extends this analysis by arguing that the New Deal helped set up an administrative presidency largely autonomous from congressional control. In addition, Jacobson (1990) argues that the executive is institutionally better suited at delivering collective goods and Congress is better at serving up "pork" and other particularistic goods.

[29] For a concurring view, see Brady et al. (1996).

dominated the party and achieved great electoral success, especially late in the Bush Administration – faced increasing concerns about their political and electoral future under Obama. In an interview with *The New York Times*, Speaker of the House Nancy Pelosi stressed how "thrilling" it was to have a Democrat entering the White House, but she also asserted, "I feel in a stronger position now. For me, my responsibility as Speaker is enormously enhanced by a president whose vision I respect and whose agenda I will help stamp.... We are an independent branch of government. The fact is that we have many ideas that will need the signature of the president" (Hulse 2009a). Unidentified congressional sources went further, saying "She has been queen of her castle for quite a while now and the face of the Democratic Party, and I think she is going to want to continue to be at least the co-face as much as possible" (Hulse 2009a).

If Obama and the congressional Democrats fail, they will have no one to blame at the ballot box but themselves. To make matters worse, the news media's fixation on balance and conflict (see Chapter 2) ensures that news of successful initiatives will be tempered by criticism and that fights within the presidential party always will be disproportionately highlighted (see Chapter 3). As discussed at the end of this chapter, many high-stakes disputes have started to rend the Democratic Party, even this early in the Obama Administration's tenure.

DIVIDED GOVERNMENT AS AN "IRONCLAD ALIBI"

In contrast, divided government provides each party with "ironclad alibis for failure" to carry out their promises (Helms 1949; see also Nicholson, Segura, and Woods 2002; Powell and Whitten 1993). Each party in divided government may fail to deliver desired outcomes to their supporters but can avoid accountability for this failure by credibly blaming the other party – exactly the lack of responsibility that political scientists feared. This "blame game" is even more elegant, however, in that the low costly and partisan credibility of the messages assigning blame (see Chapter 5) ensures that Republicans in the electorate will not believe Democratic statements blaming Republicans – and vice versa – leading to stable support along party lines.

Divided government has two other important advantages over unified government for politicians (particularly those in power). First, it enhances a party's ability to engage in "message politics" (Evans 2001) and position-taking (Mayhew 1974) by disconnecting those positions from costly policy outcomes.[30] Second and perhaps most important for this text, divided government "muzzles" criticism of the president from within his own party – criticism that was demonstrated in Chapter 5 as damaging to the governing party, particularly with regard to the president's standing among crucial swing voters.

As discussed in Chapter 1, parties use both their words and their deeds to establish a "brand name" with the public. It is virtually impossible to build a party bereft of at least some factional cleavages. There are many instances in which factional disputes within parties have spilled over into open conflicts. For example, the decades-long battle between Southern and Northern Democrats for control of the party eventually led to the exodus of most conservative Southerners from the party altogether. Liberal Republicans faced similar banishment as the Republican Party became more conservative in the same period. Such disputes are often quite visible in primary elections, which almost by definition consist of representatives of party factions fighting over who will be the party's standard-bearer in the general election. For example, in 2004 the Republican Party was roiled by disputes over whether longtime incumbent Senator Arlen Specter (R-PA) was sufficiently out of step with the party to justify a primary challenge by a more conservative opponent. Ultimately, the Republican "establishment" – apparently hopeful about Specter's ability to assist President Bush's reelection in a critical swing state – largely rallied around Specter. Nevertheless, Representative Pat Toomey (R-PA) mounted an effective primary campaign backed by conservative organizations (e.g., the Club for Growth) and came within 17,000 votes of unseating Specter (Macomber 2005). Specter apparently factored in this near-miss when he decided to abandon the Republican Party in 2009 rather than face Toomey again in a 2010 Republican primary.[31]

Once members survive an election and take office, disputes within a party should be more consequential for policy. Unfortunately for members of the governing party in unified government, their party is far more

---

[30] Evans (2001, 219) defines "message politics" as "the interrelated set of electoral, communications, and legislative strategies that congressional parties employ to advance their respective messages." His notion of party messages is similar to my conception of party "brand names" (see Chapter 1) but is not assumed to apply to the president or other party members outside of the chamber.

[31] Occasionally, primary conflicts have resulted from the party leadership initiating such challenges against rebellious members. Perhaps the most famous example of this was Franklin Roosevelt's 1938 campaign to "purge" fellow Democrats who had opposed his party leadership in favor of "100% New Dealers."

constrained in its rhetoric and legislative proposals because it knows that it alone will be held accountable for the results. For example, during the 2009 debate on health-care reform, House Republican Whip Eric Cantor (R-VA) argued, "Either this bill fails or it will change dramatically," adding, "If the bill fails it will be because of disagreements among the Democrats" (Rowley and Jensen 2009).

In contrast, parties in divided government can strategically propose policies that are certain to fail or be blocked by the opposing party – precisely because they are certain to fail or be blocked.[32] One analyst noted an example of this blame–avoidance "minuet" in the Clinton appropriations process during divided government:

> In recent years, an appropriations process that appeared chaotic was in fact adhering to something of a routine: Conservative Republicans forced adoption of a budget with a discretionary spending limit they could cite as the GOP's commitment to hold down spending. Appropriators would go to work, giving plump allocations to the first bills to move through the process, while starving others on which there was bipartisan support for generosity. . . . The appropriators knew that Clinton eventually would use vetoes or the threat of them to compel Congress to exceed its spending cap. In the end, both sides were able to address their top spending priorities, but the arrangement allowed Republicans to blame the White House for "forcing them" to exceed their budget.[33] (Parks 2001, 1128)

The opposite case also applies when a congressional party moves from minority to majority status because votes that formerly were treated as "free passes" suddenly matter. Marion Berry (D-AR) related that while he had "thought the [so-called card check] bill was a piece of junk and that he only voted for it because he knew then-President Bush would veto it" and that "the Blue Dogs told House leadership that card check wasn't a free vote for them anymore and that their constituents were giving them a lot of grief over the issue" (Sanders 2009).

In unified government, both the president and the majority party have legitimate claims to the leadership of their party. As Brooks (2004) observed following the Republican victory in the 2004 election, "There is a general sense in Congress that it is time to equalize the power relationship between the branches of government. . . . Republicans in Congress won elections of their own and have just as much right as [Bush] to shape

---

[32] See Evans (2001) for a detailed discussion of how parties can use the legislative process to advance their desired party message.

[33] Indeed, the perception that Republicans had abandoned their commitment to fiscal constraint while in control of government under George W. Bush severely damaged the party brand name among vocal segments of the Republican base (along with abortive attempts to enact "comprehensive" immigration reform).

policy." Later, a Democratic strategist wistfully (and anonymously) wondered aloud if Obama would be better served if he faced Republican majorities in Congress: "If there were a Republican Congress, there would be things that are non-starters" (York 2009).[34] From this institutional assertiveness comes the danger that each branch of the party will use its power to pursue its preferred legislative and rhetorical strategy, thereby diminishing the overall clarity, consistency, and value of the party brand name.

The nonpresidential party, conversely, has much more incentive and ability to coordinate and enforce a collective-party message in unified government: Despite its comparative weakness within the legislature, as the foremost opponent of the ruling regime, it continues to ensure its members a media venue for expressing their views. As noted previously, the out-of-power party is paradoxically aided by its institutional weakness: Members can unify around opposition to the presidential party's proposals without having to advance any of their own as alternatives. As President George W. Bush found in his attempts to reform Social Security, "Now that Republicans are in control of the presidency and both houses, Democrats – even moderates who might otherwise favor modest Social Security changes – see no reason to help Republicans dismantle any aspect of a program that is central to the Democratic legacy" (Dionne 2005). As Democratic strategists explained, there was – in their view – simply no downside to opposing Bush's plan and offering nothing in its place (Havemann 2005).[35] Representative Barney Frank (D-MA) agreed, stating that many Democrats who in the past have pushed for the party to offer explicit alternatives realized they could "more effectively communicate their message by positioning themselves in the ways they oppose Republicans" (Klein 2005b).

---

[34] The article also includes the following prognostications from an unnamed Democratic strategist: "[T]he Democrats in Congress are going to get their asses kicked in 2010. This is following a curve like the Clinton years: take on really controversial things early, fail, or succeed partially, ask Democrats to take really tough votes, and then lose. A lot of guys are going to get beat, but the president has time to recover" (York 2009).

[35] It is interesting that Brooks (2004) correctly argued that in attempting to govern following the 2004 election, Bush was "going to find himself confronting a paradox: the bigger GOP majorities will make it harder to establish one-party rule. The president will find that with Congressional Republicans increasingly discordant and assertive, he can't pass major legislation with Republican votes alone. On issues like, say, Social Security, he'll lose some Republicans whichever way he turns." However, Brooks then misread the Democrats' incentives and ability to maintain cohesion in the minority, arguing that Bush should be able to compensate by "building unlikely coalitions of the willing, including some Democrats."

Ironically, only four years later, the legislative shoe would be on the other foot as out-of-power Republicans generally reveled in their unity and freedom in the minority. In contrast to George W. Bush's increasingly damaging presence, Republicans in the Obama presidency saw a situation "where the minority can thrive, because they can sit up there while Democrats [are] forming circular firing squads" (Libit 2009). As former Speaker of the House Newt Gingrich observed from the sidelines, the Republicans' rediscovered unity did not stem from their own brilliance or leadership: "I'd like to tell you [Virginia Representative Eric] Cantor did a brilliant job, but the truth is that Pelosi and Obey pushed the members into his arms" (Nagourney 2009).[36] Compared to unified government, in divided government the presidential party's internal clashes are muted. By virtue of its minority status within the legislature, the presidential party in Congress is unable to initiate and pass much significant legislation. The ability to block legislation is considerably less potent than is the power of the president. In addition, members of the presidential party must share the media spotlight with (or, in a worst case, concede to) their president (see Chapter 4). In the media, they are constrained in their ability to establish their own brand name separate from that of the president and generally can do so only by criticizing him. The president, however, is free to pursue an active media strategy in support of his agenda and takes de facto leadership of the party brand name.

In fact, the main channel of mutual dependence in divided government flows across party lines. As one senior Democrat put it, "a president of your party tells you what *he* wants; a president of the other party asks what *you* want."[37] In such a case, the president faces the temptation to govern with the opposing party, even at the cost of his congressional party's election prospects. The president's congressional party, conversely, generally has little recourse short of publicly criticizing the

---

[36] Ironically, Democrats recognized the parallels between Bush's disastrous Social Security reform effort and their own efforts to reform health care but appeared confident that they could do better than the Republicans had. "Democrats know the rulebook. The tactics being used against them by Republican and conservative groups were perfected by the party when it set out to defeat President Bush's Social Security privatization proposals. They also know that it's easier to gin up noise against a major legislative initiative than it is to sell an initiative that isn't fully formed yet. They know the rulebook. As a Democratic strategist said to me: 'I think as Dems we learned a lot of lessons from beating Bush on privatization – we know and perfected all the tricks and tactics so we know what to expect from the tea-baggers, the insurance companies and other opponents'" (Ambinder 2009).

[37] Emphasis is in the original. Unnamed Democrat cited in Jones (2002, 149).

president – a tactic that can be the partisan equivalent of "cutting off one's nose to spite one's face" (see Chapter 5). All of this discussion suggests that while the nonpresidential party should be relatively free to communicate its desired messages in both unified and divided government, the presidential party in Congress should be far more likely to communicate cohesively when it is in a subordinate role in divided government. The following section tests this prediction.

DIVIDED GOVERNMENT AND UNIFIED PARTY COMMUNICATION

This section compares the content and likely impact of partisan communication in unified and divided government, again using the CMPA content analysis of six years of network-news statements (see Chapter 3).[38] It also relies on the analysis of the likely effect of messages based on their costly and partisan credibility (see Chapter 5). I begin this process by examining the relative prominence of different types of congressional evaluations in unified government. Table 6.3 breaks down these evaluations according to their partisan source, target, and likely persuasive impact for a member of the nonpresidential party.

The top part of Table 6.3 shows that only about one third of the messages in unified government are considered harmful (italicized in the table) to the nonpresidential party; of those messages, the vast proportion is of very low credibility (i.e., low costly and partisan credibility). Conversely, about two thirds of all messages are beneficial to the nonpresidential party, and all such messages are at least somewhat credible (i.e., high partisan or costly credibility).

The bottom part of Table 6.3 repeats this analysis for divided government and shows that, on balance, moving to divided government does not significantly change the overall proportions of beneficial or harmful messages for the nonpresidential party. Although the results for unified government show a slight increase in the proportion of "damaging" messages, the gain has largely occurred in low-credibility attacks by the presidential party. Conversely, there is also little change in the beneficial messages, in which significantly decreased infighting by the presidential party is largely offset by the nonpresidential party's increase in credible self-praise.

---

[38] Because the Chapter 3 Baum and Groeling content analysis data do not code evaluations of targets other than the president and his administration, they would be inappropriate to use here.

TABLE 6.3. *Credibility of Partisan Messages for Nonpresidential Party Viewers*

Proportion of Messages from Congressional Sources, Unified Government (n = 3,893)

Partisan Credibility for NPP Viewers

Costly Credibility	High		Low	
High	*NPP praises PP*	7%	PP attacks PP	20%
	NPP attacks NPP	3%	PP praises NPP	2%
Low	NPP attacks PP	38%	*PP attacks NPP*	8%
	NPP praises NPP	7%	*PP praises PP*	15%

Proportion of Messages from Congressional Sources, Divided Government (n = 3,605)

Partisan Credibility for NPP Viewers

Costly Credibility	High		Low	
High	*NPP praises PP*	4%↓	PP attacks PP	9%↓
	NPP attacks NPP	6%↑	PP praises NPP	1%↓
Low	NPP attacks PP	41%↑	*PP attacks NPP*	17%↑
	NPP praises NPP	15%↑	*PP praises PP*	7%↓

Notes: PP = presidential party; NPP = nonpresidential party. Italicized messages are harmful to the nonpresidential party.

Turning to the impact of messages for the presidential party, the top part of Table 6.4 highlights considerable problems for the presidential party in unified government. During this time, messages regarded as damaging to the presidential party (italicized in the table) comprise about two thirds of the total partisan evaluations. Moreover, fully one in five of the messages received at this time is from the upper-left quadrant of the table – that is, the most credible and damaging quadrant for members of the presidential party.

The bottom part of Table 6.4 repeats this analysis for the presidential party during divided government. Here, I find a less hazardous situation for the presidential party: While harmful messages still comprise about two thirds of all messages, the most harmful messages (i.e., in the upper-left quadrant) have decreased by half. The remaining harmful messages are attacks by the nonpresidential party, which are credible only to their fellow partisans in the nonpresidential party. Although the presidential party is less able to praise itself in the news, it is more able to savage the opposing party, presumably helping to shore up its standing with its fellow partisans.

In summary, divided government provides a feast of low-credibility, cross-party attacks. In unified government, the nonpresidential party still

TABLE 6.4. *Credibility of Partisan Messages for Presidential Party Viewers*

Proportion of Messages from Congressional Sources, Unified Government (n = 3,893)

Partisan Credibility for PP Viewers

Costly Credibility	High		Low	
High	PP attacks PP	20%	NPP praises PP	6%
	PP praises NPP	2%	NPP attacks NPP	3%
Low	PP attacks NPP	8%	*NPP attacks PP*	*38%*
	PP praises PP	15%	*NPP praises NPP*	*7%*

Proportion of Messages from Congressional Sources, Divided Government (n = 3,605)

Partisan Credibility for PP Viewers

Costly Credibility	High		Low	
High	*PP attacks PP*	9%↓	NPP praises PP	4%↓
	PP praises NPP	1%↓	NPP attacks NPP	6%↑
Low	PP attacks NPP	17%↑	*NPP attacks PP*	*41%↑*
	PP praises PP	7%↓	*NPP praises NPP*	*15%↑*

Note: PP = presidential party; NPP = nonpresidential party. Italicized messages are harmful to the presidential party. This excludes evaluations during the lame-duck period following a presidential election and preceding inauguration and from campaign sources during the 1992 presidential campaign.

provides significant quantities of such attacks on the presidential party. Unfortunately for the presidential party, unified government reduces the perceived authority of the nonpresidential party, thereby rendering attacks on them far less important and newsworthy (see Chapter 4).

This problem is evident in the Democratic Party's difficulties finding a credible rhetorical target after winning unified control of government in the 2008 election. Although the party initially was able to sustain itself on residual anti-Bush rhetoric, even *The New York Times* (in an article aptly titled "Blaming the Guy Who Came Before Doesn't Work Long") believed the strategy came with an expiration date (Baker 2009; Curl 2009a and b). Similarly, while the rhetorical excesses and missteps of individual Republicans in Congress allowed them to serve as rallying cries for the party, the impact faded as the original infractions left the headlines or as debate shifted to new topics.[39]

[39] A clear example of this strategy was the administration's focus on Senator Jim DeMint's (D-OH) exhortation that defeating Democratic health-care reforms would be Obama's "Waterloo," which was "used to rally the troops and money" (Tobianski 2009). An even more prominent example was the case of Representative Joe Wilson (R-SC), who

Indeed, Democrats faced no small amount of uncertainty stemming from the absence of a credible, powerful opponent around which to rally in opposition. From the earliest days of the Obama Administration, Democrats found themselves searching outside the ranks of traditional officeholders for a suitable opponent. The first and perhaps most notorious example was Rush Limbaugh, who became the focus of Democratic partisan attacks after he said shortly before the new president was sworn in that he hoped Obama would "fail." Obama advanced the narrative when he tried to build support for his economic stimulus by arguing, "You can't just listen to Rush Limbaugh and get things done.... We shouldn't let partisan politics derail what are very important things that need to get done" (Bauder 2009). Three months later, Democrats conceded they had "exhausted the use of Rush as an attention-getter" and "let the GOP get the better of [them] during the debate over pork in the budget bill" (Allen 2009).[40]

Soon afterward, heated "tea party" and town hall meeting protests against Obama Administration policies and proposals prompted the White House and allied Democrats to ramp up "efforts to make belligerent anti-Obama town hall crowds –and the media outlets that feed their resentment – the face of opposition to the president's health care agenda . . . [and] to turn that anger and material into a rallying point for proponents of reform" (Stein 2009).[41]

At the same time, Democrats also adopted "a coordinated strategy for attacking insurance companies to ward off attacks from opponents of

became the target of massive media and partisan attention after he shouted, "You lie," to President Obama during his congressional address on health care. Democrats roundly condemned Wilson's outburst and passed a resolution censuring Wilson (largely but not perfectly along party lines), in addition to using it to raise money for his prospective opponent (Phillips 2009). However, Former President Jimmy Carter then shifted the terms of debate by arguing that Wilson and other Obama critics were motivated by racism. The White House quickly distanced itself from Carter's remarks, apparently believing that "At this delicate stage of the Obama presidency, with the fate of his health-care overhaul in the balance," a heated discussion of race would be a dangerous distraction. Republicans expressed "outrage" that the Obama camp would use race to deflect legitimate policy concerns, calling it "a troubling sign about the lengths Democrats will go to disparage all who disagree with them" (Nicholas 2009).

[40] Moreover, as I will discuss in the Conclusion chapter, Democrats found that taking on media figures such as Limbaugh and Glenn Beck tends to raise their opponents' ratings and stature, while leaving them open to charges of attempting to stifle the freedom of the press.

[41] The article specifically includes Matt Drudge's drudgereport.com website as an exemplar of a "media outlet [feeding] their resentment." Democrats also mocked conservative protestors as "tea-baggers" and tried to foster news coverage of the more extreme (and allegedly violent) participants.

their health care overhaul . . . ," which Speaker Pelosi neatly summarized by stating that insurers "are the villains in this" (Soraghan 2009). In explaining the shift in message and target, House Majority Leader Steny Hoyer (D-MD) admitted that Democrats had been losing the message war "a little bit" because "We're responsible for putting together a plan" while "Republicans have been free to conjure up whatever they want" in opposition (Soraghan 2009). As Ambinder (2009) noted when discussing Democratic difficulties in rallying support for health-care reform, "[I]t's not easy to engineer a massive national congressional switchboard campaign unless there is a defined target. That's one reason why the Democrats and the White House are trying to bait the insurance companies."

In other words, without the other party providing a credible common target, the governing party's message can become muddled and ineffective. Meanwhile, as the president and factions within his party struggle for primacy and control over the party agenda, the governing party risks treating the public to a double dose of the most damaging and credible messages about that party.

DIVIDED GOVERNMENT AND A "CONSPIRACY OF INCUMBENTS"

In divided government, the president faces a powerful temptation to govern through compromise with the majority party in Congress, thereby undercutting the brand positioning of his own legislative party. As Sinclair (2002, 138) observed, the president and his legislative party are likely to "perceive their optimal strategies as conflicting because of their differences in status. Thus, the president most likely will want legislative accomplishments, but the congressional party may well see them as burnishing the reputation of the opposition congressional majority and so as a barrier to regaining majority status." In such instances, a congressional party cannot trust its president to put its interests over his own.

The presidency of Bill Clinton provides a compelling example of such conflicting incentives between a president and his legislative party. Clinton and his congressional allies were elected in 1992 with a mandate to end gridlock in Washington. After just two years of unified government, leading congressional Democrats were scrambling for distance from their erstwhile ally (see Chapter 1). Mann observed that because of Clinton's perceived missteps, the Democrats felt a "need, especially the new Democratic minority leaders in the House and Senate, to put at least some symbolic distance between themselves and the president" (CNN 8 Dec., 1994). After being selected to lead his party in the Senate, then-Minority

Leader Tom Daschle (D-SD) asserted that he would be willing to take a different path than Clinton, saying, "To the extent we can, we want very much to work with the White House. We will not be led by them. We will not view ourselves as an extension of them"[42] (ABC 1994). However, congressional Democrats found that their options for going it alone were restricted by their weak strategic position, as discussed next.

For his part, Clinton responded to the 1994 election by pursuing a strategy called "triangulation." According to adviser Dick Morris, who is credited with convincing Clinton to adopt this approach, triangulation called for the president to "create a third position, not just in between the positions of the two parties but above them as well."[43] Using this strategy, Clinton co-opted popular Republican positions on issues such as welfare reform, balancing the budget, and defense and worked with Republicans to pass the resulting legislation.[44] The strategy consciously separated Clinton not only from the Republicans but also from his own party in Congress, whose initial reaction to Clinton's new strategies was – as adviser George Stephanopoulos predicted – to "go ballistic on the Hill" (Morris 1999).

Some Democrats began speaking out against Clinton's actions shortly after the 1994 election. When asked whether there was a need for a separate party identity across branches of government, Representative Charlie Rose (D-NC) replied:

> *Rose*: I think there should be a constitutionally appropriate distance between the White House.
>
> *Borger*: Well, what does that mean?
>
> *Rose*: Well, that means not what we're doing now.... [45]

---

[42] In the same report, John Cochran concluded that "Democrats have learned that getting too close to the Clinton White House can be bad for their political health."

[43] Morris (1999) saw "triangulation as a way to change, not abandon the Democratic Party. When political activists or public officials seek to change the orientation and policies of their party, they normally work from within through persuasion or, more combatively, through primary challenges to those who espouse the orthodox view. But a president can step out ahead of his party and articulate a new position. The triangle he forms between the orthodox views of the two parties at each end of the base and his views at the apex is temporary. Either he will be repudiated by the voters and slink back into the orthodox positions or he will attract support and, eventually, bring his party with him."

[44] Clinton co-opted Republican positions on many of the collective-goods issues that (according to Jacobson 1990) gave Republicans an advantage in occupying the presidency.

[45] Borger had asked Rose the question, "Do you think you folks as leaders should distance yourselves from Bill Clinton?" Representative Kweisi Mfume (D-MD) expressed similar

Following Clinton's televised endorsement of budgetary compromise with the Republicans, in which he implicitly rebuked "those who have suggested that it might actually benefit one side or the other politically if we had gridlock and ended this fiscal year without a budget" (Clinton 1995), Representative Pete Stark (D-CA) publicly lamented that Clinton and congressional Democrats were no longer "playing on the same team.... "There is absolutely nothing we can do. The president has just absolutely cut off Democrats in the House and Senate. We're no longer a party to this" (Schieffer 1995).[46]

Despite the resentment of some congressional Democrats, Clinton stayed the course. His triangulation strategy continued, reaching its peak during the summer of 1996. At that time, Clinton was running far ahead of Bob Dole, his relatively weak rival in the presidential contest. In Congress, Republicans were hampered by public blame for the previous year's government shutdown and seemed likely to lose control of the House in November. After early legislative victories associated with the Contract with America, Republican legislation had bogged down. Stealing a page from Harry Truman, congressional Democrats eagerly attempted to hang a "do-nothing" label on congressional Republicans.

However, by early August, the strategic situation had changed dramatically. In just a few short weeks, Clinton and the Republicans in Congress collaborated in passing a series of important bills on topics such as health-care reform, anti-terrorism legislation, a minimum-wage hike, tax breaks for small businesses, environmental legislation, a taxpayers' bill of rights, defense-authorization measures, and several appropriations bills.[47] Most important, Clinton and the congressional Republicans passed the Welfare Reform Act of 1996, a massive overhaul of the welfare system.

The Welfare Reform Act was strongly opposed by many Democrats in Congress and was almost identical to Republican bills that Clinton had

sentiments on the same program, saying "I don't know if there's a need for a separate identity, if you happen to be the same party. One thing is clear – we can't have two Republican parties, just as we never could have two Democratic parties.... And I think it becomes a danger when we move to try to emulate or imitate that which we might think is successful. Republicans never do that, and I don't think Democrats should do that" (CNN 26 Nov. 1994).

[46] This is not to say that some Democratic factions did not support a more centrist brand for the Democratic Party. Indeed, the DLC, which Clinton previously headed, had been pushing for such rebranding for years.

[47] Of course, at least some congressional Democrats sincerely preferred that many of these proposals (particularly the minimum-wage hike) actually become law on policy grounds. However, such passage prior to the election likely harmed their strategies and prospects for gaining the majority within the chamber, which – as discussed previously – would have aided their agenda control, enhanced their fundraising, and so forth.

vetoed on two previous occasions. Perhaps more noteworthy, its passage amounted to what has been called "an incumbent's conspiracy" in which the partisans in power took actions that hindered the election hopes of their out-of-power peers. *Roll Call*'s Morton Kondracke noted that as Republicans cooperated with Clinton to pass the legislation, "the political losers [were] those with a vested interest in gridlock – Republican presidential nominee Bob Dole and House Democrats" (Kondracke 1996).

Dole and his campaign aides had been "dead set" against passing another welfare bill that summer, believing that Clinton's two prior vetoes handed them a juicy campaign issue (Kondracke 1996). They also believed that the bipartisan action undercut their argument that a Republican president was necessary to end gridlock. By passing the Welfare Reform Act and other significant laws, one analyst argued that Clinton was "appearing presidential and trying to show he can get things done as president . . . the same thing that Republicans in Congress are doing. He needs a record to run on, and that's what he is doing here. It was in their self-interest to help each other."[48]

Similarly, congressional Democrats saw their "do-nothing" rhetorical attack dissolve under a pile of significant legislation. Bill Archer (R-TX) stated that the burst of legislation was "the culmination of the do-something Congress" that showed the system had worked, noting it was the "Republican Congress that [had] pulled together this bipartisanship" (Henry 1996). Privately, congressional Democrats fumed, despite promises of aggressive campaigning and fundraising on their behalf by the White House.

Less than a month before the election, one political scientist predicted that Clinton would win 58% of the popular vote and that Democrats in Congress could therefore expect to ride his coattails to pick up between 25 and 30 seats in Congress (Campbell 1996). Republicans in Congress read Dole's poll numbers and again scrambled to save themselves. Press coverage at the time noted that vulnerable House Republicans felt Dole was a "drag on the ticket" and actively distanced themselves from him – with the explicit blessing of the Republican leadership[49] (Freedland 1996a). Shortly before the election, the National Republican Congressional Committee ran ads that assumed Dole's defeat by asking, "What would happen

---

[48] Neil Newhouse, Republican pollster, quoted in McGrory (1996).

[49] Newt Gingrich, in an interview with *New York Times* editors more than a month before the election, explicitly gave Republicans in marginal districts permission to distance themselves from Dole (Toner 1996).

if the Democrats controlled Congress and the White House?" (Canellos 1996). As one Republican strategist explained, "Americans like gridlock. They like Bill Clinton, but they don't want to give him a blank check" (McInturff, quoted in Freedland 1996b).

Polls at the time showed some support for this tactic: When voters believed that Clinton was assured reelection, 48% of respondents said they wanted a Republican Congress to rein him in (Sullivan 1996). ABC's Cokie Roberts said that Democrats feared the technique might actually work, concluding that she thought the election might even produce "anti-coattails," wherein "the better the President does, the worse the Democrats in Congress do...." (Roberts 1996).

On Election Day, the congressional Democrats' hopes for a 30-seat pickup in the House were dashed as they received less than a third of that amount (i.e., 9 seats). In the Senate, despite Clinton's substantial victory over Bob Dole, Democrats actually lost two seats. Republicans, in turn, maintained their majority control in both chambers. Former Senator Bill Bradley (D-NJ) summarized the Clinton presidency this way: "Clinton was president for eight years. He was the first Democrat to be reelected since Franklin Roosevelt. He was smart, skilled and possessed great energy. But what happened? At the end of his tenure in the most powerful office in the world, there were fewer Democratic governors, fewer Democratic senators, members of Congress and state legislators and a national party that was deep in debt. The president did well. The party did not" (Bradley 2005).

Although George W. Bush never appeared to be interested in running against his own party in the manner that Clinton did, the poor stewardship of the Republican brand under Bush's leadership had Republicans reeling by the end of his term. After losing 51 seats in the House and at least 14 in the Senate – and, not inconsequentially, their majorities in both chambers – the same Republicans who had benefited from a Clinton presidency could truly say to their once-vanquished Democratic legislative brethren, "We feel your pain."

In an ironic echo of Bush's problems with RINOs, political animals of a different color – the so-called Blue Dog Democrats –have strained the unity and cohesion of Democrats as they wrestle over Obama's ambitious legislative agenda. These 52 members, who tend to come from comparatively moderate or conservative districts (often carried by the Republican presidential nominee), have been at the center of contentious negotiations about the scope and nature of such legislation, particularly the debate over the so-called public option in health-care reform.

Although the Democratic surge in 2008 had swelled the ranks of Democrats by allowing challengers in nominally Republican districts to squeak into office, the electoral vulnerability of such members and the comparative conservatism of their districts put them at loggerheads with their more liberal peers. On a variety of issues – but especially on the issue of health care – disputes within the Democratic governing coalition became rancorous, including public spats in which Blue Dogs accused other Democrats of conducting "illegitimate" negotiations or outright lying (Allen, Soraghan, and Burke 2009).[50] Liberals, in turn, resented any concessions given to Blue Dogs and went so far as to run advertisements in their home district attacking them (Connolly 2009) and to advocate that such members face progressive primary challengers in the next election (O'Brien 2009b).[51]

Despite the rancor, Obama and his fellow Democrats have a powerful incentive to pass at least a minimal version of health-care reform. As journalist Daniel Balz observed, any failure to do so would be "the worst possible outcome of the health-care debate because of what it would say about the Democrats' ability to govern. That remains a powerful motivator among Democrats, and it is one reason to believe that, in the end, Congress will send some kind of health-care bill to Obama for his signature" (Balz 2009). Or, as Obama himself reportedly put it to a hesitant Democratic member of Congress, "You're going to destroy my presidency" (Edney, Hunt, and Cohn 2009). Balz then noted that "members of Congress and the president are now operating on conflicting political timetables. Obama doesn't have to worry about reelection until 2012, when the world could look quite different. Members of Congress

---

[50] Health-care reform was only the latest in a series of tough votes for the Blue Dogs, according to Representative Anthony Weiner (D-NY): "[T]he crowded legislative calendar and a bruising battle in June over a climate bill narrowly approved by the House is wearing down Democrats, particularly those in the fiscally conservative Blue Dog coalition. We had a lot of House members who cast a tough vote on energy, and thought they could catch their breath, only to have health care bear down on them" (Adamy and Weisman 2009).

[51] It is interesting that MSNBC host Keith Olbermann seemed to make similar threats toward Obama himself, arguing that because Obama had "compromised on everything so far . . . the progressive caucus and progressives would abandon him if necessary, if this was to be the policy of this administration into 2012. If it's necessary to find somebody to run against him, I think they'd do it, no matter how destructive that may seem" (Rasmussen Reports 2009). An unidentified New Jersey Republican poetically expressed the Democrats' jeopardy as follows: "If major health care fails at this point, the Democratic Party's Left might eat their center and spit out the bones" (Barnes, Cohen, and Bell 2009).

have to face the voters in 14 months and already they are nervous about what they see. Once they start worrying mostly about their own survival, Obama's hold on them will be weakened" (Balz 2009).

For most Blue Dogs, worry about 2010 is palpable, and Obama's hold does appear to be weakening. For example, in Louisiana, Representative Charlie Melancon (D-LA) aggressively emphasized his political independence from fellow Democrats, billing himself as a "pro-life, pro-gun Southern Democrat" who opposed Obama's public health insurance option. Nonetheless, his opponent in the upcoming senatorial election, incumbent Senator David Vitter (R-LA, himself damaged by an embarrassing prostitution scandal), built his campaign on a simple message: "Melancon backs the Obama presidency" (Robertson 2009). The Vitter campaign, which successfully scooped up the charliemelanconforsenate.com domain, undermined Melancon on the website by emphasizing Melancon's support for Obama and Pelosi, as well as other Democratic policies (Figure 6.1).

CONCLUSION: KEEPING ONE'S ENEMIES CLOSER

Many scholars have viewed the U.S. Constitution's system of competing institutions as a sickness and prescribed party government as a cure. As Sundquist (1992) reasoned, " . . . since redistribution of power is a zero-sum game that creates both winners and losers, one party is bound to lose [from bipartisan agreement]." In the case of 1996, however, one can clearly observe cross-party agreements in which members of both parties prospered – but at the expense of their out-of-power comrades. It is important to note that the increasing distance between the electoral fortunes of presidential and congressional party members did not occur *despite* the common party bond but rather *because* of it. Congressional Democrats bitterly resented Clinton's implicit deal with congressional Republicans, but were hobbled by their dependence on him as their party's standard-bearer going into a critical election.[52] Similarly, congressional Republicans actively worked to establish their own public image precisely because they were tethered in the public eye to likely loser Bob Dole. Although Dole was a respected and connected former senator,

---

[52] This is not to say that Democrats actually preferred a Dole victory but rather that their minority status in divided government allowed Clinton to govern and wage a campaign that specifically disadvantaged them in their efforts to unseat the Republican majority, and that there was little they could do to change this.

Melancon backs Obama presidency

Voted with Nancy Pelosi
92% of the Time.

Enter your e-mail address to
stand with David and learn more

(I Support David)

Charlie Melancon: Never Met a Bailout He Didn't Like

Charlie Melancon supported President Obama on **every vote**
to run up **more debt** in his first 100 days than every other
president over the first 219 years of our nation's history.

'If (Obama) doesn't

- Voted for the initial $700 billion Wall Street bailout
  program (House Vote 674)

win, it

will say

we will

- Voted for the final $700 billion Wall Street Bailout
  Program (House vote 681)

stay on

the same

- Voted for $14 Billion in loans to domestic
  automakers (House vote 690)

path as now.'

Charlie Melancon: Voted for Obama's Disasterous Budget That Will Bankrupt Future Generations

Charlie Melancon

U.S. Representative, D-Napoleonville

FIGURE 6.1. Fake Charlie Melancon campaign website (actually sponsored by his Republican opponent, Senator David Vitter [R-LA]).

his probable electoral defeat undercut his ability to credibly reward or punish his fellow Republicans following the election. As Daniel Schorr and Thomas Mann observed (NPR 1996):

> *Schorr*: It used to be that the standard-bearer would be pretty close to that party's contingent in Congress. A while back we suddenly found that the Democrats in Congress were moving away from President Clinton. That's

changed now. When did it start to happen that the fate of a party in Congress seemed to be so different from the fate of the standard-bearer of that party?

Mann: Indeed, it's been characteristic of the last couple of decades. That's why we've seen so many examples of divided-party government. Republicans understand well now that the chances of Bob Dole winning this election are no better than one in ten, and the bigger his deficit against Bill Clinton, the greater the probability that they will lose their majority. They feel they have to cut their losses, make decisions that will have a direct bearing on the public's image of the Republican Congress, as opposed to the Republican candidate, and they are proceeding accordingly.

This book began with a theory of how and why parties at the national level organize themselves to pursue a common party "brand name" through their words and their deeds, as well as the obstacles they face in this pursuit. Chapters 2 through 4 described the intervening role the news media play in filtering the content of this brand, particularly their overemphasis on conflict within the presidential party. Chapter 5 then demonstrated that such disputes are especially corrosive for the president's public standing, as well as that of his party.

The central point of this chapter is that unified government paradoxically undermines presidential-party unity. In fact, I conclude that parties possessing the power of the presidency might communicate a valued party image as well or even better if they were relegated to the minority in Congress. Conversely, a congressional majority may be aided in its communication and reelection efforts by the opposing party's control of the presidency, which would allow it to customize the party brand to better suit congressional rather than executive needs.[53]

This chapter opened with Woodrow Wilson's observation that in order to achieve "harmonious, consistent, and responsible party government," our government needs to connect the president as closely as possible with his party in Congress. Although parties can act to provide incentives for common action and rhetoric, there are also situations in which intense pressures push elements of the party to distance themselves from their peers and pursue a unique brand name. Although such incentives have been observed in studies describing "candidate-centered elections," "running against Congress," or other examples of individuals distancing themselves from the party, those identified here occur at the *institutional* level. In 1996, congressional Republicans had a collective party interest in

---

[53] Also, an important caveat to this statement is the assumption that a supermajority in the Senate is not included in the alternatives.

pursuing a brand name that harmed their presidential nominee. Clinton, through his famous strategy of triangulation, similarly undermined his colleagues in Congress.[54] Some congressional Republicans did the same to George W. Bush in 2001, even to the point of leaving the party.

Moreover, the belief that a party in one branch of government can "distance" itself from fellow partisans in another branch undercuts a basic motivation for party government. To the degree to which different branches of a party are willing to attempt to establish their own brand name with the public, the advantages of a single party controlling government are diminished.

All of this is not to say that the prospects for unified governing are hopeless. In the Conclusion chapter, I examine several changes to the political and media environments that I believe increase the prospects for achieving more stable, accountable party government in the future. In particular, I argue that American parties have two main hopes for unifying their brand name: (1) they can work even harder to control the messages from which the news media choose their stories; and (2) they can hope for continued changes in the media environment, particularly an expansion of more partisan news media outlets.

---

[54] There is an obvious tension between pursuing a "unified" brand and each member's "right" brand. As discussed in Chapter 1, the temptation to customize a brand often stems from the fact that a brand that works in one locale does not work in another. Throughout this book, I have tried to be agnostic about the best content of a brand, in part because circumstances change, but also because the best brand for the president might differ from that of his party. Regardless of whether the issue content of Clinton's triangulated Democratic branding was superior to the Democratic branding that preceded it, I think that Clinton damaged the prior brand by consciously denigrating it. By locating himself between (and "above," according to Morris 1999) the Democrats and Republicans, the clear implication was that he was repudiating the extremity of both parties. It is difficult to trace a causal connection between his triangulation and his party's congressional losses, but his party's congressional record was abysmal during every election except 1998, in which the Republican handling of the Monica Lewinsky scandal was a dominant issue. The failure of the Democrats to cohesively maintain Clinton's brand and the increasing marginalization of the centrist DLC following his exit from office further point to its limited utility for congressional Democrats (Berman 2005; Bradley 2005).

Conclusion: Uncircling the Firing Squad

Party Cohesion in a New Media Era

His first job, Nick Williams thought, was to separate the [Los Angeles Times] from the Republican Party, to gain some degree of independence in coverage of politics (old-time Times readers were stunned during the 1960 national campaign when the Times covered not just Richard Nixon but Kennedy as well; the idea of printing what a Democrat was saying about a Republican was unheard of).

– David Halberstam, *The Powers That Be* (1979, 286)

INTRODUCTION

During the 83rd Congress, several Republican senators died in office, giving Democrats a numerical advantage in the number of seats in the chamber. Despite their unexpected new "majority" status, however, the Democrats decided not to take official control of the chamber, uncertain that there was advantage in shouldering such responsibility.[1] Previous chapters give substantial support to this uncertainty; specifically, I argue that unified control of government has been, at best, a mixed blessing in recent years, particularly for the president's party in Congress.

The central paradox of this book is that the power associated with unified control of government makes the governing party more vulnerable: In a form of political jujitsu, the opposition party can turn the governing

---

[1] Mitchell (2001) also noted, "[I]n 1954, Senator William Knowland of California, the Republican majority leader, mourned on the floor that 'I have the responsibility of being majority leader in this body without a majority.' Democratic Senator Lyndon B. Johnson of Texas retorted, 'If anyone has more problems than a majority leader with a minority, it is a minority leader with a majority'."

party's own strength against it. The governing party is powerful enough to be held responsible for the output of government but is generally too weak to achieve its goals over the minority's objections. The minority party is too weak to serve as a credible target of attack but is able to deliver withering fire against the presidential party through the press. The presidential party is constrained in its policy proposals by the real possibility that such proposals might be enacted, while the minority party can "promise the moon" to their supporters and blame the majority for not delivering it.[2]

A main theme of this book concerns the consequences that political parties face when they "circle the firing squad" and attack one another. Although parties inevitably suffer from at least some internal squabbles, in unified government, both the president and his legislative party have legitimate claims and authority to represent their party. Because differing preferences inevitably arise – even within a party (see Chapter 1) – fellow partisans must jockey to get their preferred items onto the agenda. As one top GOP aide complained in early 2001, "We're still testing the waters to figure out who the hell is in charge, and we're learning quickly that it isn't us" (Taylor 2001b). The party's differing constituencies and electoral calendars across branches further add to the strife. As Howard Fineman (2005) observed when George W. Bush's attempts to reform Social Security stalled, "Bush remains very popular among Republican voters – Reagan-like in that respect – but GOP members of Congress grow less worried by the day about crossing him. They have their own reelections to worry about – and they are worried" – with good reason, as their 2006 drubbing demonstrated. Making matters worse, any such friction in the governing party is newsworthy and damaging to the public support for the president and his administration.

In divided government, however, the presidential party in Congress is demoted to a "junior partner" in their relationship, heavily dependent on the president to represent and fight for its interests. Divided government also can unite a party through opposition to a common foe – in metaphorical terms, it allows the presidential party to "uncircle the firing squad"

---

[2] For example, under President Clinton, the Republican leadership in Congress could rally swaying moderates by promising that "the final product once negotiated with the White House would be more to their liking" (Taylor 2001b). In unified government, moderates had to take seriously every proposal that came to the floor. As one Democratic staffer noted, "They know the line that they've always been fed, 'Please vote for this, it'll get fixed in the end' – they know that's not true any more." As one analyst summed up, "In short, [Republicans were] playing for keeps" (Taylor 2001b).

and direct its volleys at the opposing party. As discussed in previous chapters, congressional Republicans achieved high degrees of coherence and unity in the 1990s primarily through their vocal opposition to President Clinton. Former Majority Leader Trent Lott observed, "When you're in the minority, sometimes I think it's easier to come together and be very aggressive in your tactics" (Associated Press 2001). Senator Larry Craig (R-ID), former chairman of the GOP Policy Committee, argued that the loss of majority status helped "bring our conference together working as a unit again" (Lancaster 2001). The threat of Clinton had allowed "party divisions [to] be bandaged by unity against a common opponent . . . [instead of being] confronted, head on [in unified government]" (Taylor 2001b). As noted previously, Democrats in the minority under President George W. Bush had a similar experience, achieving remarkable unity in opposition to policy proposals by the governing Republicans (e.g., the 2005 effort to reform Social Security). The Democrats' ability to savage the Republicans' proposals without offering up any alternatives of their own was the partisan equivalent of a guerilla war, and Bush and the Republicans clearly struggled as a consequence: "[W]ith no high-profile political opponent as a foil, and with Democrats refusing to put forward competing proposals on issues like Social Security, the president and his policies stand on their own, with nothing to deflect partisan fire" (Stevenson 2005). The relative resurgence of the Republican brand while the party was in the minority following the 2008 election further underlines the effectiveness of this strategy.

To summarize, I contend that some members of both parties gain greater advantage by fortifying their respective institutional bunkers and lobbing the occasional grenade rather than by aggressively trying to rout their opponents in the other branch of government and seize unified power.[3] Of course, all of this belies the fact that for most of American

---

[3] This is not to say that partisans in each branch want to give up power: Partisans in Congress definitely want to serve in the majority; see, for example, the much-criticized reapportionment of Texas in 2003, inspired by House Republican Majority Leader Tom DeLay (R-TX), which resulted in a net loss of four Democratic seats and helped maintain Republican control of the House in 2004. Similarly, it is assumed that most people who run for the presidency do so precisely so that they might actually become president. This does not imply, however, that once in office, the president might not stand a greater chance of reelection if his party were in the minority, or that members of the majority party in Congress might not stand a better chance of reelection were they to face a president of the other party. For example, prior to the 2004 election, many Republicans worked exceptionally hard to defeat Senator John Kerry's (D-MA) bid for the presidency, but others within the party (particularly moderates in the Northeastern states) were far

history, parties successfully sought and maintained unified control of government (see Chapter 6). If parties successfully governed in unified government in the past, it seems reasonable that there should be some way for them to do it again.

In the remainder of this Conclusion chapter, I argue that changes in the media environment in the latter half of the 20th century severely undermined the majority party's ability to survive and prosper in unified government. I further contend that although parties can and should continue to develop internal mechanisms to increase their message cohesion, changes in the media environment – and particularly developments in new media and increased opportunities for partisans to self-select their news – are likely to prove far more consequential for the prospects of stable unified party government.

TWO FACTORS, REVISITED

In Chapter 2, I argue that the likelihood that a particular message would appear on the news was a function of two probabilities: (1) a party would offer that message, and (2) the news media would decide to air it. In turn, I argue in Chapter 5 that the persuasive impact of partisan evaluations was a function of their costliness and the party affiliation of the speaker and viewer. This implies that if parties desire to change the partisan messages received by the public, there are three options: (1) they can alter the messages they speak, (2) the media can change which messages are aired, or (3) the public can change the messages it chooses to view.

---

less helpful to the Bush effort. In particular, Senator Arlen Specter (R-PA) came under fire by conservatives within the Republican Party for his tepid support of Bush in the 2004 election. Conservatives were incensed by Specter's actions in the Senate – particularly for his stances on abortion and judicial nominees – and mounted an aggressive primary challenge to his candidacy (see Chapter 6). The challenge fell short at least in part because President Bush and the Republican leadership rallied to Specter's side, apparently because they thought his support was essential in a crucial swing state in the upcoming presidential election. In the general election, conservatives then complained that "Arlen Specter owes Bush and Santorum his career, but he isn't acting like it" and accused him of avoiding joint appearances with the president's campaign or other Republican candidates despite his safe lead in the polls (Carney 2004). Republicans were further incensed when Specter implicitly criticized Bush's judicial nominees as "extremists" and when "Kerry and Specter for Working Families" signs were widely distributed by a 527 organization headed by the former head of Specter's 1996 presidential bid (Carney 2004). Given the poor showing by Republican presidential candidates in Pennsylvania in the 2004 and 2008 presidential elections and Specter's ultimate decision to formally switch back to the Democratic Party in 2009 (see Chapter 6), Republicans were given further cause to regret their decision.

Option 1: Making Party Messages More Cohesive

From the first page, this book has been filled with numerous examples of the parties' struggles to increase internal cohesion and thereby gain greater control of the brand name they convey through the news media – and they have some successes to show for their work. Chapter 4 shows that the congressional parties' increasingly sophisticated message operations have been at least somewhat successful at reining in harmful messages directed at their peers in the chamber. Similarly, each consecutive White House press office in recent years seemingly has been crowned as the "new world champion" of message discipline and control.[4]

Unfortunately for the parties, the most pervasive failures of message discipline outlined herein have not occurred within branches but rather across them. More precisely, given the relatively scant rhetorical attention that the president typically gives to his party in the legislature (see Chapter 4), the discordant messages arise primarily from the president's party in Congress. Despite their impressive cohesion in the legislature, some members of his party will almost inevitably oppose the president (sometimes doing so cohesively with their fellow legislative partisans) – at least, on some subset of issues. Such opposition will continue to occur as long as it is in the party's or an individual member's political interest to do so.

---

[4] Former Presidents Jimmy Carter and George H. W. Bush seem to be the biggest outliers in this pattern; the latter actually received plaudits (and criticism) for the tight message control employed during the Gulf War. The Obama campaign was legendary for its message discipline throughout the 2008 election cycle. As one reporter observed, "Obama's campaign has been remarkably effective so far this year at maintaining a coherent message, built around Obama's biography and his appeal for a new kind of politics. Part of his success has been tight message discipline: The campaign has been virtually leak-free, and the line of control from Obama to his chief strategist David Axelrod to campaign manager (and Axelrod business partner) David Plouffe is unchallenged" (Smith 2008). Of course, successful political operations usually produce less leaking, finger-pointing, and recrimination than those confronting failure (as the saying goes, "Success has a thousand parents, but failure is an orphan"). While the Obama Administration (and particularly its press office) has generally emulated the campaign's emphasis on disciplined messaging, internal disputes between officials at the heart of the administration have begun to bubble into the press as this manuscript enters final production. One such dispute has divided supporters and opponents of White House Chief of Staff Rahm Emanuel. It is interesting that part of the imbroglio centers on whether Emanuel leaked accounts of key administration decisions that burnished his reputation at the expense of others in the administration (including Obama himself). Wading into this debate, David Broder took the unusual step of lambasting both Emanuel and supportive writers from his own newspaper in an article titled "The Fable of Emanuel the Great" (Broder 2010).

Unfortunately, Madison (1787) was probably prescient with regard to the ability to prevent factional disagreements. As he noted in *Federalist #10*, the only two sure methods to prevent such disagreement were "by destroying the liberty which is essential to its existence; the other, by giving to every citizen the same opinions, the same passions, and the same interests."

Given the news media's preference to highlight discord within a governing party, even small disputes are nearly certain to be magnified. Preventing internal disagreements, in turn, is nearly impossible, especially with officeholders facing different constituencies and electoral calendars across branches of government. As discussed in Chapter 1, it is therefore unsurprising that many modern party systems outside of the United States have chosen to use Madison's first strategy. Much like strong commercial franchisors (e.g., McDonald's Corporation), such parties vest tremendous power in centralized party organizations that reduce the liberty of party members and enforce stringent message discipline.

Chapter 1 also highlighted that American parties, in contrast, traditionally appear to be franchises with exceptionally weak central control. In American parties, many obstacles prevent the central Republican and Democratic franchisors from asserting similar central power over their members. In their modern incarnations, the parties have had limited power to sanction officeholders. More important, American parties have limited control over who does and does not run under their brand name, and they have great difficulty "firing" party members who do not "toe the party line," particularly across branches of government.

Similarly, although both the president and his congressional delegation may sometimes share common opinions, passions, and interests, the chances of this occurring all the time are exceedingly remote, even in the most cohesive parties. Unfortunately, like a bickering couple, the president and his party may hate arguing and crave agreement but strongly prefer that the solution be reached by having the *other* side concede. This is not to say that the president and his legislative party are unable to take steps to increase the commonality of their interests. The 1980 Governing Team Day is an example of this type of attempt (see Chapter 1). Of course, it was no accident that the exercise took place when both Reagan and his congressional peers were out of power and that a similar attempt failed to get off the ground in 1992 when a Republican was in the White House.

President George W. Bush's exceptionally aggressive campaigning for his congressional party in the 2002 midterm elections apparently was another attempt to forge these cross-chamber bonds. Although seemingly successful in the short term, the longer-term impact of being closely tied to an increasingly unpopular Bush and his policies clearly seems to have been a net negative to his legislative party in the disastrous 2006 and 2008 elections.

Option 2: Controlling Message Distribution

Madison's second prescription for dealing with the mischief of faction was to treat the effects rather than the cause. Unfortunately for parties, the negative effects of their factionalization on public perception stem largely from the choices of two entities that they do not control: the news media and the viewers. If parties could gain greater control over which partisan messages are distributed through the mass media or which messages viewers choose to consume (as I discuss in the next section), they might be able to increase public exposure to favorable intraparty evaluations or at least limit the damage caused by breakdowns in party message discipline.

The degree to which parties value control over mass-media distribution of desired messages can be seen by examining the resources that parties pour into "paid media" during election cycles. From 2007 to 2008, the TNS Media Intelligence Campaign Media Analysis Group concluded that candidates and groups spent a record-setting $2.5 billion on advertising in that year's elections – $800 million more than the comparable figure for 2004, which also had been a record (Fitzgerald 2008; TNS Media Intelligence 2004). Citizens, scholars, and politicians bemoaned the increasing cost of advertising-centered campaigns and decried the consequences of such campaigns on American politics. What generally is unaddressed in such discussions is *why* politicians go to such great lengths to purchase advertising in the mass media. Clearly, part of the answer lies with the powerful persuasive impact of these media, particularly negative ads. This discussion, however, suggests that politicians have been forced to rely heavily on paid mass media because they face such difficulties in getting their desired messages distributed through the "free" news media.

I argued in Chapter 2 that the core difficulties for the parties lie not in partisan bias on the part of the news media. In fact, my predictions rely on an explicit assumption that journalists are nonpartisan and unbiased. Ironically, in the following section, I argue that not only is increasing the partisanship in the mass media the most likely route for achieving more stable unified control of government, it is also largely a moot point: Such changes are already underway. As a cursory glance at cable news or the Internet reveals, partisan news outlets are proliferating in

the 21st century, even as the nonpartisan mainstream media are suffer-
ing losses in their audience share and credibility (Pew Research Center
2004; Zurawik 2004). Indeed, a 2008 Pew Research Center study reveals
double-digit declines in the credibility of most major news organizations
in the prior decade. CNN, which had the highest credibility rating of the
organizations in the study, actually dropped 12 points in that time frame
in the percentage of those who "believe all or most of what [the] organization says" (i.e., 42% in 1998 compared to 30% in 2008b). Indeed, the
same study shows that media stalwarts like *The New York Times* (18%)
and even the AP (16%) had fewer than one in five Americans willing to
believe all or even most of their coverage (Pew Research Center 2008a). It
is somewhat surprising that those figures were below both the Fox News
Channel (23%) and MSNBC (24%), which had established reputations
as being more partisan alternatives to mainstream outlets, particularly in
the 2008 campaign. In the next section, I examine the historical role of
such partisan-tilted outlets in American partisan politics.

The Partisan Press Is Dead. Long Live the Partisan Press

From almost the beginning of the American Republic, parties and the
press were deeply intertwined. Until the rise of the "penny press" in
the mid-19th century, most newspapers had symbiotic relationships with
political parties and governmental officials (Cook 1989; Hamilton 2004).
Members of the "partisan press" took pride in their skill as "cheerlead-
ers" for their side rather than their prowess in gathering news. They often
received financial inducements, patronage, loans, printing contracts, cir-
culation assistance, and other benefits as a consequence of their party
boosterism (Smith 1977).

Such subsidies soon were dwarfed by commercial opportunities posed
by the mass-advertising revenue model (Schudson 1978). However, even
as newspapers became detached from their formal party ties, they were
still quite partisan in much of their coverage. Despite the increasing
professionalism of journalism as a discipline in the late 19th and early
20th centuries (Schudson 1978), large swaths of newspapers continued to
remain stubbornly partisan well into the 20th century.[5] One of the most
famous partisan holdovers was the *Los Angeles Times*.

[5] For example, Mott (1944) attempted to catalog the political leanings of papers for the
nation's history thus far, including their largely anti-Roosevelt campaigning more recent
elections. In an appendix to its 1939 survey on press attitudes, *Fortune* magazine provided
a fascinating "Five Minute Tour" of "press geography" in the United States, region by
region, identifying the major newspapers and their prevailing stands on the partisan issues

Prior to the late 1950s, the *Times* had exemplified pro-Republican partisanship. In fact, Halberstam (1979, 108) argues that from 1890 to 1960, "[T]he *Times* was not just a voice of anti-unionism, but an outspoken, relentless instrument for all conservative policies and candidates, wedded to the Republican Party, but wary of the party lest it become too soft." The *Times* was famous for its enthusiastic boosterism of Republican candidates, especially Richard Nixon. Halberstam (1979, 261) argues that during the 1950s, the *Times* gave Nixon "wonderful coverage, his every attack on the Reds printed, applauded, his deeds written large and heroically."[6]

of the day. For example, in its description of the papers of the Pacific Northwest, *Fortune* observed:

In the Northwest the character of the press is fairly well diversified. For example, there is the Seattle *Times*, which hasn't been able to stomach and which practically never backs a winning candidate or legislative issue. There is Hearst's Seattle *Post-Intelligencer*, unlike any other Hearst paper anywhere, run by the President's son in law John Boettiger, who doesn't have to print anything from Hearst unless he feels like it – and who often does not feel like it. The *P-I* is the most pro–New Deal paper in the Pacific Northwest, is consistently on the popular side in local issues. In Spokane there are the *Spokesman-Review* and *Chronicle*, which, while they support many a New Deal enterprise (notably Grand Coulee), are heavily conservative – in a section of the state where conservatism and Republicanism seem to be on the upbeat.

To the south there is the superbly edited Portland *Oregonian*, whose traditional Republicanism was approved by the voters, last fall when they returned Oregon to the Republican column. The *Oregonian* is becoming somewhat more liberal, and was the only important paper in the state to oppose flatly the anti-picketing bill – which the voters passed by a large majority. Its opposition, the *Journal*, is less out-spoken, pulls its editorial punches. Nominally Democratic, it has turned against the New Deal in most policies. (Fortune 1939, 78)

Partisan affiliations were so overt that editors would attend conventions of like-minded partisan editors to coordinate their activities. For example, in 1955, Former President Harry Truman spoke to the annual convention of the Indiana Democratic Editors Association and lamented that his party seemed to have a continuing disadvantage in news partisanship to the Republicans, complaining that "in the process of our vast economic expansion we have failed to remedy one of our serious shortages – the shortage of Democratic newspapers. I hope that some day soon this shortage will be overcome" (*Los Angeles Times* 1955). Truman continued, clarifying (perhaps rhetorically) that "I am sure that you realize that when I say Democratic newspapers, I don't mean violent, partisan, distorted newspapers, like so much of the Republican press. Democrats don't want that kind of press nor do the American people" (*Los Angeles Times* 1955).

[6] Of course, Nixon was not the only beneficiary of the *Times*' favorable coverage. Republicans across local, state, and national coverage could count on almost sycophantic coverage in the *Times*' pages. For example, in a front-page article titled "New Attorney General Quiet Guardian of Law: Simple in Word and Deed, Mr. Stone Is Described as Man People Can Put Full Trust In," the *Times* went to almost comical lengths in its effusive praise of

The *Los Angeles Times* was not alone in its continuing partisanship, at least at first. Table C.1 illustrates the gradual decline of partisan newspapers in the latter half of the 20th century.[7] The table illustrates that following an increase from 1940 to 1950, partisan newspapers were on the decline throughout the United States for the remainder of the 20th century.

The decline of partisan newspaper outlets coincided with the rise of a new and powerful news and entertainment medium: television. Like radio before it, television relied on the public airwaves for transmission and, as such, was regulated by the FCC to ensure service of "the public interest, convenience, or necessity." Since their beginning, television and radio were more regulated and less partisan than their rough-and-tumble peers in the press. In fact, for part of the 20th century, the FCC explicitly banned editorializing over broadcast outlets, although that decision was later reversed to allow editorializing if broadcasters provided "a reasonable opportunity for the presentation of contrasting viewpoints on such issues" (FCC 1985).[8]

what appears, in retrospect, to have been a fairly nondescript government figure (Bennett 1924). Stone, who described himself in the story as "not much of a phrase-maker," confessed to "sawing wood" rather than attending to the reporter's first question. The intrepid reporter favorably interpreted this as indicating "a massive sort of repose [that] held him laconic through the visit." The headlines on the continuation of the article trumpeted Stone as "quiet but forceful in all his utterances" and noted that he "comes of [the] same sturdy race as [the] president" (Bennett 1924, 3).

[7] These numbers present party self-identification by newspapers in the *Editor and Publisher Annual Yearbook* surveys. I combined the "Independent-Republican" and "Independent-Democrat" categories into the Republican and Democratic categories, respectively. Lawrence (1928, 894) argued that such self-identifications undercount partisanship:

Every time you send a questionnaire to newspapers listed in the newspaper directory, and ask them for their political affiliations, they invariably reply 'independent'; and there is no way to get away from that classification.... I mention this because, much as we might not like to admit it, the news content of the newspapers of today depends to no small extent on the editorial policies of those papers ... and hence a very good thing is frequently relegated to some inside page or the waste-basket if it is favorable to the cause they are opposing, while the meritorious thing about the candidate they are supporting is usually put on the first page and given all the prominence necessary. That is a very important factor in political campaigns.

[8] The FCC's "Fairness Doctrine" (Section 315 of the Communication Act) evolved significantly in its content and interpretation over time. For example, in the famous Mayflower decision (1941), the FCC ruled that "A broadcaster cannot be an advocate," effectively ruling out any expression of editorial opinion by stations. The FCC argued in its decision that "as one licensed to operate in the public domain, the licensee has assumed the obligation of presenting all sides of important public questions, fairly, objectively and without bias" (Friendly 1976, 42). The decision was reversed seven years later, allowing

TABLE C.1. *Proportion of Counties That Had Partisan (Republican or Democratic) Newspapers, by Region, 1940–2000*

1940	Democratic	Republican	N
Midwest	12.4%	33.5%	629
Northeast	9.3%	40.8%	397
South	62.6%	5.0%	521
West	12.3%	27.3%	300
1950	Democratic	Republican	N
Midwest	13.2%	37.9%	659
Northeast	7.8%	38.2%	411
South	59.3%	5.5%	587
West	12.2%	29.2%	336
1960	Democratic	Republican	N
Midwest	11.4%	35.0%	571
Northeast	3.3%	38.0%	332
South	51.5%	5.5%	511
West	8.2%	29.5%	292
1970	Democratic	Republican	N
Midwest	8.6%	28.7%	593
Northeast	2.8%	30.4%	319
South	39.9%	5.4%	539
West	5.5%	20.4%	289
1980	Democratic	Republican	N
Midwest	6.6%	17.6%	561
Northeast	1.9%	14.3%	314
South	18.7%	3.2%	566
West	3.0%	10.1%	296
1990	Democratic	Republican	N
Midwest	3.1%	14.1%	511
Northeast	1.1%	8.5%	283
South	10.3%	2.4%	535
West	1.7%	5.6%	288
2000	Democratic	Republican	N
Midwest	2.2%	9.1%	494
Northeast	0.8%	5.8%	243
South	6.2%	1.2%	484
West	1.2%	2.3%	256

Note: Sample excludes counties that were not home to a least one daily newspaper.
Source: Editor & Publisher annual yearbooks, compiled by the author.

By 1963, television news already had surpassed newspapers as Americans' primary source of news (Stanley and Niemi 1998, Table 4.5). Nonpartisan news outlets continued to expand their scope and influence throughout most of the 1970s and 1980s.[9] As discussed in Chapter 2, the implication of such dominant nonpartisan coverage of politics was to severely curtail the opportunities for parties to promote themselves in the news, increasingly forcing them to rely instead on a consistent strategy of cross-party attacks. However, beginning in the late 1980s, the market for political news began to shift again. Fineman (2005) described the shift as follows: "The notion of a neutral 'mainstream' national media gained a dominant following only in World War II and in its aftermath, when what turned out to be a temporary moderate consensus came to govern the country.... Still, the notion of a neutral, nonpartisan mainstream press was, to me at least, worth holding onto. Now it's pretty much dead, at least as the public sees things." Fineman's eulogy for his so-called media party may be premature, but there is no question that recent years have seen a striking resurgence of news sources aligned with the parties. While it is by no means clear that the increasing partisan activism across media in recent years will grow to resemble anything like the pervasively partisan press of the past, it seems that the mainstream media's hegemonic dominance of both the rules and content of American news has been undermined. If a party can succeed in its struggle to manage its internal disputes and generate a consistent brand name, it should now have a far easier time communicating that brand, particularly to committed supporters.

Back to the Future

The vanguard of the increasingly partisan American mass media was undoubtedly "talk radio." Influential conservative talk-show hosts including Rush Limbaugh, Sean Hannity, and Bill O'Reilly draw audiences by the millions. Since he was first nationally syndicated in 1988,

---

editorial positions, provided that the broadcaster followed "the principles of balance and fairness in providing time for discussions of controversial issues." Two years later, the FCC issued the Seek Out Opposition Rule, in which stations were viewed as having a "duty to seek out opposing points of views and encourage opposing views" if a station editorialized on controversial issues. This rule was rescinded in 1959, instead requiring that the station make an effort to provide a "reasonable" opportunity for the expression of opposing views whenever a station expressed its opinion. Finally, in 1987, the FCC repealed the Fairness Doctrine entirely.

[9] See Groeling and Engstrom (2009) for a discussion of the causes of this shift toward nonpartisan news, as well as an analysis of its impact on voting behavior.

Limbaugh alone has amassed a cumulative weekly audience that surpasses that of most newscasts (Talkers 2003).[10] It is not surprising that scholarly evidence already shows that listening to conservative talk radio substantially increases vote preference for Republican candidates (Barker 1999; but see also Jones 1998). This concern led liberals to push forward their own competing radio network in 2004, Air America, which recently collapsed as a result of weak ratings, ownership changes, bankruptcy, and a series of financial scandals (Mainelli 2005; Stein 2008).

In television news, the hegemony of the three major network evening newscasts also has been challenged by news with a partisan point of view. In fact, the 2004 election marked a watershed of sorts for network news programs: After serving as the country's single most dominant and trusted news sources for more than 30 years (Stanley and Niemi 1998), network newscasts have lost much of their influence. In fact, the recent trend is so dramatic that Thomas Rosenstiel (2004, B07) of PEJ declared that 2004 marked "The end of 'network news.'"

Rosenstiel's immediate judgment was prompted by the stunning revelation that ratings for the Republican National Convention on the upstart Fox News cable channel had surpassed those of each of the three major networks covering the same convention. An earlier Pew Research Center survey, however, had already indicated that the newscasts were losing their hold over partisan communication. In that survey, fewer than one in five Republican respondents reported believing "all or most" of what they saw on each of the broadcast networks. In contrast, about twice as many Republican respondents reported believing all or most of what they saw on Fox. Democrats viewed CNN as the most believable network (i.e., 45% indicated belief in "all or most" of the channel's news), whereas only 26% of Republicans agreed (Pew Research Center 2004). More interesting, perhaps, is the rapid change in partisan opinion about the channels: Only four years before, nearly twice as many Republicans viewed the three major networks as believable, while that same year, more Democrats than Republicans viewed Fox as believable (i.e., 27% versus 26%) (Pew Research Center 2004). The trend toward partisanship continued in the 2008 election cycle, with a 15-point partisan gap in the perceived believability of Fox (i.e., 34% of Republicans believed all or most of Fox's

---

[10] See Farhi (2009) for an attempt to quantify Limbaugh's audience size. Limbaugh claims to reach 20 million people per week, although other estimates cited in the story range from 14 million to 25 million. In contrast, the network evening newscasts were each watched by a nightly average of 6 million to 8 million people (Gorman 2009).

news versus only 19% of Democrats); a 13-point gap for CNN (i.e., 22% of Republicans versus 35% of Democrats); and a 15-point gap for traditional network NBC (i.e., only 16% of Republicans versus 31% of Democrats).

The changes led some to suggest in 2004 that at least one other cable news channel might "break off from the pack and decide to become the liberal alternative to Fox" (Rosen 2004; Zurawik 2004). That change arguably has come to pass in recent years with MSNBC's very public shift to the left – most notably through the efforts of Keith Olbermann and his protégé Rachel Maddow, as well as *Hardball* host Chris Matthews, who famously confessed to getting a "thrill up his leg" after seeing Barack Obama speak. Unlike the financially untenable Air America effort, however, MSNBC's leftward tilt proved financially lucrative. As one media commentator noted, "Without a doubt, Olbermann and his spirited Bush-bashing have been the primary engine of the network's ratings growth (including a primetime audience increase of more than 50 percent in the year's first half) . . . " (Bercovici 2008).[11]

An interesting implication of this revival of overtly partisan news sources is that some of their broadcasters increasingly have served as de facto party representatives. However, in summer 2009, it became clear that some of these partisan media figures were actually beginning to help steer the course of their respective parties, especially among Republicans. Although Democrats appeared to welcome the opportunity to pair Republicans with the image of Rush Limbaugh in the first days of the Obama Administration (see Chapter 6), by summer 2009, some observers concluded that "the real opposition party to Obama right now is the conservative grassroots that draws its energy from Fox News, talk radio, and the Drudge Report, and often leaves Republican elected officials scrambling to catch up" (Smith and Henderson 2009). That summer, such media figures had helped launch the so-called Tea Party protest movement (i.e., CNBC's Rick Santelli); force the resignation of a close Obama advisor, Van Jones (i.e., Fox's Glenn Beck); organize a mass protest in Washington, DC (i.e., mostly Beck again); and force Democrats to

---

[11] As this book goes to press, some observers have begun to note softening in Olbermann's ratings in the Obama era. Bercovici (2010) reports that by the end of Obama's first year in office, Olbermann had lost 44% of his viewers among the key demographic of adults 25 to 54 years old. Some of this decline can probably be explained by the Democrats' unified control of government, which made out-of-power Republicans less credible, important, and interesting targets of attack than was the case when George W. Bush was president.

dissociate from and vote down funding for ACORN, one of their most prolific grassroots organizations (i.e., Andrew Breitbart's BigGovernment.com blog) (Smith and Henderson 2009).

The latter case is especially interesting because it appears to be an example of what I call an "organizational counterforce" strategy, in which rival political organizations mobilize to target the infrastructure of a competing grassroots organizer. Because political officeholders often cannot strike back directly at these organizations without appearing to be stifling free speech or suppressing turnout or free association, attacking them now seems to be the province of their own grassroots organizations in an interesting form of proxy warfare. Further examples of such attacks include the liberal boycott of Glenn Beck advertisers (Siemaszko 2009); Republican exposés on apparent Obama Administration attempts to use National Endowment for the Arts funding to support pro-administration artwork (Courrielche 2009); and liberal calls for greater "balance," "accountability," and "localism" in radio broadcasting (i.e., targeted at conservative talk radio), (Calderone 2009a and b; Uliano 2009).

Option 3: Self-Selected Sources and Seeing No Evil

Of course, one of the most interesting shifts in partisan communication in the 21st century has been the ability of partisans to circumvent journalists, particularly online. Although parties always had this ability through the use of paid advertising or expensive face-to-face outreach, digital technology increasingly allows partisans to use "cheap speech" to distribute their views, from the parties to the public as well as peer to peer (Volokh 1995). Due to tremendously inexpensive transmission costs and exceptionally low unit costs, parties can communicate with their partisans more directly and cheaply than ever before, facilitating activities such as recruitment, fundraising, and grassroots mobilization.

Presidential campaigns already have been early adopters of technological innovations such as e-mail, candidate websites, online fundraising, computerized turnout modeling, and digital video. In many cases, this communication takes forms that are indistinguishable from expensive television ads. In 2004, for example, both major parties edited highly polished commercials that could be accessed directly by visitors to their respective sites. The Democratic National Committee's "Dem TV" site featured videos with titles including "Fortunate Son," "Halliburton," and "Mission Not Accomplished"; Republicans countered with a video called "Kerry on Iraq," which they claimed was viewed by more than seven million people.[12] However, the 2008 election set a new standard in such digital outreach by partisans, combining prior tools and new ones (e.g., YouTube, social networking, and text messaging) into a cohesive communication and targeted mobilization effort. Andrew Rasiej, a commentator on Internet and political issues, concluded that "Obama's success online is as much about how our society has changed, how our media ecology has changed, just in the past four years. . . . Obama's Internet team is doing a hell of a job taking advantage of all these changes. They've basically leapfrogged not just the Clinton and McCain campaigns but also the mainstream media when it comes to reaching their supporters" (quoted in Vargas 2008).

Midway through the campaign, the videos on McCain's custom YouTube channel had been viewed 9.5 million times – an impressive tally in any prior election. However, Obama's channel dwarfed McCain's over the same period, attracting more than five times as many views (Vargas 2008). These videos allowed both candidates an escape from the filtering and time constraints of traditional media as well as increased participation from their supporters. Kate Albright-Hanna, who ran Obama's video team, was a former Emmy-winning member of CNN's political unit and confessed to reveling in the new format's comparative freedom:

I guess I've kind of been rebelling from my CNN days, where video had to be a certain length, a certain format with a certain sensibility. Where I came from, there's a lot of concern about ratings and about what they think people, everyday people, are interested in watching. . . . One of our goals is to get people talking about what's going on in their lives and why they're supporting Barack – and hopefully not only will they watch the videos but also comment on them and forward them to relatives and friends and co-workers. (Quoted in Vargas 2008)

That reliance on the peer-to-peer redistribution of the candidate's message is one of the most crucial innovations of the Obama campaign. Candidate supporters previously had been able to influence others through forwarding e-mails, conducting "meet-ups," and blogging about candidates; however, the Obama campaign took these efforts to another level of integration. As one journalist observed shortly before Election Day, "Obama is the first to successfully integrate technology with a revamped model of political organization that stresses volunteer participation and feedback on a massive scale, erecting a vast, intricate machine set to fuel

---

[12] This claim appeared on the main gop.com homepage on September 14, 2004. The page further claimed that this tally surpassed the "Viewership of [Michael Moore's anti-Bush documentary] Fahrenheit 911 Opening Weekend."

an unprecedented get-out-the-vote drive ... " (Stirland 2008). The experience of Jeanette Scanlon, an Obama supporter, shows how deeply the campaign integrated technology into traditional get-out-the-vote efforts:

Scanlon organized [a streetcorner rally for Obama in Florida] – and 24 others since September – through Obama's social networking site, my.BarackObama.com. Similarly, she used the site's Neighbor-to-Neighbor tool in September to find registered voters in her own neighborhood, so she could canvass them for Obama. And this weekend, Scanlon and another 75 or so Plant City volunteers will be phoning thousands of Floridians to urge them to vote, using a sophisticated database provided by the Obama campaign to ensure they don't call McCain supporters by mistake. (Stirland 2008)

The Obama campaign's strategy also can be seen in its famous iPhone application, which was one of the most popular downloads at the iTunes Application Store during the campaign.

The application, parts of which are shown in Figure C.1, beautifully illustrates the integrated potential of modern technology for parties seeking to effectively reach their followers (and potential followers). As shown on the "home" screen of the application (i.e., top left in Figure C.1), Obama supporters who downloaded the application immediately had several ways to increase their engagement with the campaign. The "Media" option (i.e., bottom left) allowed supporters to quickly access the types of multimedia discussed previously in this chapter. Similarly, the News tab (i.e., upper left) allowed supporters to peruse various (presumably pro-Obama) developments on an ongoing basis or to request those and similar updates from the campaign via e-mail or text messages. Because the iPhone is location-aware, users also could track Local Events (i.e., upper left) and learn of local ways to "get involved" without contacting the campaign or navigating through irrelevant options that applied to other geographic areas.

Perhaps the most interesting development of the application, however, is the Call Friends option, prominently displayed at the top of the list. As the screen shown in the upper right of Figure C.1 illustrates, the option encouraged supporters to "help Barack Obama get elected by calling people you already know." By doing so, the application actually accessed the contents of the supporter's existing iPhone phonebook of personal contacts and phone numbers, sorting and prioritizing them by how competitive Obama was in the state in which the contact resided. It then tracked whether each contact had been called, and reported to the Obama campaign the total number of calls made by that supporter.

FIGURE C.1. The 2008 Obama campaign's iPhone social-networking program.

In the context of this book, it seems obvious that having an army of diverse supporters representing the candidate and his positions to their peers has the potential to harm the consistency of the party brand name. However, the Obama campaign apparently anticipated this possibility and therefore included key "talking points" for callers on a variety of issues that could be accessed on the iPhone during a phone call.

As a result of this tightly integrated mobilization effort, the Obama campaign reaped tremendous benefits. Such efforts allowed the campaign to take advantage of specific knowledge and expertise undoubtedly lacking in its existing databases – extensive as they may have been. Friends and colleagues likely had a more personal and deeper understanding of the drives and concerns of their peers than a stranger working at an impersonal phone bank. Even more important, relying on supporters to distribute partisan messages had an important implication for the credibility of those messages: Such messages should be inherently more credible to the recipient, as they could rely on the credibility of the person who was choosing to redistribute it rather than just the partisan candidate. By building on these peer-based redistribution channels, the Obama campaign simultaneously widened the distribution of its messages and targeted them to people selected by local experts (i.e., their friends and colleagues), who in turn used their personal credibility to boost the likelihood that the message would be believed.

Of course, it is uncertain whether these powerful campaign tools will be similarly effective as tools of governing. Because such efforts rely heavily on activists, they will likely wax and wane in their impact depending on the enthusiasm of those supporters. As an insurgent candidate, Obama likely benefited from the factors discussed in Chapter 6 that allow the opposition party in government to increase its cohesion when out of power. However, those same benefits might not accrue to the efforts of President Obama (particularly when his party also controls Congress). Indeed, although many of the groups that supported Obama during the campaign continued supporting his efforts once he was in office, they were outclassed and "caught flat-footed" by opposition activists, who seized the initiative with their grassroots rallies against Obama's policies. Judith Le Blanc, coordinator of the activist group United for Peace and Justice, explains: "We were in opposition mode for so many years that it became a struggle to get reoriented to the historic break in right-wing rule" (Potter 2009). Even Obama's 13-million–member grassroots campaign organization – now called Organizing for America and operating independently of the White House – currently appears to be far less effective at mobilizing supporters than during the campaign (Przybyla 2009; Zeleny 2009).

The decrease in engagement also seemed to affect Obama supporters in the general public, who appeared far less interested in monitoring his new media communication after the election. For example, one study of traffic statistics on political websites indicated that in the sampled left-of-center sites, page views decreased 64% between October 2008 and

May 2009 (Owens 2009).[13] Similarly, post-inauguration traffic to the official Obama YouTube channel also plummeted, dropping from almost a million daily viewers after his inauguration to only about 42,000 eight months later (Sifry 2009). Moreover, about half of the viewed videos were "oldies" from the campaign rather than newer videos. Even more worrisome for prospective mobilization: The most popular post-2008 video showed Obama killing a fly during an interview, with more than four million views across different versions of the video. In contrast, his September 10, 2009, speech before a joint session of Congress on health reform logged only 4,123 weekly views (Sifry 2009).

In contrast to his surprisingly limited success in attracting potential supporters through new media once in office, Obama has done shockingly well at commandeering the attention of traditional media. According to data from Martha Joynt Kumar, Obama took part in three times as many sit-down television interviews in his first eight months in office than his two predecessors *combined* (Hurt 2009). Similarly, Obama gave 36 interviews with print outlets – almost double the combined Bush and Clinton tallies (Hurt 2009). This suggests that although parties have made tremendous strides in attempts to make information that is favorable to their party available to viewers through new media, it is still difficult to get all but the truest believers to reliably consume that information outside the hubbub of campaigns. Moreover, any media outlet that becomes too closely identified with a particular party will begin to lose credibility with independent viewers or those from the other party, equivalent to the partisan credibility persuasion effects discussed in Chapter 5.[14]

CLOSING THOUGHTS

I selected the title of this book (*When Politicians Attack*) because I thought it neatly referenced two different but complementary questions that I hoped to answer through my research. The first reference is to the implied question, "*When* do *politicians attack?*" while the second invokes the consequences of such attacks ("What happens *when politicians attack?*").[15] Although this chapter has provided some "green

---

[13] In contrast, page views among the sampled right-of-center sites decreased only 37% during that same period (Owens 2009).

[14] For more discussion of the implication of partisan credibility as applied to specific news outlets, see Baum and Groeling (2008).

[15] The title also alludes to *When Animals Attack*, a famous 1990s-era "shockumentary" reality series on Fox that featured graphic animal attacks caught on video.

shoots" of optimism for the current Democratic unified government, the continuing inability of governing parties to "paper over" internal disputes or shield them from public view provides answers to these questions that make any party's prospects of maintaining control of government appear dim – at least in the near future.

References

ABC. 1994. *World News Tonight with Peter Jennings*. 2 December.

Abramson, Phyllis. 1990. *Sob Sister Journalism*. Westport, CT: Greenwood Press.

Abramson, Paul, John Aldrich, and David Rohde. 1996. *Change and Continuity in the 1994 Elections*. Washington, DC: Congressional Quarterly Press.

Abramson, Paul, John Aldrich, and David Rohde. 2002. *Change and Continuity in the 2000 Elections*. Washington, DC: Congressional Quarterly Press.

Adamy, Janet, and Jonathan Weisman. 2009. "Health-Care Anger Has Deeper Roots." *The Wall Street Journal*, 1 September. www.online.wsj.com/article/SB125176363081674373.html.

Advertising Age. 2008. "Power Players 2008." 13 October. www.adage.com/article?article_id=131580.

Agranoff, Robert. 1976. *The New Style in Election Campaigns*. Boston: Holbrook Press.

Alchian, Armen A., and Harold Demsetz. 1972. "Production, Information Costs, and Economic Organization." *The American Economic Review* 62: 777–95.

Aldrich, John H. 1995. *Why Parties?: The Origin and Transformation of Political Parties in America*. Chicago: University of Chicago Press.

Aldrich, John, and David W. Rohde. 1996. "A Tale of Two Speakers: A Comparison of Policy Making in the 100th and 104th Congresses." Paper presented to the 1996 annual meeting of the American Political Science Association.

Alexander, Delroy. 2003. "Upgrade Edict by McDonald's Faces Challenge: Owner-Operators to Hire Law Firm." *Chicago Tribune*, 3 September.

Allen, Jared, Mike Soraghan, and Lauren Burke. 2009. "House Healthcare Talks Break Down in Anger." *The Hill*, 24 July. www.thehill.com/leading-the-news/house-healthcare-talks-break-down-in-anger-2009-07-24.html.

Allen, Mike. 2001. "Bush Brain Trust Hears Criticism: Cadre of Aides Blasted by Both Parties as Out of Touch in Wake of Jeffords Switch." *The Washington Post*, 27 May: A14. www.washingtonpost.com/wp-dyn/articles/A82298-2001May26.html. Accessed: May 27, 2001.

Allen, Mike. 2004. "Next Question: Reporters Walk Line Between Deference and Diligence in Quizzing Bush." *The Washington Post*, 1 December.

Allen, Mike. 2005. "DeLay Ethics Allegations Now Cause of GOP Concern." *The Washington Post*, 14 March.

Allen, Mike. 2009. "Obama Launches Message War." *Yahoo! News*, 14 March. www.news.yahoo.com/s/politico/20090314/pl_politico/20007/p...= X30DMTB1MjgxN2UzBHBvcwMxNARzZWMDdG9vbHMtdG9wBHNsaw NwcmludA-.

Allpolitics, Jonathan Karl, and the Associated Press. 1998. "Livingston Bows out of the Speakership: He Makes a Stunning Announcement on House Floor; Clinton Urges Him to Reconsider." *CNN/Allpolitics.Com*. www.cnn.com/ALLPOLITICS/stories/1998/12/19/livingston.quits.

Althaus, Scott L. 2003. "When News Norms Collide, Follow the Lead: New Evidence for Press Independence." *Political Communication* 20: 381–414.

Altman, Douglas G. 1991. *Practical Statistics for Medical Research*. Boca Raton, FL: Chapman & Hall/CRC.

Ambinder, Marc. 2009. "Are Democrats in for an August Slaughter?" *The Atlantic*, 3 August. www.politics.theatlantic.com/2009/08/are_democrats_in_for_an_august_slaughter.php.

American Political Science Review (APSA). 1950. "News and Notes." 44: 154–76.

Aristotle. n.d. *On Rhetoric*. Translation by W. Rhys Roberts. www.ac-nice.fr/philo/textes/Aristotle-Works/22-Rhetoric.pdf.

Arterton, Christopher. 1984. *Media Politics: The News Strategies of Presidential Campaigns*. Lexington, MA: D.C. Heath.

Asch, Soloman. 1952. *Social Psychology*. New York: Prentice-Hall.

Associated Press. 2001. "Jeffords Calls Bush 'One-Term'." www.dailynews.netscape.com/mynsnews/story.tmpl?table=n&cat=50700&2.00105251232e+20. Accessed: May 25, 2001.

Associated Press. 2005. "Clinton Adviser: Kerry Ran Inconsistent Campaign." *Boston Herald*, 17 March.

Atkinson, Claire. 2008. "2008 Political Ads Worth $2.5 Billion to $2.7 Billion." *Broadcasting & Cable*, 12 December.

Babington, Charles. 2004. "Hastert Launches a Partisan Policy." *The Washington Post*, 27 November.

Bacon, Perry, Jr. 2006. "Don't Mess with Nancy Pelosi." *Time*, 27 August. www.time.com/time/printout/0,8816,1376213,00.html.

Baker, Peter. 2009. "Blaming the Guy Who Came Before Doesn't Work Long." *The New York Times*, 11 June. www.nytimes.com/2009/06/12/us/politics/12memo.html?_r=1&src=sch.

Baker, Peter, and Jeff Zeleny. 2009. "Emanuel Wields Power Freely, and Faces the Risks." *The New York Times*, 16 August. www.nytimes.com/2009/08/16/us/politics/16emanuel.html.

Balutis, Alan P. 1977. "Congress, the President, and the Press," *Journalism Quarterly* 53: 509–15.

Balz, Dan. 2009. "After a Bruising August, Time for Obama Team to Regroup." *The Washington Post*, 2 September. www.washingtonpost.com/wp-dyn/content/article/2009/09/01/AR2009090103741_pf.html.

Barker, D. C. 1999. "Rushed Decisions: Political Talk Radio and Vote Choice, 1994–1996." *Journal of Politics* 61: 27–540.

Barnes, James A., Richard E. Cohen, and Peter Bell. 2009. "Insider Poll." *National Journal*, 19 September. www.nationaljournal.com/njmagazine/print_friendly.php?ID=ip_20090919_1849.

Bartels, Larry. 1996. "Politicians and the Press: Who Leads and Who Follows?" Paper presented to the 1996 annual convention of the American Political Science Association.

Bartlett, John, comp. 1919. *Familiar Quotations*, 10th ed., rev. and enl. by Nathan Haskell Dole. Boston: Little, Brown and Company. *Bartleby.com*, 2000. www.bartleby.com/100.

Barwise, P., A. Dunham, and M. Ritson. 2000. "Ties That Bind." In *Brand New*, ed. Jane Pavitt. London: V&A Publications.

Bauder, David. 2009. "Rush Limbaugh Challenging Notion of New Politics." *Breitbart.com*. 30 January. www.breitbart.com/article.php?id=D961JE5G0&show_article=1.

Baum, Matthew. 2002. "The Constituent Foundations of the Rally-Round-the-Flag Phenomenon." *International Studies Quarterly* 46 (June): 263–98.

Baum, Matthew, and Tim Groeling. 2004. "Crossing the Water's Edge: Elite Rhetoric, Media Coverage, and the Rally-Round-the-Flag Phenomenon, 1979–2003." Paper presented at the 2004 annual meeting of the American Political Science Association, Chicago, IL: 2–5 September.

Baum, Matthew A., and Tim Groeling. 2008. "Shot by the Messenger: Partisan Cues and Public Opinion Regarding National Security and War." *Political Behavior* 31: 157–86.

Baumann, Gregory C. 1997. "Baltimore McDonald's Franchisee Loses 'Oversaturation' Lawsuit." *The Daily Record*, 14 February: 3A.

BBC. 2003. /3205889.stm. "Galloway Expelled by Labour." *BBC News*, 24 October. www.news.bbc.co.uk/2/hi/uk_news/politics.

BBC. 2005. "Paxman v Galloway." *BBC News*, 6 May. www.news.bbc.co.uk/2/hi/uk_news/politics/vote_2005/blog/4519553.stm.

Beaumont, Thomas. 2005. "Iowa's Top Statesmen Have Low U.S. Profile." *The Des Moines Register* (online edition), 10 October.

Bennett, James O'Donnell. 1924. "New Attorney General Quiet Guardian of Law: Simple in Word and Deed, Mr. Stone Is Described as Man People Can Put Full Trust In." *Los Angeles Times*, 27 April: 1.

Bennett, W. Lance. 1990. "Toward a Theory of Press-State Relations in the United States." *Journal of Communication* 40: 103–25.

Bennett, W. Lance. 1997. *News: The Politics of Illusion*, 3rd ed. New York: Longman.

Bennett, W. Lance. 2003. "The Burglar Alarm That Just Keeps Ringing: A Response to Zaller." *Political Communication* 20 (April/June): 131–8.

Bennett, W. Lance, Regina Lawrence, and Steven Livingston. 2006. "None Dare Call It Torture: Indexing and the Limits of Press Independence in the Abu Ghraib Scandal." *Journal of Communication* 56: 467–85.

Bercovici, Jeff. 2008. "Mixed Media: Maddow Hire Speeds MSNBC's Leftward Drift." *Conde Nast Portfolio.com*. 20 August. www.portfolio.com/views/blogs/mixed-media/2008/08/20/maddow-hire-speeds-msnbcs-leftward-drift.

Bercovici, Jeff. 2010. "Is America Getting Over Keith Olbermann?" *AOL Daily Finance*. 29 January. www.dailyfinance.com/story/media/is-america-getting-over-keith-olbermann/19337944.

Berke, Richard L. 2001. "Democrats See a Party Adrift as Presidential Loss Sinks In." *The New York Times*, 16 February: A18.

Berman, Ari. 2005. "Going Nowhere: The DLC Sputters to a Halt." *The Nation*, 4 March.

Best, Kathleen. 1994. "350 GOP Candidates Make Vow." *St. Louis Post-Dispatch*, 28 September.

Billings, Erin. 2003. "Democrats Clash on Communications." *Roll Call*, 5 November.

Blechman, Barry M., and Stephen S. Kaplan. 1978. *Force without War: U.S. Armed Forces as a Political Instrument*. Washington, DC: The Brookings Institution.

Bond, Jon R., and Richard Fleisher. 2000. *Polarized Politics: Congress and the President in a Partisan Era*. Washington, DC: Congressional Quarterly Press.

Bovitz, Gregory, James Druckman, and Arthur Lupia. 2002. "When Can a News Organization Lead Public Opinion? Ideology versus Market Forces in Decisions to Make News." *Public Choice* 113: 127–55.

Bradley, Bill. 2005. "A Party Inverted." *The New York Times*, 30 March.

Bradley, Lian, and John Oneal. 1993. "Presidents, the Use of Military Force, and Public Opinion." *Journal of Conflict Resolution* 37 (2): 277–300.

Brady, David, John Cogan, Brian Gaines, and Douglas Rivers. 1996. "The Perils of Presidential Support: How the Republicans Took the House in the 1994 Midterm Elections." *Political Behavior* 18: 345–67.

Broder, David. 2001a. "Bush's Tougher Leadership Challenge." *The Washington Post*, 25 May: A01. www.washingtonpost.com/wp-dyn/articles/A74601-2001May24.html. Accessed: May 27, 2001.

Broder, David. 2001b. "A Crack in Bush's Governance." *The Washington Post*, 27 May. www.washingtonpost.com/wp-dyn/opinion/columns/broderdavid/A80283-2001May26.html. Accessed: May 27, 2001.

Broder, David. 2010. "The Fable of Emanuel the Great." *The Washington Post*. 4 March. www.washingtonpost.com/wp-dyn/content/article/2010/03/03/AR2010030301776.html. Accessed: March 8, 2010.

Brody, Richard A. 1989. *Assessing the President: The Media, Elite Opinion, and Public Support*. Stanford, CA: Stanford University Press.

Brooks, David. 2004. "Strength in Disunity." *The New York Times*, 23 November.

Brownstein, Ronald. 1992. "Some GOP Hopefuls Hedge Bets with Clinton Tie-Ins." *Los Angeles Times*, 26 October.

Brownstein, Ronald. 2009. "The Parliamentary Challenge." *National Journal Magazine*, 12 September. www.nationaljournal.com/njmagazine/print_friendly .php?ID=nj_20090912_2821.

Buckley, Christopher. 2008. "Sorry, Dad, I'm Voting for Obama." *The Daily Beast*, 10 October. www.thedailybeast.com/blogs-and-stories/2008-10-10/ the-conservative-case-for-obama.

Bunting, Madeline. 2001. "The New Gods." *The Guardian (UK)*. 9 July. www. guardian.co.uk/media/2001/jul/09/marketingandpr.g22.

Burns, James MacGregor. 1963. *The Deadlock of Democracy: Four-Party Politics in America*. Englewood Cliffs, NJ: Prentice-Hall.

C-SPAN. 1999. *American Profiles*. Interview with Newt Gingrich. www.cspan .org/guide/americanprofiles/newt_transcript1.asp. Accessed May 11, 2000.

Calderone, Michael. 2009a. "Sen. Stabenow Wants Hearings on Radio 'Account-ability'; Talks Fairness Doctrine." *Politico.com*. 5 February. www.politico.com/ blogs/michaelcalderone/0209/Sen_Stabenow_wants...hearings_on_radio_ accountability_talks_fairness_doctrine.html?showall.

Calderone, Michael. 2009b. "Clinton Wants 'More Balance' on Airwaves." *Politico.com*. 12 February. www.politico.com/blogs/michaelcalderone/02/09/ Clinton_wants_more_balance_on_the_airwaves.html).

Cameron, Charles, William Howell, and E. Scott Adler. 1997. "Toward an Under-standing of the Institutional Performance of Congress in the Postwar Era: Structural Explanations for Surges and Slumps in the Production of Significant Legislation, 1945–1994." Presented at the Midwest Political Science Associa-tion annual meeting, Chicago, IL: 10–13 April.

Campbell, Angus, Philip E. Converse, Warren E. Miller, and Donald E. Stokes. 1960. *The American Voter*. New York: John Wiley & Sons, Inc.

Campbell, James E. 1993. *The Presidential Approach to Congressional Elections*. Lexington: University Press of Kentucky.

Campbell, James. 1996. As quoted on NPR's "All Things Considered." 17 Octo-ber.

Canellos, Peter S. 1996. "New TV Ad Mentions a GOP Unmentionable." *The Boston Globe*, 29 October.

Cappella, Joseph N., and Kathleen Hall Jamieson. 1997. *Spiral of Cynicism: The Press and the Public Good*. New York: Oxford University Press.

Carney, Timothy. 2004. "Thank You, Arlen: We Reelected the Worst Republican Senator, and Still Lost Pennsylvania." *National Review Online*, 3 November.

Carty, R. Kenneth. 2004. "Parties as Franchise Systems: The Stratarchical Orga-nizational Imperative." *Party Politics* 10: 5–24.

Cater, Douglas. 1959. *The Fourth Branch of Government*. Boston: Houghton Mifflin.

Cattani, Richard J. 1980. "Reagan, Congressional Republicans Display Unified Front; President Fights Political Brush Fires at the White House; GOP's 'Gov-erning Team Day' Shows New Togetherness in Minority Party." *The Christian Science Monitor*, 16 September.

Chiou, Fang-Yi, and Lawrence Rothenberg. 2003. "When Pivotal Politics Meets Partisan Politics." *American Journal of Political Science* 47: 503–22.

Clinton, William Jefferson. 1995. "Battle over the Budget; Clinton's Statement on Plan to Balance Federal Budget by 2005." *The New York Times*, 14 June. query.nytimes.com/gst/fullpage.html?res=990CE3DE133FF937A25755Co A963958260&sec=&spon=&pagewanted=2.

"CMPA Coding Guidebook." 1997. File "TRACK1.BOK," August: 120.

CNN. 1994. *Inside Politics*. 8 December.

CNN. 1994. *Newsmaker Saturday*. 26 November.

CNN. 2000. Transcript #00112702V54, CNN Live Event/Special, 27 November. LexisNexis: 4 December.

CNN. 2006. "Elections 2006, Rhode Island Senate Exit Poll." www.cnn.com/ ELECTION/2006/pages/results/states/RI/S/01/epolls.0.html.

CNN. 2010. "CNN Poll: Most Americans Applaud Democrats' Loss of Supermajority." 25 January. politicalticker.blogs.cnn.com/2010/01/25/cnn-poll-most-americans-applaud-democrats-loss-of-supermajority.

Cohen, Bernard. 1963. *The Press and Foreign Policy*. Princeton, NJ: Princeton University Press.

Coleman, John J. 1999. "Party Images and Candidate-Centered Campaigns in 1996: What's Money Got to Do with It?" In *The State of the Parties: The Changing Role of Contemporary American Parties*, 3rd ed., eds. John C. Green and Daniel M. Shea. Lanham, MD: Rowman & Littlefield Publishers, Inc.

Coleman, Kevin, Joseph Cantor, and Thomas Neale. 2000. *Presidential Elections in the United States: A Primer*. Washington, DC: Congressional Research Service.

Condon, Stephanie. 2009. "Obama's Political Group Pushes Health Reform in Ad." *CBSNews.com*, 15 July. www.cbsnews.com/blogs/2009/07/15/politics/ politicalhotsheet/entry5161695.shtml.

Congressional Quarterly Almanac. 1996. Washington, DC: Congressional Quarterly, Inc. P. C-15.

Connelly, William F., and John J. Pitney. 1994. *Congress's Permanent Minority?* Lanham, MD: Rowman & Littlefield Publishers, Inc.

Connolly, Ceci. 2009. "Obama Urges Groups to Stop Attacks." *The Washington Post*, 4 July. www.washingtonpost.com/wp-dyn/content/article/2009/07/03/ AR2009070302309_pf.html.

Cook, Thomas, and Donald Campbell. 1979. *Quasi-Experimentation*. Chicago: Rand McNally.

Cook, Timothy E. 1986. "House Members as Newsmakers: The Effects of Televising Congress." *Legislative Studies Quarterly* 11: 203–26.

Cook, Timothy E. 1989. *Making Laws and Making News: Media Strategies in the U.S. House of Representatives*. Washington, DC: The Brookings Institution.

Cook, Timothy E. 1998. *Governing with the News: The News Media as a Political Institution*. Chicago: University of Chicago Press.

Cooper, Kenneth J. 1994. "GOP Offers a 'Contract' to Revive Reagan Years." *The Washington Post*, 28 September.

Coraso, Ryan. 2008. "Biden's Traveling Press Corps Finds Little Opportunity to Ask Him Questions." CBSnews.com. 22 October. www.cbsnews.com/blogs/ 2008/10/22/politics/fromtheroad/entry4539166.shtml.

Courrielche, Patrick. 2009. "Explosive New Audio Reveals White House Using NEA to Push Partisan Agenda." *Big Hollywood*, 21 September. www.bigholly wood.breitbart.com/pcourrielche/2009/09/21/explosive-new-audio-reveals-white-house-using-nea-to-push-partisan-agenda.

Cox, Gary, and Sam Kernell. 1991. "Introduction: Governing in a Divided Era." In *The Politics of Divided Government*. Boulder, CO: Westview Press.

Cox, Gary, and Eric Magar. 1999. "How Much Is Majority Status in the U.S. Congress Worth?" *American Political Science Review* 93: 299–309.

Cox, Gary, and Mathew McCubbins. 1993. *Legislative Leviathan: Party Government in the House*. Berkeley: University of California Press.

Crawford, Vincent P., and Joel Sobel. 1982. "Strategic Information Transmission." *Econometrica* 50: 1431–51.

Cronkite, Walter. 1998. "Reporting Presidential Campaigns: A Journalist's View." In *The Politics of News: The News of Politics*, eds. D. Graber, D. McQuail, and P. Norris. Washington, DC: Congressional Quarterly Press: 57–69.

Curl, Joseph. 2009a. "Obama Still Cashing in on Bush's Failings." *The Washington Times*, 29 July. www.washingtontimes.com/news/2009/jul/29/obama-still-cashing-in-on-bushs-economic-failings/print.

Curl, Joseph. 2009b. "Dems Still Run against Bush in N.J., Va.: Voters Transition to Judge Obama on own Record." *The Washington Times*, 22 September. www.washingtontimes.com/news/2009/sep/22/bush-as-rival-risky-tactic.

Cusack, Bob, and Hans Nichols. 2003. "Pelosi's August Recess Memo Takes the Cake." *The Hill*, 6 August: 1.

Cutler, Lloyd. 1988. "Some Reflections about Divided Government." *Presidential Studies Quarterly* 18: 485–92.

Dahl, Robert A. 1961. *Who Governs? Democracy and Power in an American City*. New Haven, CT: Yale University Press.

De Chernatony, Leslie, and Malcolm McDonald. 2000. *Creating Powerful Brands in Consumer, Service, and Industrial Markets*. Oxford: Butterworth-Heinemann.

Delli Carpini, Michael X., and Scott Keeter. 1996. *What Americans Know about Politics and Why It Matters*. New Haven, CT: Yale University Press.

Dionne, E. J. Jr. 2005. "A GOP Plan to 'Fix' the Democrats." *The Washington Post*, 10 May.

Dole, Bob. 1993. Interview on *This Week with David Brinkley*. 22 August.

Donohew, Lewis. 1965. "Publishers and Their 'Influence' Groups." *Journalism Quarterly* 42: 112–14.

Downs, Anthony. 1957. *An Economic Theory of Democracy*. New York: Harper and Row.

Druckman, James. 1999. "The Limits of Political Manipulation: Psychological and Strategic Determinants of Framing." Ph.D. Dissertation, University of California, San Diego.

Druckman, James. 2001. "Framing and Deliberation: How Citizens' Conversations Limit Elite Influence." *American Journal of Political Science* 47: 729.

Druckman, James. 2004. "Political Preference Formation: Competition, Deliberation, and the (Ir)relevance of Framing Effects." *American Political Science Review* 98: 671.

Dutton, Donald. 1973. "The Maverick Effect: Increased Communicator Credibility as a Result of Abandoning a Career." *Canadian Journal of Behavioral Science* 5: 145–51.

Eagly, Alice H. 1981. "Recipient Characteristics as Determinants of Responses to Persuasion." In *Cognitive Responses and Persuasion*, eds. R. Petty, T. Ostrom, and T. Brok. Hillsdale, NJ: Erlbaum.

Eagly, Alice H., Wendy Wood, and Shelly Chaiken. 1978. "Causal Inferences about Communicators, and Their Effect on Opinion Change." *Journal of Personality and Social Psychology* 36: 424–35.

Edney, Anna, Kasie Hunt, and Peter Cohn. 2009. "Dems Start to Push Back Hard to Prevent a 'Waterloo'." *National Journal*, 22 July. www.nationaljournal.com/congressdaily/hca_20090722_6620.php.

Edsall, Thomas B., and David Broder. 2001. "A Defection Highlights GOP's Fragile Coalition." *The Washington Post*, 26 May: A1. www.washingtonpost.com/wp-dyn/articles/A79602-2001May25.html. Accessed: May 27, 2001.

Edwards, George C., and B. Dan Wood. 1999. "Who Influences Whom? The President and the Public Agenda." *American Political Science Review* 93: 327–44.

Edwards, George C., III, Andrew Barrett, and Jeffrey Peake. 1997. "The Legislative Impact of Divided Government." *American Journal of Political Science* 41 (2): 545–63.

Eilperin, Juliet. 2000. "GOP Moderates Fend off Attacks from Right." *The Washington Post*, 17 March: A04.

Entman, Robert. 1989. *Democracy without Citizens: Media and the Decay of American Politics*. New York: Oxford University Press.

Entman, Robert. 2004. *Projections of Power: Framing News, Public Opinion, and U.S. Foreign Policy*. Chicago: University of Chicago Press.

Entman, Robert M. 2005. "Media and Democracy without Party Competition." In *Mass Media and Society*, eds. James Curran and Michael Gurevitch. New York: Oxford University Press.

Entman, Robert, and Benjamin Page. 1994. "The News Before the Storm." In *Taken by Storm: The Media, Public Opinion, and U.S. Foreign Policy in the Gulf War*, eds. Lance W. Bennett and David Paletz. Chicago: University of Chicago Press.

Epstein, Edward. 1973. *News from Nowhere: Television and the News*. New York: Random House.

Erbe, Bonnie. 2008. "Parties Switch Roles." *Metrowest Daily News*, 1 August. www.metrowestdailynews.com/opinion/x280666137/Erbe-Parties-switch-roles.

Evans, C. Lawrence. 2001. "Committees, Leaders, and Message Politics." In *Congress Reconsidered*, 7th ed., eds. Lawrence C. Dodd and Bruce I. Oppenheimer. Washington, DC: Congressional Quarterly Press.

Evans, C. Lawrence, and Daniel Lipinski. 2005. "Obstruction and Leadership in the U.S. Senate." In *Congress Reconsidered*, 8th ed., eds. Lawrence Dodd and Bruce Oppenheimer. Washington, DC: Congressional Quarterly Press.

Evans, C. Lawrence, and Mark J. Oleszek. 1999. "Procedural Features of House Republican Rule." In *New Majority or Old Minority?: The Impact of Republicans on Congress*, eds. Nicole C. Rae and Colton C. Campbell. Lanham, MD: Rowman & Littlefield Publishers, Inc.

Evans, C. Lawrence, and Mark J. Oleszek. 2001. "Message Politics and Partisan Theories of Congress." Paper presented to the 2000 convention of the Midwest Political Science Association. Chicago, IL: 19–22 April.

Farhi, Paul. 2009. "Limbaugh's Audience Size? It's Largely up in the Air." *The Washington Post*, 7 March. www.washingtonpost.com/wp-dyn/content/article/2009/03/06/AR2009030603435_pf.html.

Farnsworth, Stephen, and S. Robert Lichter. 2004. "Source Material: New Presidents and Network News: Covering the First Year in Office of Ronald Reagan, Bill Clinton, and George W. Bush." *Presidential Studies Quarterly* 34: 674–90.

Federal Communications Commission (FCC). 1985. "The General Fairness Doctrine Obligations of Broadcast Licensees." 102 F.C.C. 2d 145, 146.

Fenno, Richard F. 1978. *Home Style: House Members in Their Districts*. Boston: Little, Brown and Company.

Ferraro, Thomas. 2001. "New Democratic Voice May Be Heard Tuesday." Reuters Online, 26 October. dailynews.yahoo.com/h/nm/20010226/pl/democrats/dc_5.html.

Festinger, Leon. 1957. *A Theory of Cognitive Dissonance*. Evanston, IL: Row, Peterson.

Fineman, Howard. 2005. "That Bush Political Capital Thing: When to Spend It and What's the Payback?" *MSNBC News*, 27 April.

Fiorina, Morris. 1981. *Retrospective Voting in American National Elections*. New Haven, CT: Yale University Press.

Fitzgerald, Toni. 2008. "Dollar-Wise, 2008 Elections Fall Short: Total Ad Spending is Likely to Come in at $2.5 Billion." *Media Life Magazine*, 4 November. www.medialifemagazine.com/artman2/publish/Television_44/Dollar-wise_2008_elections_fall_short.asp.

Fletcher, Martin. 1994. "Democrat Hold on House Attacked." *The Times of London*, 28 September.

Foerstel, Karen. 2000. "Choosing Chairmen: Tradition's Role Fades." *Congressional Quarterly Weekly Report*, 9 December.

Foerstel, Karen. 2001. "Democrats See Brighter Days in a Shared Spotlight." *Congressional Quarterly Weekly Report*, 14 April.

Fordham, Benjamin, and Christopher Charles Sarver. 2001. "Militarized Interstate Disputes and United States Uses of Force." *International Studies Quarterly* 45 (3): 455–66.

Fortune. 1939. "The Press and the People – A Survey." August 1939, 70: 64–78.

Franklin, Charles H. 1991. "Eschewing Obfuscation? Campaigns and the Perception of U.S. Senate Incumbents." *The American Political Science Review* 85(4): 1193–214.

Franz, Michael, and Kenneth Goldstein. 2002. "Following the (Soft) Money: Party Advertisements in American Elections." In *The Parties Respond*, 4th ed., ed. Sandy Maisel. Boulder, CO: Westview Press.

Freedburg, Louis. 2002. "Personal Perspective: Democrats v. Democrats." *San Francisco Chronicle*, 18 November.

Freedland, Jonathan. 1996a. "US Election: With One Week to Go, the Battle Shifts to Congress: Hopeful Clinton's Weak Underbelly; The House Staring Defeat in the Face. Mr. Dole Is Now Limping on for His Party's Sake." *The Guardian* (London), 20 October.

Freedland, Jonathan. 1996b. "Republicans to Put Their Hopes in Congress." *The Guardian* (London), 25 October.

Friendly, Fred. 1976. *The Good Guys, The Bad Guys, and the First Amendment*. New York: Random House.

Galtung, Johan, and Marl Ruge. 1965. "The Structure of Foreign News." *Journal of Peace Research* 2: 64–90.

Gans, Herbert J. 1979. *Deciding What's News: A Study of* CBS Evening News, NBC Nightly News, Newsweek *and* Time. New York: Random House.

Garfield, Bob. 2005. "How Sweet the Beat." NPR/WNYC's "On the Media," 21 January.

Geer, John, ed. 1998. *Politicians and Party Politics*. Baltimore, MD: The Johns Hopkins University Press.

Germain, David. 2009. "No More Docs? Moore Mulls Post-'Capitalism' Career." *Associated Press*, 15 September. www.google.com/hostednews/ap/article/ALeq M5iRmEDXX8SS3TDoHcP4SZF021S7vAD9ANMQ4O0.

Gieber, Walter. 1956. "Across the Desk: A Study of 16 Telegraph Editors." *Journalism Quarterly* 31: 61–8.

Gieber, Walter. 1960. "How 'Gatekeepers' View Local Civil Liberties News." *Journalism Quarterly* 37: 199–205.

Gigot, Paul. 1999. "The News Hour with Jim Lehrer," 28 May. www.pbs.org/ newshour/shields&gigot/may99/sg_5-28.html. Accessed: May 31, 1999.

Goldberg, Jeffrey. 2005. "The Unbranding: Can the Democrats Make Themselves Look Tough?" *The New Yorker*, 18 March.

Goodsell, Paul. 1994. "Christensen Signs GOP Pact; Hoagland Sees Flaws in Agenda GOP Pledge." *Omaha World-Herald*, 28 September.

Gorman, Bill. 2009. "NBC *Nightly News* Wins 2008–9 Season." *TV by the Numbers*, 22 September. www.tvbythenumbers.com/2009/09/22/nbc-nightly-news-wins-2008-9-season/28124.

Graber, Doris. 1997. *Mass Media and American Politics*. Washington, DC: Congressional Quarterly, Inc.

Green, Joshua. 2005. "The Enforcer." *Rolling Stone*, 20 October. www.rolling stone.com/politics/story/8091986/the_enforcer.

Groeling, Tim. 1999. "Virtual Discussion: Web-Based Discussion Forums in Political Science." Los Angeles: University of California, Department of Communication Studies/Speech. Unpublished manuscript. escholarship.org/uc/item/ 99d387c8.

Groeling, Tim. 2008. "Who's the Fairest of Them All? An Empirical Test for Partisan Bias on ABC, CBS, NBC, and Fox News." *Presidential Studies Quarterly* 38: 631–57.

Groeling, Tim, and Matthew Baum. 2006. "Rally 'Round the Opposition: Presidential Rallies in Unified and Divided Government." In *The Public Domain:*

Presidents and the Challenge of Public Leadership, eds. Diane Heath and Lori Cox Han. Albany, NY: SUNY Albany Press.

Groeling, Tim, and Matthew Baum. 2008. "Crossing the Water's Edge: Elite Rhetoric, Media Coverage, and the Rally-Round-the-Flag Phenomenon." *Journal of Politics* 70: 1065–85.

Groeling, Tim, and Matthew Baum. 2009. "Journalists' Incentives and Media Coverage of Elite Foreign Policy Evaluations." *Conflict Management and Peace Sciences* 26: 437–70.

Groeling, Tim, and Erik Engstrom. 2009. "Who Cleans up When the Party's Over? The Decline of Partisan Media and Rise of Split-Ticket Voting in the 20th Century." Paper presented at the 2009 annual meeting of the American Political Science Association. Toronto, Canada: 3–9 September.

Groeling, Tim J., and Samuel Kernell. 1998. "Is Network News Coverage of the President Biased?" *The Journal of Politics* 60: 1063–87.

Grossman, Michael Baruch, and Martha Joynt Kumar. 1981. *Portraying the President*. Baltimore, MD: The Johns Hopkins University Press.

Grossman, Michael Baruch, and Francis E. Rourke. 1976. "The Media and the Presidency: An Exchange Analysis." *Political Science Quarterly* 91: 455–70.

Grynaviski, Jeffrey D. 2002. "McDonald's, Martin van Buren, and the American Mass Party." Durham, NC: Duke University. Unpublished dissertation.

Halberstam, David. 1979. *The Powers That Be*. New York: Alfred A. Knopf.

Hallin, Daniel. 1986. *The "Uncensored War": The Media and Vietnam*. Berkeley: University of California Press.

Hamilton, James. 2004. *All the News That's Fit to Sell: How the Market Transforms Information into News*. Princeton, NJ: Princeton University Press.

Hamilton, Lee. 1999. Introductory remarks to "Two Decades of House Television: For Better or Worse?" A seminar on March 19, 1999, at the Woodrow Wilson International Center for Scholars, Washington, DC.

Hardin, Garrett. 1968. "The Tragedy of the Commons." *Science* 162: 1243–48.

Hart, Roderick P. 2000. *Campaign Talk: Why Elections Are Good for Us*. Princeton, NJ: Princeton University Press.

Harwood, John. 2009. "The President's Best Hope in the G.O.P." *The New York Times*, 20 September. www.nytimes.com/2009/09/21/us/politics/21caucus.html.

Havemann, Joel. 2005. "Most Democrats Opt Against Social Security Brainstorming." *Los Angeles Times*, 7 May.

Hecht, Peter. 2009. "GOP Moves to Punish Members Who Backed Budget." *The Sacramento Bee*, 23 February. www.sacbee.com/capitolandcalifornia/story/1644908.html.

Helms, E. Allen. 1949. "The President and Party Politics." In "The Presidency in Transition." *The Journal of Politics*. 11(1): 42–64.

Henry, Ed. 1996. "What the 104th Congress Did; Gloating Democrats and Burned-Out Republicans Learned the Same Lesson: Don't Bite Off More Than You Can Chew." *Cleveland Plain Dealer*, 8 August.

Hernandez, Raymond. 2005. "Bush's Plan for Retirement Leaves G.O.P. in a Quandary." *The New York Times*, 23 May. www.nytimes.com/2005/05/23/nyregion/23social.html.

Herrnson, Paul 2003. *Congressional Elections: Campaigning at Home and in Washington*, 4th ed. Washington, DC: Congressional Quarterly Press.

Hess, Stephen. 1986. *The Ultimate Insiders: U.S. Senators in the National Media.* Washington, DC: The Brookings Institution.

Hess, Stephen. 1991. *Live from Capitol Hill*. Washington, DC: The Brookings Institution.

Hofstadter, Richard. 1969. *The Idea of a Party System: The Rise of Legitimate Opposition in the United States, 1780–1840.* Berkeley: University of California Press.

Hollings, Ernest. 2006. "Stop the Money Chase." *The Washington Post*, 19 February.

Hook, Janet. 2004. "Bush on Notice Despite Win in Congress." *Los Angeles Times*, 9 December.

Hovland, Carl I., Irving L. Janis, and Harold H. Kelly. 1953. *Communication and Persuasion*. New Haven, CT: Yale University Press.

Hovland, Carl, and Walter Weiss. 1951–1952. "The Influence of Source Credibility on Communication Effectiveness." *Public Opinion Quarterly* 15: 635–50.

Hulse, Carl. 2009a. "Speaker Makes Room for New No. 1 Democrat." *The New York Times*, 4 January. www.nytimes.com/2009/01/05/us/politics/05Pelosi.html.

Hulse, Carl. 2009b. "Democrats Eye (Shh!) Reconciliation." *The New York Times*, 1 August. www.nytimes.com/2009/08/02/us/politics/02hulse.html.

Hurt, Charles. 2009. "On-the-Air Prez Seems Like Endless 'Infomercial.'" *New York Post*, 21 September. www.nypost.com/p/news/national/on_the_air_prez_seems_like_endless_QNYXXyakSyHi8h306QRAKL.

Hutchings, Vincent. 2003. *Public Opinion and Democratic Accountability: How Citizens Learn about Politics*. Princeton, NJ: Princeton University Press.

Iyengar, Shanto. 1991. *Is Anyone Responsible?: How Television Frames Political Issues*. Chicago: University of Chicago Press.

Iyengar, Shanto, and Donald R. Kinder. 1987. *News That Matters: Television and American Opinion*. Chicago: University of Chicago Press.

Jackson, K. O. 2004. "Racism Still Wins Votes in Tennessee." *Mansfield (Ohio) News Journal*, 8 August. www.mansfieldnewsjournal.com/news/stories/20040808/localnews/1003970.html.

Jacobson, Gary. 1990. *The Electoral Origins of Divided Government: Competition in U.S. House Elections 1946–1988*. Boulder, CO: Westview Press.

Jacobson, Gary. 2004. *The Politics of Congressional Elections*, 6th ed. New York: Pearson Longman.

Jacobson, Gary. 2005. "Polarized Politics and the 2004 Congressional and Presidential Elections." *Political Science Quarterly* 120: 199–218.

Jacobson, Gary. 2008. *A Divider, Not a Uniter: George W. Bush and the American People – The 2006 Election and Beyond*. New York: Pearson Longman.

Jamieson, Kathleen Hall. 1984. *Packaging the Presidency: A History and Criticism of Presidential Campaign Advertising*. New York: Oxford University Press.

Jamieson, Kathleen Hall. 1992. *Dirty Politics: Deception, Distraction, and Democracy*. New York: Oxford University Press.

Janowitz, Morris. 1975. "Professional Models in Journalism: The Gatekeeper and the Advocate." *Journalism Quarterly* 52: 618–26, 662.

Jarvis, Sharon. 2005. *The Talk of the Party: Political Labels, Symbolic Capital, and American Life*. Lanham, MD: Rowman & Littlefield Publishers, Inc.

Jeffords, James. 2001. Speech given on May 24, 2001. www.washingtonpost .com/wpsrv/onpolitics/transcripts/jeffordstext_052401.htm. Accessed: May 27, 2001.

Jones, Charles O. 1970. *The Minority Party in Congress*. Boston: Little, Brown and Company.

Jones, Charles O. 1994. *The Presidency in a Separated System*. Washington, DC: The Brookings Institution Press.

Jones, Charles O. 2002. "Presidential Leadership in a Government of Parties: An Unrealized Perspective." In *Responsible Partisanship? The Evolution of American Political Parties Since 1950*, eds. John C. Green and Paul Herrnson. Lawrence: University Press of Kansas.

Jones, Douglas A. 1998. "Political Talk Radio: The Limbaugh Effect on Primary Voters." *Political Communication* 15: 367–81.

Kane, Paul. 2008. "2 Democrats to Submit Compromise on Lieberman: Connecticut Senator Would Be Sanctioned for Backing GOP Ticket but Could Keep Key Committee Post." *The Washington Post*, 18 November: A13.

Kane, Paul, Ben Pershing, and Perry Bacon Jr. 2009. "Deeply Divided House Democrats Return to Work – and the Same Set of Problems." *The Washington Post*, 8 September. www.washingtonpost.com/wp_dyn/content/article/ 2009/09/07/AR2009090701988_pf.html.

Kaplan, Jonathan E. 2007. "Emanuel Tells Freshmen to Avoid Stephen Colbert." *The Hill*, 15 March.

Kaplowitz, Stan A., Edward L. Fink, James Mulcrone, David Atkin, and Saleh Dabil. 1991. "Disentangling the Effects of Discrepant and Disconfirming Information." *Social Psychology Quarterly* 54: 191–207.

Katz, Elihu, and Paul Lazarsfeld. 1955. *Personal Influence: The Part Played by People in the Flow of Mass Communication*. New York: The Free Press.

Kedrowski, Karen. 1996. *Media Entrepreneurs in the United States Congress*. Cresskill, NJ: Hampton.

Kelly, Sean Q. 1993. "Divided We Govern: A Reassessment." *Polity* 25 (1): 475–84.

Kernell, Samuel. 1977. "Presidential Popularity and Negative Voting: An Alternative Explanation of the Midterm Congressional Decline of the President's Party." *American Political Science Review* 71: 44–66.

Kernell, Samuel. 1997. *Going Public: New Strategies of Presidential Leadership*, 3rd ed. Washington, DC: Congressional Quarterly Press.

Kernell, Samuel, and Gary C. Jacobson. 1987. "Congress and the Presidency as News in the Nineteenth Century." *Journal of Politics* 49: 1016–35.

Kesten, Lou. 2005. "Shays: DeLay Should Quit as House Leader: GOP Congressman Tells AP That Texas Rep. Tom DeLay Should Step Down as House Majority Leader." *Associated Press*, 10 April. www.abcnews.go.com/Politics/wireStory?id=658259&CMP=OTC-RSSFeeds0312.

Key, V. O. 1966. *The Responsible Electorate*. New York: Vintage.

Kiewiet, D. Roderick, and Mathew D. McCubbins. 1991. *The Logic of Delegation: Congressional Parties and the Appropriations Process*. Chicago: University of Chicago Press.

Kinder, Donald, and Thomas Palfrey, eds. 1993. *Experimental Foundations of Political Science*. Ann Arbor: University of Michigan Press.

King, Gary, Michael Tomz, and Jason Wittenberg. 2000. "Making the Most of Statistical Analyses: Improving Interpretation and Presentation." *American Journal of Political Science* 44: 341–55.

Kingdom, John. 1999. *Government and Politics in Britain: An Introduction. 2nd Edition*. Cambridge, UK: Polity Press.

Kingdon, John W. 1984. *Agendas, Alternatives, and Public Policies*. Boston: Little, Brown and Company.

Kingdon, John W. 1989. *Congressmen's Voting Decisions*, 3rd ed. Ann Arbor: University of Michigan Press.

Klein, Rick. 2005a. "House GOP Seen Straying from Pledges in 'Contract'." *The Boston Globe*, 10 January.

Klein, Rick. 2005b. "Foes Cite Progress vs. Bush Agenda: Say Strategy Fuels GOP Infighting." *The Boston Globe*, 11 April.

Koeske, Gary F., and William D. Crano. 1968. "The Effect of Congruous and Incongruous Source-Statement Combinations upon the Judged Credibility of a Communication." *Journal of Experimental Social Psychology* 4: 384–99.

Kondracke, Morton. 1996. "Strange Bedfellows in Washington." *The San Diego Union-Tribune*, 7 August.

Krehbiel, Keith. 1996. "Institutional and Partisan Sources of Gridlock: A Theory of Divided and Unified Government." *Journal of Theoretical Politics* 8 (1): 7–40.

Krehbiel, Keith. 1998. *Pivotal Politics: A Theory of U.S. Lawmaking*. Chicago: University of Chicago Press.

Kuhn, David Paul, and Jonathan Martin. 2007. "Republican Candidates Begin Snubbing Bush." *Politico.com*, 19 June.

Kuklinski, James H., and Norman L. Hurley. 1996. "It's A Matter of Interpretation." In *Political Persuasion and Attitude Change*, eds. Diana C. Mutz, Paul M. Sniderman, and Richard A. Brody. Ann Arbor: University of Michigan Press.

Kuklinski, James, and Lee Sigelman. 1992. "When Objectivity Is Not Objective: Network Television and the 'Paradox of Objectivity.'" *Journal of Politics* 54: 810–33.

Kurtz, Howard. 1998. *Spin Cycle: How the White House and the Media Manipulate the News*. New York: The Free Press.

Kurtz, Howard. 2000. "Feeding the Media Beast: Leaks, Rats, and BlackBerrys." *The Washington Post*, 17 December: C1.

Kurtz, Howard. 2004. "Republican Convention Gets Under Way; Kerry Interviewed on 'The Daily Show.'" *CNN's Reliable Sources*, 29 August. www.cnn.com/TRANSCRIPTS/0408/29/rs.00.html. Accessed: August 31, 2004.

Lakoff, George. 1996. *Moral Politics: What Conservatives Know That Liberals Don't.* Chicago: University of Chicago Press.

Lamb, Brian. 1995. C-SPAN Interview with Newt Gingrich, "To Renew America." *Book Notes*, 23 July. www.booknotes.org/transcripts/10148.htm. Accessed: August 21, 2004.

Lambro, Donald. 2005. "Centrist Democrats Warn Liberals." *The Washington Times*, 4 April.

Lancaster, John. 2001. "Senate Republicans Try to Regroup; GOP Caucus Unites Behind Lott as Leader in the Wake of Jeffords's Defection." *The Washington Post*, 26 May: A18.

Langdon, Steve. 1994. "Clinton's High Victory Rate Conceals Disappointments: President Lost on Few Votes, but Some Big Issues Never Made It to the Floor of Either Chamber." *Congressional Quarterly Weekly Review*, 31 December: 3619.

Lasorsa, Dominic, and Stephen Reese. 1990. "News Source Use in the Crash of 1987: A Study of Four National Media." *Journalism Quarterly* 67: 60–3.

Lauter, David. 1994. "Clinton Holds out His Record as Election Issue Politics: In Risky Move, He Urges Voters to Choose Between His Policies and What the GOP Is Proposing." *Los Angeles Times*, 8 October: 1.

Lawrence, David. 1928. "Reporting the Political News at Washington." *The American Political Science Review* 22: 893–902.

Levine, John M., and Ronald S. Valle. 1975. "The Convert as a Credible Communicator." *Social Behavior and Personality Journal* 3: 81–90.

Libit, Daniel. 2009. "GOP Warns Dems of September Heat." *Politico.com*. 1 September. www.dyn.politico.com/printstory.cfm?uuid=734A2CF2-18FE-70B2-A83836F45AFBA867.

Lichter, S. Robert, and Daniel Amundson. 1994. "Less News Is Worse News: Television News Coverage of Congress." In *Congress, the Press and the Public*, eds. Thomas E. Mann and Norman Ornstein. Washington, DC: American Enterprise Institute and The Brookings Institution.

Lichter, S. Robert, and Richard E. Noyes. 1995. *Good Intentions Make Bad News: Why Americans Hate Campaign Journalism.* Lanham, MD: Rowman and Littlefield Publishers, Inc.

Lichter, S. Robert, Stanley Rothman, and Linda S. Lichter. 1986. *The Media Elite.* Bethesda, MD: Adler and Adler.

Limbaugh, Rush. 2005. "Judges Are GOP Litmus Test." *The Rush Limbaugh Show.* 9 May. www.rushlimbaugh.com/home/daily/site_050905/content/rush_warning.guest.html.

Linsky, Martin. 1986. *Impact: How the Press Affects Federal Policymaking.* New York: Norton & Company.

Lipinski, Daniel. 1999. "Communicating the Party Record: How Congressional Leaders Transmit Their Messages to the Public." Paper prepared for delivery at the 1999 Annual Meeting of the American Political Science Association. Atlanta, GA: 2–5 September.

Lipinski, Daniel. 2004. *Congressional Communication: Content and Consequences*. Ann Arbor: University of Michigan Press.

Lipinski, Daniel. n.d. *A New Theory of Congressional Party Government*. Unpublished manuscript.

Lipman, Larry. 1999. "Fellow Democrats Don't Want Medicare Reform." *Palm Beach Post*, 12 May: 16A.

Lippmann, Walter. 1920. *Liberty and the News*. New York: Harcourt, Brace and Howe.

Los Angeles Times. 1949. (Unsigned Article.) "McGrath to Crack Down on Dixiecrats." 9 May.

Los Angeles Times. 1955. (Unsigned Article.) "Truman's Address to Indiana Group." 28 August.

Los Angeles Times. 1997. "McDonald's Franchisees Join the McFight; Fast Food: Disgruntled Owner-Operators Back Federal 'Good Faith' Legislation." 22 May: 8.

Love, John F. 1986. *McDonald's: Behind the Arches*. New York: Bantam Books.

Lupia, Arthur. 1994. "Shortcuts Versus Encyclopedias: Information and Voting Behavior in California Insurance Reform Elections." *The American Political Science Review*, 88 (1): 63–76.

Lupia, Arthur, and Mathew D. McCubbins. 1998. *The Democratic Dilemma: Can Citizens Learn What They Need to Know?* Cambridge: Cambridge University Press.

Macomber, Shawn. 2005. "Campaign Crawlers: The Toomey Revolution." *The American Spectator*, 7 January.

Madison, James. 1787. "Federalist No. 10: The Same Subject Continued: The Union as a Safeguard Against Domestic Faction and Insurrection." *New York Packet*, 23 November. www.thomas.loc.gov/home/histdox/fed_10.html. Accessed: March 7, 2010.

Madison, James. 1788. "Federalist No. 51: The Structure of the Government Must Furnish the Proper Checks and Balances Between the Different Departments." *New York Packet*, 8 February. Accessed: March 7, 2010. www. thomas.loc.gov/home/histdox/fed_51.html.

Mainelli, John. 2005. "Radio $.O.$ Signal." *New York Post*, 27 September.

Maltzman, Forrest, and Lee Sigelman. 1996. "The Politics of Talk: Unconstrained Floor Time in the U.S. House of Representatives." *Journal of Politics* 58: 810–21.

Maraniss, David, and Michael Weisskopf. 1996. *Tell Newt to Shut Up! Prizewinning Washington Post Journalists Reveal How Reality Gagged the Gingrich Revolution*. New York: Touchstone.

Martin, Jurek. 1994. "Resurgent Republicans Eye the Polls." *Financial Times*, 28 September.

Martis, Kenneth C. 1989. *The Historical Atlas of the Political Parties in the United States Congress: 1789–1989*. New York: Macmillan.

Master-McNeil, Inc. 2003. "Brand Name." Glossary. www.naming.com/resources .html. Accessed August 6, 2004.

Matthews, Donald R. 1960. *U.S. Senators and Their World*. Chapel Hill: University of North Carolina Press.

Mayhew, David R. 1974. *Congress: The Electoral Connection*. New Haven, CT: Yale University Press.

Mayhew, David R. 1991. *Divided We Govern: Party Control, Lawmaking, and Investigations 1946–1990*. New Haven, CT: Yale University Press.

McDonald's Corporation. 2003. "2003 Financial Report." Oak Brook, IL.

McDonald's Corporation. 2004. "Franchising." www.media.mcdonalds.com/secured/company/franchising/usfactsheet/media/franpt1.pdf. Accessed: August 6, 2004.

McGrory, Brian. 1996. "President's Party Basks as He Signs Wage Bill." *The Boston Globe*, 21 August.

McGrory, Mary. 2001. "Aftershocks." *The Washington Post*, 27 May: B1. www.washingtonpost.com/wp-dyn/opinion/columns/mcgrorymary/A80309-2001May26.html. Accessed: May 27, 2001.

McManus, John. 1992. "What Kind of Commodity Is News?" *Communication Research*, 19: 787–805.

Michigan Court of Appeals. 2000. (Unpublished Opinion.) "Dawn N. Ison, as Personal Representative of the Estate of Tenika Hiter, V William Pickard, Bearwood Management Company, Inc., and Braille Corporation and McDonald's Corporation." No. 207199, Wayne Circuit Court, LC No. 95-53 5765, 24 March. www.michbar.org/opinions/appeals/2000/032400/6620.html. Accessed: August 9, 2004.

Milkis, Sidney. 1993. *The President and the Parties: The Transformation of the American Party System since the New Deal*. New York: Oxford University Press.

Milligan, Susan. 2001. "Centrists Hold Sway, to Leader's Chagrin." *The Boston Globe*, 4 May: A2.

Mills, Jim. 2000. "Spooky Stuff." *Roll Call*, 27 October.

Mirrlees, James A. 1976. "The Optimal Structure of Incentives and Authority within an Organization." *The Bell Journal of Economics* 7: 105–31.

Mitchell, Alison. 2001. "Musical Chairs: Democrats Take Their Turn in the Hot Seat." *The New York Times*, 27 May.

Morris, Dick. 1999. *Behind the Oval Office: Getting Reelected Against All Odds*. Los Angeles: Renaissance Books.

Mott, Frank Luther. 1944. "Newspapers in Presidential Campaigns." *Public Opinion Quarterly* 8: 348–67.

Mueller, John E. 1970. "Presidential Popularity from Truman to Johnson." *American Political Science Review* 64: 18–34.

Mueller, John E. 1973. *War, Presidents, and Public Opinion*. New York: John Wiley & Sons, Inc.

Murphy, Cullen, and Todd S. Purdum. 2009. "Farewell to All That: An Oral History of the Bush White House." *Vanity Fair* (February). www.vanityfair.com/politics/features/2009/02/bush-oral-history200902?printable=true&currentPage=all.

Mutz, Diana. 1992. "Mass Media and the Depoliticization of Personal Experience." *American Journal of Political Science* 36: 483–508.

Nagourney, Adam. 2006. "Democratic Hard Chargers Try to Return Party to Power." *The New York Times*, 30 April.

Nagourney, Adam. 2009. "In Gingrich Mold, a New Voice for Solid Resistance in Republican Party." *International Herald Tribune*, 15 February. www.iht.com/bin/printfriendly.php?id=20195088.

Needham, Catherine. 2002. "Branding Public Policy: Marketed Government under Clinton and Blair." Paper presented at the 2002 Annual Meeting of the American Political Science Association. Boston, MA: 29 August–1 September.

Needham, Catherine. 2005. "Brand Leaders: Clinton, Blair and the Limitations of the Permanent Campaign." *Political Studies* 53: 343–61.

Neustadt, Richard E. 1990. *Presidential Power and the Modern Presidents: The Politics of Leadership from Roosevelt to Reagan*. New York: The Free Press.

Newport, Frank. 2009. "Americans More Likely to Say Government Doing Too Much." *Gallup*, 21 September. www.gallup.com/poll/123101/Americans-Likely-Say-Government-Doing-Too-Much.aspx.

Nicholas, Peter. 2009. "Obama Team Keeps Distance from Carter's Charges of Racism." *Los Angeles Times*, 17 September. www.latimes.com/news/nation world/nation/healthcare/la-na-carter-obama17-2009sep17,0,4980703.story.

Nichols, Hans. 2005. "Soros Says Be Patient." *The Hill*, 20 April.

Nicholson, Stephen P., Gary M. Segura, and Nathan D. Woods. 2002. "Presidential Approval and the Mixed Blessing of Divided Government." *The Journal of Politics* 64: 701–20.

Nie, Norman, Sidney Verba, and John Petrocik. 1976. *The Changing American Voter*. Cambridge, MA: Harvard University Press.

Norquist, Grover. 1999. "Politics: The Chairman's Candidates – A Candid Assessment of the GOP Presidential Field." *The American Spectator*, June. www.atr.org/opeds/tas/tas0699.html. Accessed: September 10, 2004.

Novak, Robert. 2001. "New Dem on the Block Chips Away at Gridlock." *Chicago Sun-Times*, 25 January. www.suntimes.com/output/novak/novak251.html.

Novak, Robert. 2004. "Dictated by Bush." *CNN Inside Politics*. www.cnn.com/2004/ALLPOLITICS/08/26/novak.bush/index.html. Accessed September 5, 2004.

Novak, Robert. 2005. "Quest to Get a Republican to Fight DeLay May Have Crossed a Line." *Chicago Sun-Times*, 11 April.

NPR. 1996. "Weekend Edition Saturday," 28 September.

O'Brien, Michael. 2009a. "Congressman: Centrist Dems Talking Healthcare Coalition with GOP." *The Hill's Blog Briefing Room*, 18 July. www.briefing room.thehill.com/2009/07/18/congressman-centrist-dems-approached-gop-to-form-healthcare-coalition.

O'Brien, Michael. 2009b. "Waters Blames Rahm for Recalcitrant Dems on Healthcare." *The Hill's Blog Briefing Room*, 28 July. www.briefingroom.thehill.com/2009/07/28/waters-blames-rahm-for-recalcitrant-dems-on-healthcare.

Olsen, Stefanie. 2003. "Online Ad Outlook Brightens." *CNET News*, 21 April. www.news.com.com/2100-1024-997369.html?part=dht&tag=ntop. Accessed: August 6, 2004.

Olson, Mancur. 1965. *The Logic of Collective Action*. Cambridge, MA: Harvard University Press.

Oneal, John R., Bradley Lian, and James H. Joyner, Jr. 1996. "Are the American People 'Pretty Prudent?' Public Responses to U.S. Uses of Force, 1950–1988." *International Studies Quarterly* 40: 261–280.

Orne, M. T. 1962. "On the Psychology of the Psychology Experiment." *American Psychologist* 17: 776–83.

Osborne, David. 1984. "Newt Gingrich: Shining Knight of the Post-Reagan Right." *Mother Jones* (November/December). www.bsd.mojones.com/mother_jones/ND84/index.html. Accessed: October 31, 1999.

Ostrom, Elinor. 1990. *Governing the Commons: The Evolution of Institutions for Collective Action*. New York: Cambridge University Press.

Owens, Simon. 2009. "May '09 Political Blog Readership 53% Lower Than It Was in October '08." *Bloggasm.com*. 11 June. www.bloggasm.com/may-09-political-blog-readership-53-lower-than-it-was-in-october-08.

Page, Benjamin. 1996. *Who Deliberates?* Chicago: University of Chicago Press.

Paletz, David L., and Robert M. Entman. 1981. *Media Power Politics*. New York: The Free Press.

Parker, Sarah. 2008. "Palin Problem: She's out of Her League." *National Review Online*, 26 September. article.nationalreview.com/?q=MDZiMDhjYTU1NmI5Y2MwZjg2MWNiMWMyYTUxZDkwNTE=.

Parks, Daniel J. 2001. "Will Bush Turn His Veto Pen on a Fiscally Wayward GOP?" *CQ Weekly Report*, 19 May: 1128.

Patterson, Thomas E. 1996. "Bad News, Period." *PS: Political Science and Politics* 29: 17–20.

Patterson, Thomas E. 2000. "Doing Well and Doing Good." *Research Report*. Cambridge, MA: Joan Shorenstein Center on the Press, Politics, and Public Policy, Harvard University.

Patterson, Thomas E. 2003. "The Search for a Standard: Markets and the Media." *Political Communication* 20: 139–43.

Petrocik, John. 1996. "Issue Ownership in Presidential Elections, with a 1980 Case Study." *American Journal of Political Science* 40: 825–50.

Petrocik, John, William Benoit, and Glenn Hansen. 2003. "Issue Ownership and Presidential Campaigning, 1952–2000." *Political Science Quarterly* 118: 599–626.

Pew Research Center. 2004. "News Audiences Increasingly Politicized: Online News Audience Larger, More Diverse." Pew Research Center for the People and the Press, 8 June www.people-press.org/reports/display.php3?ReportID=215. Accessed: August 17, 2004.

Pew Research Center. 2008a. "Audience Segments in a Changing News Environment: Key News Audiences Now Blend Online and Traditional Sources." Pew Research Center for the People and the Press, 17 August.

Pew Research Center. 2008b. "Internet's Broader Role in Campaign 2008: Social Networking and Online Videos Take Off." Pew Research Center for the People and the Press, 11 January.

Phillips, Kate. 2009. "Republicans Slam Democrats for Planned Wilson Rebuke." *The New York Times*, 15 September. www.thecaucus.blogs.nytimes .com/2009/09/15/republicans-slam-democrats-for-planned-wilson-rebuke.

Popkin, Samuel L. 1991. *The Reasoning Voter: Communication and Persuasion in Presidential Campaigns*. Chicago: University of Chicago Press.

Potter, Mitch. 2009. "How Barack Obama Lost his Mojo." *The Star*, 6 September. www.thestar.com/news/insight/article/691563.

Povich, Elaine. 1996. "Partners and Adversaries: The Contentious Connection Between Congress and the Media." Arlington, VA: Freedom Forum. www .freedomforum.org/FreedomForum/resources/media_and_soc/congress_and_ media/ Accessed: October 31, 1999.

Powell, G. Bingham Jr., and Guy D. Whitten. 1993. "A Cross-National Analysis of Economic Voting: Taking Account of the Political Context." *American Journal of Political Science* 37: 391–414.

Preston, Mark. 2006. *Republicans and Democrats Head Home with Talking Points*. www.cnn.com/2006/politics/06/30/mg.fri/CNN.com. Accessed: June 30, 2006.

Printers' Ink. 1933. Unsigned Article. "Hitler on Advertising: 'See with Eyes of the Masses' Is Advice of Germany's New Dictator." 20 July.

Project for Excellence in Journalism (PEJ). 2002. "Local TV News Project–2002." www.journalism.org/resources/research/reports/localTV/2002/public.asp. Accessed: September 10, 2004.

Przybyla, Heidi. 2009. "Obama Campaign Activists Find Health Care Harder Sell (Update1)." *Bloomberg*. www.bloomberg.com/apps/news?pid=20670001& refer=&sid=arSw7zOwyxKo. Accessed: June 17, 2009.

Quirk, Paul J., and Bruce Nesmith. 1995. "Divided Government and Policy Making: Negotiating the Laws." In *The Presidency and the Political System*, 4th ed., ed. Michael Nelson. Washington, DC: Congressional Quarterly Press.

Rae, Nichol. 1998. "Party Factionalism, 1946–96." In *Partisan Approaches to Postwar American Politics*, ed. Byron E. Shafer. Chatham, NJ: Chatham House.

Raju, Manu. 2009. "Republicans Chew on DeMint." *Politico.com*, 27 January.dyn.politico.com/printstory.cfm?uuid=15B18F32-18FE-70B2-A8EAFE8949E9B160.

Ranney, Austin. 1954, *Doctrine of Responsible Party Government*. Urbana: The University of Illinois Press.

Ranney, Austin. 1983. *Channels of Power: The Impact of Television on American Politics*. New York: Basic Books.

Rasmussen Reports. 2009. "Does Obama Face a 2012 Challenge in His Own Party?" 4 September. www.rasmussenreports.com/public_content/politics/ obama_admin . . . n/september_2009/does_obama_face_a_2012_challenge_in_ his_own_party.

Reagan, Ronald. 1990. *An American Life*. New York: Pocket Books, Simon & Schuster, Inc.

Reuters News Service. 2001. "Streisand Calls Bush 'Destructive'." *San Diego Union-Tribune*, 3 April: A-6.

Reynolds, John F. 2006. *The Demise of the American Convention System, 1880–1911*. New York: Cambridge University Press.

Roberts, Cokie. 1993. *This Week with David Brinkley*. 17 October.

Roberts, Cokie. 1996. As quoted on ABC's *World News Tonight with Peter Jennings*. 18 October.

Robertson, Campbell. 2009. "Obama Factor Plays to Senator's Advantage." *The New York Times*, 10 September. www.nytimes.com/2009/09/11/us/11vitter.html?_r=1&src=sch.

Robins, Lynton, and Bill Jones. 1997. *Half a Century of British Politics*. Manchester, UK: Manchester University Press.

Robinson, Michael J. 1976. "Public Affairs Television and the Growth of Political Malaise." *American Political Science Review* 70: 409–32.

Robinson, Michael J., and Kevin R. Appel. 1979. "Network News Coverage of Congress." *Political Science Quarterly* 94: 407–18.

Robinson, Michael J., and Margaret A. Sheehan. 1983. *Over the Wire and on TV: CGS and UPI in Campaign '80*. New York: Russell Sage Foundation.

Roff, Peter. 2009. "Democrats' Healthcare Censorship Shows How Desperate They've Become." *U.S. News*, 27 July. www.usnews.com/blogs/peter-roff/2009/07/24/democrats-healthcare-censorship-shows-how-desperate-theyve-become.html.

Rohde, David. 1991. *Parties and Leaders in the Postreform House*. Chicago: University of Chicago Press.

Rohde, David, John H. Aldrich, and Michael Tofias. 2007. "One D Is Not Enough: Measuring Conditional Party Government in 1887–2002." In *Process, Party and Policy Making: Further New Perspectives on the History of Congress*, eds. David W. Brady and Mathew D. McCubbins. Stanford, CA: Stanford University Press.

Rosen, Jay. 2004. "Are We Headed for an Opposition Press?" *Press Think Online*, 3 November. www.journalism.nyu.edu/pubzone/weblogs/pressthink.

Rosenstiel, Tom. 2004. "The End of 'Network News.'" *The Washington Post*, 12 September: B07.

Rothenberg, Stuart. 1998. "Analysis: A Small but Historic Shift for the Democrats: What Will the Shift Mean for Both Parties?" CNN On-Politics. www.cnn.com/ALLPOLITICS/stories/1998/11/03/election/house/roundup.

Rowley, James, and Kristin Jensen. 2009. "Hoyer Says House May Leave Before Health-Care Vote (Update3)." *Bloomberg*, 21 July. www.bloomberg.com/apps/news?pid=20601087&sid=aEAi6zSd837c.

Rozell, Mark J. 1994. *Executive Privilege: The Dilemma of Secrecy and Democratic Accountability*. Baltimore, MD: The Johns Hopkins University Press.

Russert, Tim. 2005a. "Guest: Howard Dean, Chairman of the Democratic Party." *NBC News: Meet the Press*. 22 May.

Russert, Tim. 2005b. "Transcript for October 2: John Abizaid, Rahm Emanuel, Thomas Reynolds, Dan Balz, and John Harwood." *NBC News: Meet the Press*, 2 October. www.msnbc.msn.com/id/9542948.

Rutkus, Denis Steven. 1991. *Newspaper and Television Network News Coverage of Congress during the Summers of 1979 and 1989: A Content Analysis*. Washington, DC: Congressional Research Service.

Sabato, Larry J. 1991. *Feeding Frenzy: How Attack Journalism Has Transformed American Politics.* New York: The Free Press.

Sabato, Larry J., and Bruce A. Larson. 2002. *The Party's Just Begun*, 2nd ed. New York: Longman.

Salant, Jonathan D. 2008. "Obama Leveraged Record Fundraising, Spending to Defeat Rivals." *Bloomberg*, 4 November. www.bloomberg.com/apps/news?pid=2060 1087.

Sammon, Bill. 2009. "Bush Says He Refused to Bail out Republicans with Iraq Withdrawal." *Fox News*, 11 January. www.foxnews.com/politics/2009/01/10/bush-says-refused-bail-republicans-iraq-withdrawal.

Sanders, David J. 2009. "Blue Dog Democrats Oppose Card Check." *Arkansas News*, 18 February. www.arkansasnews.com/?p=26290.

Sawyer, Jon. 1996. "Races Indicate Democrats Face Election Struggles; Congressional Hopefuls Low on Funds in South." *St. Louis Post-Dispatch*, 15 August.

Schattschneider, E. E. 1942. *Party Government.* New York: Rinehart.

Schattschneider, E. E. 1960. *The Semi-Sovereign People.* Hinsdale, IL: Dryden Press.

Schieffer, Bob. 1995. "President Clinton's Budget Proposal Draws Criticism on Capitol Hill by Fellow Party Members." *CBS This Morning*, 14 June.

Schlesinger, Joseph. 1984. "On the Theory of Party Organizations." *The Journal of Politics* 46: 369–400.

Schlosser, Eric. 2001. *Fast Food Nation.* New York: Houghton Mifflin.

Schneider, Judy. 2001. "Special Order Speeches: Current House Practices." *Congressional Research Service Report.* www.house.gov/rules/rl30136.pdf.

Schramm, Wilbur. 1949. "The Nature of News." *Journalism Quarterly* 26: 259–69.

Schudson, Michael. 1978. *Discovering the News: A Social History of American Newspapers.* New York: Basic Books.

Seelye, Katharine Q., Stephen Engelberg, and Jeff Gerth. 1995. "Birth of a Vision: Files Show How Gingrich Laid a Grand G.O.P. Plan." *The New York Times*, 3 December.

Sellers, Patrick. 2005. "Constructing News in Congress: The Response of the Rank and File." Paper presented to the 2005 meeting of the American Political Science Association. Washington, DC: 1–3 September.

Sellers, Patrick, and Brian Schaffner. 2007. "Winning Coverage in the U.S. Senate." *Political Communication* 24: 377–91.

Shapiro, Walter. 2005. "Democrats Won't Win by Whining." *The Los Angeles Times*, 3 January. www.articles.latimes.com/2005/jan/03/opinion/oe-shapiro3.

Sharkey, Mary Anne. 1994. "GOP Contract Is Hokum and the Voters Know It." *The (Cleveland) Plain Dealer*, 28 September.

Shaw, David. 2003. "The More Pernicious Bias Is Less Substance, More Fluff." *Los Angeles Times*, 19 January.

Siemaszko, Corky. 2009. "Advertisers Continue to Abandon Glenn Beck after Pundit Had Called President Obama a 'Racist.'" *New York Daily News*, 3 September. www.nydailynews.com/money/2009/09/03/2009-09-03_advertisers_.html.

Sifry, Micah. 2009. "The Obama Roadblock: Why He's Sagging Online." *Techpresident.com*. 21 September. www.techpresident.com/blog-entry/obama-roadblock-why-hes-sagging-online.

Sigal, Leon V. 1973. *Reporters and Officials: The Organization and Politics of Newsmaking*. Lexington, MA: D.C. Heath and Company.

Sigal, Leon V. 1986. "Sources Make the News." In *Reading the News: A Pantheon Guide to Popular Culture*, eds. R. K. Manoff and M. Shudson. New York: Pantheon Books.

Simon, Herbert A. 1957. *Models of Man: Social and Rational*. New York: John Wiley & Sons, Inc.

Sinclair, Barbara. 1989. "The Transformation of the U.S. Senate." Baltimore, MD: The Johns Hopkins Press.

Sinclair, Barbara. 1997. *Unorthodox Lawmaking: New Legislative Processes in the U.S. Congress*. Washington, DC: Congressional Quarterly Press.

Sinclair, Barbara. 2002. "The Dream Fulfilled? Party Development in Congress, 1950–2000." In *Responsible Partisanship? The Evolution of American Political Parties Since 1950*, eds. John C. Green and Paul Herrnson. Lawrence: University Press of Kansas.

Singer, Jane. 1997. "Still Guarding the Gate? The Newspaper Journalist's Role in an On-line World." *Convergence: The Journal of Research into New Media Technologies* 3: 72–89.

Smith, Ben. 2008. "Obama: Don't Fund Independent Groups." *Politico.com*. 13 May. www.dyn.politico.com/printstory.cfm?uuid=E3B0286A-3048-5C12-002C0EDCA4CE3CF7.

Smith, Ben, and Nia-Malika Henderson. 2009. "Glenn Beck Up, Left Down and Van Jones Defiant." *Politico.com*. 7 September. www.politico.com/news/stories/0909/26813.html.

Smith, Culver. 1977. *The Press, Politics, and Patronage*. Athens: University of Georgia Press.

Smoller, Frederic T. 1990. *The Six O'Clock Presidency: A Theory of Presidential Press Relations in the Age of Television*. New York: Praeger.

Snider, Paul. 1967. "'Mr. Gates' Revisited: A 1966 Version of the 1949 Case Study." *Journalism Quarterly* 44: 419–27.

Sniderman, Paul, Richard Brody, and Philip Tetlock. 1991. *Reasoning and Choice: Explorations in Political Psychology*. New York: Cambridge University Press.

Soraghan, Mike. 2009. "Dem Memo Plots Message War on Insurers." *The Hill*, 30 July. www.thehill.com/leading-the-news/dem-memo-plots-message-war-on-insurers-2009-07-30.html.

Spence, A. Michael. 1973. *Market Signaling*. Cambridge, MA: Harvard University Press.

Spilotes, Constantine, and Lynn Vavreck. 2002. "Campaign Advertising: Partisan Convergence or Divergence?" *Journal of Politics* 64: 249–61.

Squire, Peverill. 1988. "Who Gets National News Coverage in the U.S. Senate?" *American Politics Quarterly* 16: 139–56.

Stanley, Alessandra. 2004. "The TV Watch: Just Barely Off Broadway, the G.O.P. Puts on a Show." *The New York Times*, 2 September.

Stanley, Harold W., and Richard G. Niemi. 1998. *Vital Statistics on American Politics, 1997–1998*. Washington, DC: Congressional Quarterly, Inc.

Stanley, Harold W., and Richard G. Niemi. 2000. *Vital Statistics on American Politics, 1999–2000*. Washington, DC: Congressional Quarterly, Inc.

Stein, Sam. 2008. "Air American Is Changing Ownership." *The Huffington Post*, 21 February. www.huffingtonpost.com/2008/02/21/air-america-is-changing-o_n_87765.html.

Stein, Sam. 2009. "Obama and DNC Try Turning Angry Mobs and Drudge into Benefits." *The Huffington Post*, 4 August. www.huffingtonpost.com/2009/08/04/obama-and-dnc-try-turning_n_250890.html.

Stevenson, Richard. 2001. "News Analysis: Bush's Capitol Hill Two-Step." *The New York Times*, 6 May. www.nytimes.com/2001/05/06/politics/06BUSH.html.

Stevenson, Richard. 2005. "Some in GOP Call on Bush to Focus on Governing." *The New York Times*, 27 June.

Stevenson, Richard, and Robin Toner. 2005. "2 Top GOP Lawmakers Buck Bush on Social Security." *The New York Times*, 18 February.

Stewart, Charles H. 1991. "Lessons from the Post–Civil War Era." In *The Politics of Divided Government*, Gary Cox and Samuel Kernell. Boulder, CO: Westview Press.

Stirland, Sarah Lai. 2008. "Obama's Secret Weapons: Internet, Databases and Psychology." *Wired.com*, 29 October. www.blog.wired.com/27bstroke6/2008/10/obamas-secret-w.html.

Stolberg, Sheryl G. 2004. "The Keynote Speaker: Disaffected Democrat Who Is Now a G.O.P. Dream." *The New York Times*, 1 September.

Sullivan, Andrew. 1996. "Do They Want Bill 1 or Bill 2?" *The Sunday Times of London*, 27 October.

Sundquist, James. 1988. "Needed: A Political Theory for the New Era of Coalition Government in the United States." *Political Science Quarterly* 103: 613–35.

Sundquist, James. 1992. *Constitutional Reform and Effective Government* (rev. ed.). Washington, DC: The Brookings Institution Press.

Talkers. 2003. "Top Talk Radio Audiences by Size." *Talkers Magazine*. Fall.

Taylor, Andrew. 2001a. "A Senate of Singular Personalities and Possibilities." *CQ Weekly Report*, 27 January: 212.

Taylor, Andrew. 2001b. "GOP Members Grapple with Roles as Bush Team Players." *CQ Weekly Report*, 3 February: 269.

Taylor, Andrew J. 2005. *Elephant's Edge: The Republicans as a Ruling Party*. Westport, CT: Greenwood.

Thrush, Glenn. 2009. "Big Dem Cash Dump on Eve of Climate Vote." *Politico.com*, 17 July. www.politico.com/blogs/glennthrush/0709/Big_Dem_cash_dump_on_eve_of_climate_vote.html?showall.

Tidmarch, Charles M., and John J. Pitney, Jr. 1985. "Covering Congress." *Polity* 17: 463–83.

TNS Media Intelligence. 2004. "U.S. Political Advertising Spending Reaches $1.45 Billion Reports TNS Media Intelligence/CMR." Press release. www.tns-mi.com/news/11012004.htm.

Tobianski, Sarah. 2009. "Obama Rallies the Troops and Money with DeMint's 'Waterloo.'" *ABC News: Political Punch*, 21 July. www.blogs.abcnews.com/politicalpunch/2009/07/obama-rallies-the-troops-and-money-with-demints-waterloo-.html.

Toner, Robin. 1996. "Put Re-Election Before Dole, Gingrich Advises." *The New York Times*, 4 October.

Toner, Robin, and Carl Hulse. 2005. "In the Partisan Power Struggle, a New Underdog Tries New Tricks." *The New York Times*, 11 April.

Tuchman, Gaye. 1972. *Making News: A Study in the Construction of Reality*. New York: MacMillan.

Tufte, Edward R. 1975. "Determinants of the Outcomes of Midterm Congressional Elections." *American Political Science Review* 69: 812–26.

Uliano, Dick. 2009. "Dems Target Right-Wing Talk Radio." *CNN: Political Ticker*, 13 February. www.politicalticker.blogs.cnn.com/2009/02/13/dems_target_right_wing_talk_radio.

Unsigned Commentary. 1994. "Our Perspective: Newtspeak; Will Voters Swallow Reagan Redux?" *Minneapolis Star Tribune*, 28 September.

Unsigned Editorial. 1994. "The G.O.P's Deceptive Contract." *The New York Times*, 28 September.

Upbin, Bruce. 1999. "Beyond Burgers." *Forbes* Magazine, 1 November.

Vargas, Jose Antonio. 2008. "Obama's Wide Web: From YouTube to Text Messaging, Candidate's Team Connects to Voters." *The Washington Post*, 20 August: C01.

Vieth, Warren, and Janet Hook. 2004. "White House Admits Social Security 'Fix' Means Borrowing." *Los Angeles Times*, 7 December.

Vinson, C. Danielle. 2005. "Congress Goes Public: Who Is Using the Media for Policymaking Goals?" Paper presented to the 2005 annual convention of the American Political Science Association.

Viser, Matt, and Andrew Ryan. 2009. "Senate Republicans Halt Debate on Bill for a Kennedy Fill-in." *The Boston Globe*, 19 September. www.boston.com/news/local/massachusetts/articles/2009/09/19/senate_republicans_halt_debate_on_bill_for_kennedy_fill_in.

Volokh, Eugene. 1995. "Cheap Speech and What It Will Do." *The Yale Law Journal*, May. www.adager.com/VeSoft/CheapSpeech.html. Accessed: March 10, 2002.

Walster, E., E. Aronson, and D. Abrahams. 1966. "On Increasing the Persuasiveness of a Low Prestige Communicator." *Journal of Experimental Social Psychology* 2: 325–42.

Washington, George. 1796. "Farewell Address." www.avalon.law.yale.edu/18th_century/washing.asp. Accessed: January 9, 2009.

Washington School of CPAs. n.d. Washington Association of CPAs online glossary: "Franchise" in "Accounting Glossary." www.wscpa.org/wscpa/acctg-terms.cfm. Accessed: August 6, 2004.

Washington Times. 2004. "Who Is Barack Obama?" 2 August.

Wattenberg, Martin P. 1996. *The Decline of American Political Parties: 1952–1994*. Cambridge, MA: Harvard University Press.

Weaver, David H., and G. Cleveland Wilhoit. 1974. "News Magazine Visibility of Senators." *Journalism Quarterly* 51: 67–72.

Weaver, David, Doris Graber, Maxwell McCombs, and Chaim Eyal. 1981. *Media Agenda-Setting in a Presidential Election*. New York: Praeger.

Weisman, Jonathan, and Naftali Bendavid. 2009. "New Rx for Health Plan: Split Bill." *Wall Street Journal*, 20 August. online.wsj.com/article/SB125072573848144647.html.

Weisman, Jonathan, and Jim VandeHei. 2005. "GOP Is Divided on Social Security Push." *Washington Post*, 7 January.

West, Darrell. 2001. *Air Wars: Television Advertising in Election Campaigns, 1952–2000*. Washington, DC: Congressional Quarterly Press.

Westin, Drew. 2007. *Political Brain: The Role of Emotion in Deciding the Fate of the Nation*. Cambridge, MA: Perseus Book Group.

Westley, Bruce, and Malcolm MacLean. 1957. "A Conceptual Model for Communications Research." *Journalism Quarterly* 34: 31–8.

Westlye, Mark C. 1991. *Senate Elections and Campaign Intensity*. Baltimore, MD: The Johns Hopkins University Press.

White, David. 1950. "The Gatekeeper: A Case Study in Selection of News." *Journalism Quarterly* 27: 383–90.

White, John Kenneth, and Jerome Mileur. 2002. "In the Spirit of Their Times: 'Toward a More Responsible Two-Party System' and Party Politics." In *Responsible Partisanship? The Evolution of American Political Parties Since 1950*, eds. John C. Green and Paul Herrnson. Lawrence: University Press of Kansas.

Wilson, Woodrow. 1908. *Constitutional Government*. New York: Columbia University Press.

Wilson, Woodrow. 1911. *Constitutional Government in the United States*. New York: Columbia University Press.

Wilson, Woodrow. "Mr. Cleveland's Cabinet." In *Public Papers*, I: 221–2. Quoted in Austin Ranney, 1954, *Doctrine of Responsible Party Government*. Urbana: The University of Illinois Press.

Wolfsfeld, Gadi. 1991. *Media, Protest, and Political Violence: A Transactional Analysis*. Columbia, SC: Association for Education in Journalism and Mass Communication.

Wormser, Michael D. 1982. *Guide to Congress*, 3rd ed. Washington, DC: Congressional Quarterly Press.

York, Byron. 2009. "GOP Thinks the Unthinkable: Victory in 2010." *Washington Examiner*, 14 August. www.washingtonexaminer.com/politics/GOP-thinks-the-unthinkable-Victory-in-2010-8103193-53174842.html.

Zaller, John. 1992. *The Nature and Origins of Mass Opinion*. New York: Cambridge University Press.

Zaller, John. 1997. "A Model of Communication Effects at the Outbreak of the Gulf War." In *Do the Media Govern?: Politicians, Voters, and Reporters in America*, eds. Shanto Iyengar and Richard Reeves. Thousand Oaks, CA: Sage Publications, Inc.

Zaller, John. n.d. *A Theory of Media Politics*. Chicago: University of Chicago Press.

Zaller, John, and Dennis Chiu. 2000. "Government's Little Helper: U.S. Press Coverage of Foreign Policy Crises, 1946–1999. In *Decision Making in a Glass House*, eds. Brigitte L. Nacos, Robert Y. Shapiro, and Pierangelo Isernia. New York: Rowman & Littlefield Publishers, Inc.

Zeleny, Jeff. 2009. "Health Debate Fails to Ignite Obama's Grass Roots." *The New York Times*, 14 August. www.nytimes.com/2009/08/15/health/policy/15ground.html?src=sch.

Zuckman, Jill. 1994. "GOP Musters for House Control; Party Promises Voters a Very Different Future." *The Boston Globe*, 28 September.

Zurawik, David. 2004. "Captains of TV Weigh the Future of the Anchor: Personnel Changes Could Open Door to Newscasts Driven by Ideology." *Baltimore Sun*, 28 November.

Index

CPSIA information can be obtained
at www.ICGtesting.com
Printed in the USA
LVOW04s1628281215

468133LV00008B/135/P